fantasia
AN ALGERIAN CAVALCADE

raid on horseback

1985

L'Amour fantasia

fantasia

AN ALGERIAN CAVALCADE

ASSIA DJEBAR

Translated by Dorothy S. Blair

Heinemann
Portsmouth, NH

Heinemann
A division of Reed Elsevier Inc.
361 Hanover Street
Portsmouth, NH 03801-3912
Offices and agents throughout the world

Fantasia: An Algerian Cavalcade
is the first volume of a quartet.
The second volume is
A Sister to Scheherazade

First U.S. Printing 1993
First Published in English by Quartet Books Limited
A member of the Namara Group
27/29 Goodge Street, London W1P 1FD
First published in France by Editions Jean-Claude Lattès 1985
as L'amour, la fantasia

Copyright © by Assia Djebar 1985
Translation and Introduction copyright © by Dorothy S. Blair

Library of Congress Cataloging–in–Publication Data
Djebar, Assia, 1936–
    [Amour, la fantasia. English]
    Fantasia, an Algerian cavalcade / Assia Djebar : translated by
Dorothy S. Blair.
        p. cm.
    Sequel: A sister to Scheherazade.
    ISBN 0–435–08621–9
    1. Women—Algeria—History—Fiction. I. Title.
PQ3989.2.D57A813 1993
843—dc20   92–42700
                                                               CIP

Typeset by MC Typeset Limited, Gillingham, Kent
Printed in the United States of America on Acid-Free Paper
94 95 96 97 5 4 3 2

CONTENTS

GLOSSARY

açaba   a diadem, tiara, jewelled fillet

Aga (Agha)   (Turk.), Minister in charge of Sultan's armed
                     forces; in Algeria, an officer superior to a *caïd*

alim   one who has knowledge

aman   mercy (to plead for a. = to surrender, ask for
                     assurance of safe conduct)

Amir (Emir)   title of Muslim sovereign ruler, here the Sultan
                     Abd al-Qadir

attatich   (Turk.) palanquin

bach-kateb   secretary (term derived half from Turkish, half
                     Arabic)

bessita   multiple necklaces, covering the whole bust,
                     down to the waist

Bey   (Turk.) Governor of a *beylik* (q.v.) in Regency
                     of Algiers with three principal vassals:
                     governors of Oran, Constantine and Titteri

beylik   (Turk.) one of the provinces of Regency of
                     Algiers

burnous   long, loose, woollen cloak, woven in one piece

cadi (qadi)   Muslim judge, interpreter of law of Islam

Caïd (Qaïd)   Arab administrator, chief or civil judge
                     appointed by government

Caliph   successor of Mohamed, Muslim civil and
                     religious chief, Sultan (see *Amir*)

chaouch   (Turk.) usher

chikhat (cheikat) fem. of sheikh, here 'lady-musicians'; term
                     used here to denote respect for their age and
                     the religious nature of their chants

chengal   pendant earrings

deira	retinue, lit. 'circle', i.e. roving capital of Abd al-Qadir
Dey	(Turk.) ruler of Regency of Algiers before French conquest in 1830
Divan	(Turk.) council of state in Regency of Algiers
douar	hamlet or settlement, clan, extended family
'Etlag el Goum!'	battle-cry, 'Forward gallop!', lit. 'Drop the reins!'
fatiha	introduction to recital of *sura* (q.v.)
fellah, fellaheen (pl.)	peasant, derogatory term used by the French to refer to the partisans
fraction	part of tribe or village
'France'	the French army, expression used by the Algerian peasants during the War of Independence
galam	wooden stylus used in Quranic school for writing verses from the Quran on wooden tablets
goum	Arab military unit, allied to the French
goumier	Arab soldier who has enlisted with the French
guelta	stream
guerba	goatskin for carrying water, holding about twenty litres
hadri	citizen, town-dweller
haïk	all-enveloping, woollen square of cloth in which Middle Eastern women cover themselves out of doors, leaving only one eye visible
hammam	Turkish bath
janizary (janissary)	(Turk.) infantry constituting the Sultan's guard and main part of Turkish standing army
jebel	mountain
jemmaa	council of elders
jihad	holy war waged on behalf of Islam
kachabia	cloak worn by peasants and maquisards in winter to protect them from the cold; worn by a girl in the maquis so that the enemy soldiers will take her for a man
kanoun	brazier

kasbah	citadel or fortress; in Algiers, fortified Turkish seat of government
Khalifa	deputy to the Caliph
khalkhal (*khelkhal*)	ankle bracelet (anklet)
Khasnaji	(Turk.) Minister of Finance
khatiba	a company of maquisards (approx. 100)
khoja	(Turk.) clerk, secretary
Kulughli (*Kouloughli*)	(Turk. = son of the slave) i.e. son of Turkish father and native Algerian woman
marabout	Muslim holy man, saint
Méchouar	usually the Council Chamber, here the city fortress which is the headquarters of the military guard
meddah	a poet who chants his poetry, a bard
medina	old part of an Arab city
medresa	Quranic school
mejnoun	mad, in the sense of possessed by demons
Moujahidine	partisans, the most dedicated and fanatical of the freedom-fighters
nay	a very old type of flute
naylette	dancer and prostitute
seroual (*saroual*)	loose, baggy trousers
setla	goblet, elaborate drinking cup
Sharif	tribal ruler who claims descent from the Prophet
Sheikh	(i) chief of a tribal *fraction*; (ii) chief of a religious order; (iii) head of family
smala	Arab chief's retinue, cf. *deira*
spahi	member of native Algerian cavalry in French service, recognized by their scarlet capes
Sultan	ruling sovereign
sura	a verse of the Quran, recited during the daily prayers
taleb	disciple of *marabout*, teacher in a Quranic school
terrace	in N. Africa, the flat roof where the women congregate for social gatherings or to sit in the cool
thuya	a species of conifer

wadi	river or dry river bed
wali	(i) a saint; (ii) the saint's tomb, a sanctuary; (iii) a representative or 'prefect'
yatagan	(Turk.) sword, without guard, often double-edged
zaouia (zawiyah)	headquarters of an Islamic brotherhood

CHRONOLOGY

1510	Beginning of Turkish rule in Algeria
29 April 1827	Hussein, the Dey of Algiers, strikes the French consul, starting a crisis in the relations between the two countries, French begin naval blockade of Algiers
November 1829	France decides to send military expedition to Algeria, with a view to the conquest of Algiers
2 March 1830	Charles X announces decision to invade Algiers
May 1830	Bourmont prepares to sail from Toulon
14 June 1830	French land at Sidi Ferruch
5 July 1830	French troops capture Algiers and Dey Hussein capitulates
30 July 1830	Revolution in Paris forces Charles X to abdicate. Louis-Philippe proclaimed king. Bourmont, loyal to Charles, withdraws his troops from Bône and Oran, resigns his command and goes into exile in Spain. Clauzel takes over command in Algiers from Bourmont and pursues a policy of colonization which continues for ten years into the hinterland of Algiers and the Mitidja plain
4 January 1831	French occupy Oran

22 November 1832	Abd al-Qadir elected supreme Commander of the Faithful; establishes military base at Mascara; emerges as leader of resistance against French
March 1833–September 1834	Colonization of Mitidja plain progresses rapidly, with 6,000 troops stationed at Blida
26 February 1834	Gen. Desmichels, commander of French forces in Oran, and Abd al-Qadir sign treaty ending hostilities, and recognizing the Amir's jurisdiction over territory in neighbourhood of Oran
22 July 1834	Position of Governor-General of French Possessions in N. Africa established
1835	Abd al-Qadir continues attacks on French posts
December 1835	Field-Marshal Clauzel attacks Mascara, the Amir's capital
1835–36	Continued clashes between French forces and those of the Amir
November 1836	Attempt to take Constantine by force fails, the French losing about 1,000 men
May 1837	Gen. Bugeaud signs treaty with Abd al-Qadir
July 1837	Hostilities resumed
October 1837	French capture Constantine
October 1839	Field-Marshal Valée leads military column towards Algiers
November 1839	The Amir retaliates by invading Mitidja plain
December 1840	Governor-General Valée replaced by Gen. Bugeaud. Gen. Lamoricière appointed in Oran
1840–7	Bugeaud pursues policy of total occupation and war takes on cruel

character. Four recorded incidents of French officers ordering burning of defeated groups of Muslims in caves

November 1843	The Amir seeks asylum in Morocco
21 December 1847	Abd al-Qadir surrenders to the French
1848–52	He is held in French prison, despite promise of safe conduct to the East
1852	Napoleon III orders Abd al-Qadir's release
1883	Abd al-Qadir dies in Damascus
1939	Outbreak of Second World War
1940	German occupation of France
1945	End of Second World War in Europe
1954	Start of the Algerian War of Independence
1962	End of Algerian War. De Gaulle grants Algeria independence
1968	Abd al-Qadir's remains transferred from Damascus to Algiers for burial

INTRODUCTION

When Assia Djebar published *L'amour, la fantasia* in 1985, she had already established her reputation as the major woman writer from the Maghreb, with four novels in French to her name by the time she was thirty. She then announced that she was abandoning fiction writing – in particular, writing in French – and from 1962 devoted herself to teaching history at the University of Algiers. However, during the ensuing twelve years of 'silence', she tried to tackle the problem of the passage from writing in French to writing in Arabic, to which she found a partial solution in the cinema with her film *La Nouba des femmes du Mont Chenoua* which was awarded the Critics' Prize at the Venice Biennale 1979. The film, in which musical sequences alternate with testimonies in Arabic, is based on the experiences of Algerian peasant women during the War of Independence – material which the author introduces into the second part of *L'amour, la fantasia*, in the chapters which she entitles 'Voice'. When Assia Djebar returns to fiction writing, the result of this long maturation period is to be seen in the originality and complexity and also in the interwoven themes of her works. After a volume of short stories, published in 1980, specifically dealing with the lives of contemporary urban Algerian women: *Femmes d'Alger dans leur appartement*, came the first two parts of a projected *Algerian Quartet*, published in 1985 and 1987 respectively.

Assia Djebar's work has, up till now, only been known to the English reader through the translation of her first novel *La Soif* (1957) under the title of *The Mischief*. *L'amour, la fantasia*, translated here as *Fantasia: an Algerian Cavalcade*, is in fact the first part of the Quartet, the second volume, *A Sister to Scheherazade*, having already appeared. But the order is immaterial to the appreciation of the works, for although both are constructed on the same contrapuntal pattern, with echoes of characterization and incident in each, and both refer to the travels in Algeria of the French artist and novelist Eugène Fromentin, each of the novels has an independent texture and anecdotal autonomy. The link between them is the narrator of *Fantasia*, with whom Isma in the second work can be identified. In the former, the chapters in the first person are admittedly autobiographical, whereas Isma, who shares the author's headstrong, passionate nature, her background and many of her experiences, is intended to typify the dilemma of the emancipated Algerian woman in general, in contrast to the illiterate cloistered Hajila. *A Sister to Scheherazade* begins and ends with Isma leaving at dawn with her six-year-old daughter Meriem, in search of her roots in her native city of Cherchel, where Assia Djebar was born in 1936. The first chapter of *Fantasia*, which begins with the author's father taking her to school for the first time, ends with the phrase which will be echoed in the second novel: '. . . I cut myself adrift. I set off at dawn with my little girl's hand in mine.' *Fantasia: An Algerian Cavalcade* is an historical pageant, a dialectic between written (French) and oral (Arabic) personal accounts, an inquiry into the nature of the Algerian identity, and a personal quest.

An historical pageant of the vicissitudes of her native country, it covers the capture of Algiers in 1830 to the War of Independence of 1954–62: for the chapters devoted to the War of Colonization, Djebar, the historian, draws on the archives, and disinters little-known eye-witness accounts written at the time by artists, obscure officers, publicists (whom we would now call war correspondents) and various camp-followers. They write, sometimes for publication in the metropolis, but just as often simply to share their experiences in letters to their families at home, or jotting down impressions hot from the battle for official records or private journals. These episodes include acts of barbarism by the French, who exterminated whole tribes, and individual experiences – particularly of women – highlighting their pride and obdurate courage in the face of invaders and conquerors. The hero of the Algerian resistance to the French conquests was the legendary Sultan Abd al-Qadir, but the episodes which stand out here are those featuring the sufferings of women: victims of the ruthless 'fumigations' of rebel tribes in the Dahra caves, dancing girls caught up in the fighting, anonymous women whose hands and feet are amputated for their jewelled ornaments, and the dignified young 'Bride of Mazuna'. To these Djebar adds the account of the humble but no less proud Pauline Rolland, who was among the ten French women transported to Algiers in 1852 for their part in the 1848 Revolution. Without inventing incident, the author calls on her rich poetic imagination and exceptional descriptive powers to conjure up the atmosphere, the colour, the tumult of these historical events, as well as the presence and psychology of the authentic historical characters.

Whereas the episodes from nineteenth-century history are based on research into contemporary writings in French, and are deliberately written in a very colourful style, the second historical sequence, devoted to the War of Independence, relies on the oral testimony of the women who took part in the struggle. The author travelled into the mountains that had been the scene of guerrilla warfare, recorded the women's stories, and reproduces them here in their own words, with their sobriety of tone, staccato, laconic expression and popular turns of phrase, which I have made no attempt to 'polish' in the English version. So, for example, these peasant women say 'France came up to the village', meaning 'the French army' . . . The transcription into French (and now into English) of these unedited accounts explains the distinct and deliberate difference in linguistic style of the chapters devoted to the women's stories from the author's own virtuoso use of the French language, and is an important element in the antiphonal structure of the work: dialogue between recent and more distant past; between personal and national experience; between writing and orality; between the conflicting claims of the author's 'father and mother tongues'.

If Algerian Woman in all her complexity and historical reality is the protagonist of Assia Djebar's most ambitious and original work of fiction, this is also an attempt to wrest her own identity as an Algerian woman from the warring strands of her Arabo-Berber origins and her Franco-European education. The traditional reticence of an Arab woman, discouraged from speaking of herself, is a barrier to the composition of an autobiography, so she calls this work 'a preparation for an autobiography'. While the last part of the book is a dialogue between the author and the peasant women whose voices she reproduces, throughout the work she intervenes 'with nomad memory and intermittent voice' to create a polyphony of the incidents from her own girlhood and early womanhood interwoven into the fabric of the historical sequences from 1830 to the present day.

While Arabic is Assia Djebar's mother tongue, she calls French both her 'father tongue', since it was her schoolteacher father who introduced her to it and also her 'step-mother tongue', with which she maintains a love-hate relationship. She resents the fact that her early exposure to a French education made her a cultural, linguistic and, for a time a literal exile from the land of her origins; at the same time she appreciates that French has been the gateway to freedom, denied to many of her countrywomen. She is clearly in love with the musicality of French, which she exploits in those passages of prose poetry printed in italics, and in which she makes the prose approximate to music, both structurally and sonically. At other times, in a conscious effort to escape from the shackles of writing in 'the enemy's language', she seems to be colonizing the language of the colonizers. She does violence to it, forcing it to give up its riches and defying it to hand over its hidden hoard, in compensation for the treasure looted from Algiers in 1830, and also to compensate her personally for being dispossessed of her Arabic heritage. She thus has at her command, and uses effortlessly, an astonishing variety of vocabulary, drawing on archaisms, rare esoteric words, medical, scientific and musical terms, in an exuberance of metaphor which it is often difficult to accommodate in English prose, with its normal economy of imagery. This may well deter the English reader, unaccustomed to such verbal extravagance. But the result is both an extraordinary attention to detail of atmosphere, an appeal to all the senses, the evocation of emotion and the perfection of a prose style in which the sentences fill their own space and establish their own rhythm.

The *Fantasia* (derived from the Arabic *fantaziya* [meaning ostentation]), is in North Africa a set of virtuoso movements on horseback executed at a gallop, accompanied by loud cries and culminating in rifle shots; the *Fantasia*, associated with ceremonial occasions and military triumphs, forms the *leitmotif* of the novel as well as providing its title. But a *Fantasia* (Italian for 'fantasy' or 'fancy') is also a musical composition in which, according to the definition given in Kennedy's *Concise Oxford Dictionary of Music*, 'form is of secondary importance . . . in the sixteenth and seventeenth centuries such compositions were usually contrapuntal and in several sections, thus being an early form of variations . . . compositions, in which the character of the music suggested an improvisational character or the play of free fancy'. The author uses Beethoven's instruction to his Sonatas 1 and 2, '*Quasi una fantasia . . .*' as the epigraph to Part Three of her novel, so establishing the title unambiguously as a serious word-play on the double character of the work, and highlighting its strong musical associations of form and style. Moreover the third part of the novel, in which the musical references are most insistent, is divided into five 'movements', to which is added a coda in the form of a short chapter entitled 'Air on a *Nay*' (an ancient kind of flute), where the strands of sound, episode and imagery are drawn together.

Assia Djebar is not only a musical and visual writer, but she is also startlingly physical. The first element of the original French title, *L'amour, la fantasia*, is omitted from the English title for stylistic reasons, but the love theme is both implicit and explicit in the text. In the autobiographical chapters, the author discreetly analyses the emotional torments of her first love affairs, but eschews the eroticism with which she evokes the sensual ecstasies of her alter ego, Isma, in *A Sister to Scheherazade*. While she avoids expression of the intimacy of sexuality, she suggests the abandonment of consummated love by association – again having recourse to a play on words: '*L'amour, ses cris, (s'écrit)*'. Love that is written, like the cries uttered at the height of orgasm, makes the writer vulnerable; in this she is compared to her cloistered sisters who live their hidden lives behind their veils and their illiteracy, but are mistresses of a body language which 'seeks some unknown shore as destination for its message of love'. The emancipated woman, who has broken out of the harem, is still reticent in this work about the physical union, whereas her preoccupation with the *physical act* of writing forms one of the original aspects of her work and becomes a metaphor for her dichotomy. She compares the cramped posture she adopts when writing in French with the sensual act of writing in Arabic, when the movements of her body seem to echo the scrolls, the curlicues, the rhythms of the calligraphy. In the very first pages of the novel, she ironically announces the theme of the repercussions of writing: '. . . there is more danger in love that is committed to paper than love that languishes behind enclosing walls', since the written word, the surreptitious, forbidden correspondence, is the key to the outside world for the cloistered Arab virgin. And the remarkable fact of the author's father having actually written to her mother, during a short absence from home, establishes their mutual love on a different plane from the relationship of feminine submission to male dominance obtaining in the Arab society of her youth. For the author herself, the love-letter is more of a trap than a talisman, because it crystallizes the overt expression of emotions that the reticence of her mother-tongue would half conceal. There is an analogy between love-letters and the correspondence despatched from the encampments by forgotten captains participating in the conquest of Algeria; both are the occasion for self-analysis and result in insight into the ambiguity of emotions: '. . . it is as if these parading warriors, around whom cries rise up which the elegance of their style cannot diminish, are mourning their unrequited love for my Algeria'. The theme of the love-letter is thus another link between the historical and the autobiographical dimensions of the novel as well as a basic part of its structure. The antiphony between the written and the oral elements, between '*l'écrit*' and '*les cris*', is introduced by the love-letters (*L'amour s'écrit* in the original), but the final response is given to the cries of the *Fantasia*.

Dorothy S. Blair, 1989

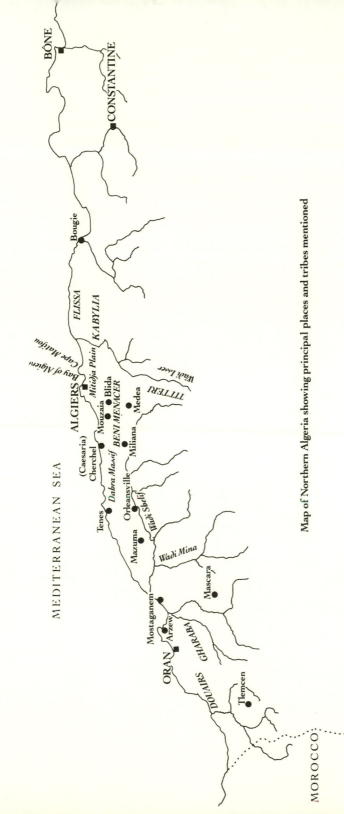

Map of Northern Algeria showing principal places and tribes mentioned

A heart-rending cry arose – I can hear it still as I write to you – then the air was rent with screams, then pandemonium broke loose . . .

Eugène Fromentin
A Year in the Sahel

PART ONE

THE CAPTURE OF THE CITY

or

Love-letters

Our sentinels were gaining in experience: they were learning to distinguish the footsteps and voices of the Arabs from the sounds made by the wild beasts that prowled around the camp in the dark.

Barchou de Penhoën
Expedition to Africa, 1835

A Little Arab Girl's
First Day at School

A little Arab girl going to school for the first time, one autumn morning, walking hand in hand with her father. A tall erect figure in a fez and a European suit, carrying a bag of school books. He is a teacher at the French primary school. A little Arab girl in a village in the Algerian Sahel.

Towns or villages of narrow white alleyways and windowless houses. From the very first day that a little girl leaves her home to learn the ABC, the neighbours adopt that knowing look of those who in ten or fifteen years' time will be able to say 'I told you so!' while commiserating with the foolhardy father, the irresponsible brother. For misfortune will inevitably befall them. Any girl who has had some schooling will have learned to write and will without a doubt write that fatal letter. For her the time will come when there will be more danger in love that is committed to paper than love that languishes behind enclosing walls.

So wrap the nubile girl in veils. Make her invisible. Make her more unseeing than the sightless, destroy in her every memory of the world without. And what if she has learned to write? The jailer who guards a body that has no words – and written words can travel – may sleep in peace: it will suffice to brick up the windows, padlock the sole entrance door, and erect a blank wall rising up to heaven.

And what if the maiden does write? Her voice, albeit silenced, will circulate. A scrap of paper. A crumpled cloth. A servant-girl's hand in the dark. A child, let into the secret. The jailer must keep watch day and night. The written word will take flight from the patio, will be tossed from a terrace. The blue of heaven is suddenly limitless. The precautions have all been in vain.

At seventeen I am introduced to my first experience of love through

3

a letter written by a boy, a stranger. Whether acting thoughtlessly or out of bravado, he writes quite openly. My father, in a fit of silent fury, tears up the letter before my eyes and throws it into the waste-paper basket without letting me read it.

As soon as term ends at my boarding school, I now spend the summer holidays back in the village, shut up in the flat overlooking the school playground. During the siesta hour, I piece together the letter which has aroused my father's fury. The mysterious correspondent says he remembers seeing me go up on to the platform during the prize-giving ceremony which took place two or three days previously, in the neighbouring town. I recall staring at him rather defiantly as I passed him in the corridors of the boys' high school. He writes very formally suggesting that we exchange friendly letters. In my father's eyes, such a request is not merely completely indecent, but this invitation is tantamount to setting the stage for rape.

Simply because my father wanted to destroy the letter, I interpreted the conventional French wording used by this student on holiday as the cryptic expression of some sudden, desperate passion.

During the months and years that followed, I became absorbed by this business of love, or rather by the prohibition laid on love; my father's condemnation only served to encourage the intrigue. In these early stages of my sentimental education, our secret correspondence is carried on in French: thus the language that my father had been at pains for me to learn, serves as a go-between, and from now a double, contradictory sign reigns over my initiation . . .

As with the heroine of a Western romance, youthful defiance helped me break out of the circle that whispering elders traced around me and within me . . . Then love came to be transformed in the tunnel of pleasure, soft clay to be moulded by matrimony.

Memory purges and purifies the sounds of childhood; we are cocooned by childhood until the discovery of sensuality, which washes over us and gradually bedazzles us . . . Voiceless, cut off from my mother's words by some trick of memory, I managed to pass through the dark waters of the corridor, miraculously inviolate, not even guessing at the enclosing walls. The shock of the first words blurted out: the truth emerging from a break in my stammering voice. From what nocturnal reef of pleasure did I manage to wrest this truth?

I blew the space within me to pieces, a space filled with desperate voiceless cries, frozen long ago in a prehistory of love. Once I had discovered the meaning of the words – those same words that are revealed to the unveiled body – I cut myself adrift.

I set off at dawn, with my little girl's hand in mine.

I

Dawn on this thirteenth day of June 1830, at the exact moment when the sun suddenly blazes forth above the fathomless bowl of the bay. It is five in the morning. As the majestic fleet rends the horizon the Impregnable City sheds her veils and emerges, a wraith-like apparition, through the blue-grey haze. A distant triangle aslant, glinting in the last shreds of nocturnal mist and then settling softly, like a figure sprawling on a carpet of muted greens. The mountain shuts out the background, dark against the blue wash of the sky.

The first confrontation. The city, a vista of crenelated roofs and pastel hues, makes her first appearance in the rôle of 'Oriental Woman', motionless, mysterious. At first light the French Armada starts its slow glide past, continuing its stately ballet until noon spills its spangled radiance over the scene. No sound accompanies this transformation – this solemn moment of anticipation, breathless with suspense, the moment before the overture strikes up. But who are to be the performers? On which side shall we find the audience? Five in the morning. A Sunday; and what is more, it is the Feast of Corpus Christi in the Christian calendar. The first lookout, wearing the uniform of a frigate captain, stands on the poop of one of the craft of the reserve fleet which will sail past ahead of the battle squadron, preceding a hundred or so men-o'-war. The name of the lookout man is Amable Matterer. He keeps watch and that same day will write, 'I was the first to catch sight of the city of Algiers, a tiny triangle on a mountain slope.'

Half past five in the morning. The immense flotilla of frigates, brigs and schooners, bedecked with multicoloured pennons, streams endlessly, three by three, into the entrance to the bay, from which all traces of night and threats of storm have vanished. It has been decided

6

that the decks of the *Provence*, the admiral's flagship, shall be cleared for action.

Units of able-seamen and soldiers clatter up in their thousands on to the decks and swarm on forecastle and poop. The scene is suddenly blanketed in silence, as if the intense silken light, squandered so lavishly in dazzling pools, were about to be rent with a strident screech. Nothing stirs in the Barbary city. Not a quiver disturbs the milky dazzle of the terraced houses that can gradually be distinguished on the slopes of the mountain whose mass is now clearly silhouetted in a series of gentle emerald-green undulations.

Officers and men are drawn up in tight formation close to the rails and stanchions, taking care that their swords do not rattle at their sides; silence save for an occasional interjection, a muffled oath, a throat being cleared, an expectoration. The host of men waiting to invade, stand and watch amidst the jumble of hammocks, in between pieces of artillery and big guns drawn up in their firing position, like circus animals waiting under the spotlights, ready to perform. The city faces them in the unchanging light which absorbs the sounds.

Amable Matterer, first officer of the *Ville de Marseille*, does not stir, nor do his companions. The Impregnable City confronts them with its many invisible eyes. Although they had been prepared for its skyline – here a dome reflected in the water, there the silhouette of a fortress or the tip of a minaret – nevertheless the dazzling white panorama freezes before them in its disturbing proximity.

Thousands of watchful eyes there are doubtless estimating the number of vessels. Who will pass on the number? Who will write of it? Which of all these silent spectators will live to tell the tale when the encounter is over? Amable Matterer is at his post in the first squadron which glides slowly westward; he gazes at the city which returns his gaze. The same day he writes of the confrontation, dispassionately, objectively.

I, in my turn, write, using his language, but more than one hundred and fifty years later. I wonder, just as the general staff of the fleet must have done, whether the Dey Hussein has gone up on to the terrace of his kasbah, telescope in hand. Is he personally watching the foreign armada approach? Does he consider this threat beneath contempt? So many foes have sailed away after a token bombardment or two, just as Charles V of Spain did in the sixteenth century! . . . Is the Dey at a loss? Is he unmoved? Or is he giving vent to one of his dramatic rages, such as he recently displayed when the King of France sent his envoy with a demand for unreasonable apologies: the Dey's reply is enshrined in legend: 'The King of France may as well demand my wife!'

I can imagine Hussein's wife neglecting her dawn prayer to climb up too on to the terrace. How many other women, who normally only retreated to their terraces at the end of the day, must also have gathered there to catch a glimpse of the dazzling French fleet.

When the squadron left Toulon, there were four painters, five draughtsmen and about a dozen engravers on board . . . The battle is not yet joined, they are not yet even in sight of their prey, but they are already anxious to ensure a pictorial record of the campaign. As if the imminent war were to be considered as some sort of festivity.

As this day dawns when the two sides will come face to face, what are the women of the town saying to each other? What dreams of romance are lit in their hearts or are extinguished for ever, as they gaze on the proud fleet tracing the figures of a mysterious ballet? . . . I muse on this brief respite; I slip into the antechamber of this recent past, like an importunate visitor, removing my sandals according to the accustomed ritual, holding my breath in an attempt to overhear everything . . .

On this thirteenth day of June 1830, the confrontation continues for two, three hours, well into the glare of the afternoon. As if the invaders were coming as lovers! The vessels sail so slowly, so quietly westward, that they might well have been planted there above the glassy surface of the water, by the eyes of the Impregnable City, blinded by mutual love at first sight.

And the silence of this majestic morning is but the prelude to the cavalcade of screams and carnage which will fill the ensuing decades.

Three Cloistered Girls

Three girls live cloistered in an airy house in the middle of the tiny Sahel village, surrounded by vast vineyards, where I come to spend my spring and summer holidays. My stay there, shut up with these three sisters, is my 'visit to the country'. I am ten, then eleven, then twelve . . .

All through the summer I play with the youngest of these girls who is a year or two older than me. We spend hours together on the swing at the bottom of the orchard near the farmyard. Now and then we break off from our games to peep through the hedge at the village women shouting from the neighbouring small-holdings. At dusk the farm gate opens to let in a flock of goats. I learn to milk the most docile ones. Then I drink from the skin bottle, whose tarry smell makes me rather nauseous. Not being allowed to wander in the dusty lanes of the village is no hardship to me.

The house is large. There are many cool shady rooms filled with mattresses piled up on the floor, and hung with Saharan tapestries woven in the past by the then mistress of the house – a relative by marriage of my mother, who herself comes from the nearby town.

I never go into the end room: a senile old relative of the family squats there in permanent darkness. Sometimes the youngest sister and I venture as far as the doorway, petrified by the sound of her cracked voice, now moaning, now uttering vague accusations, denouncing imaginery plots. What hidden drama do we touch on, resurrected, revived by the ravings of the old crone in her second childhood, violently denouncing some past persecution in a voice that paralyses us. We do not know the magical formulas, the passages from the Quran, that the grown-ups recite aloud to exorcize these outbursts.

The presence of this ancient, with one foot already in the grave, ensures that the other women of the household never miss one of their

9

daily prayers. They gather in the largest room, next to the kitchen or pantry; one of them sews or embroiders, while another squats on the floor, busily sorting chickpeas or lentils, spread out on white cloths. Suddenly five or six slight figures, their veils covering their heads and shoulders, silently straighten up, keeping their eyes lowered. Frail phantoms, both strengthened and weakened by the propitiatory liturgy, they prostrate themselves several times in unison . . . Sometimes my mother forms part of this group of pious women, making their obeisances, brushing the cold floor tiles with their lips.

We little girls take refuge beneath the medlar trees. To shut out the old woman mumbling to herself, the others' fervent whisperings. We go to count the pigeons in the loft or savour the smell of carobs in the shed, and of the hay trampled under the mare's hooves when she was let out into the fields. We compete to see who can swing highest. Oh! the exhilaration of swinging rhythmically, now high, now low, up over the house and the village! To soar with our legs higher than our heads, till the sounds of the animals and women are all swallowed up behind us.

In a gap in my memory, I suddenly recall one torrid, interminable summer. The raving old crone must have died the previous winter. There are fewer women of the family around: that same season there have been a great number of circumcisions and marriages in the nearby town – so many new brides to be comforted, congratulated, consoled by the band of frustrated females accompanying them . . . I find the girls of the hamlet practically alone.

In the little farmyard, in spite of the carobs and the pigeons in the loft, I wish I were back at school; I miss the companionship of the other boarders, I describe the basketball games to the three country girls. I must be now about twelve or thirteen. I seem older; probably because I'm too tall, too thin. The eldest of the sisters keeps on bringing up the occasion when I first attended a gathering in the town and I was wearing the veil, and one of the city ladies came buzzing round me like a bee.

'Her son must have fallen in love with your silhouette and your eyes! You'll soon be hearing news of your first proposal!'

I stamp my feet in childish anger exacerbated by an ambiguous unease. I sulk for days on end, refusing to speak to the eldest sister.

During that same summer, the youngest sister and I manage to open the bookcase belonging to the absent brother, which up till then had

10

always been kept locked. He works as an interpreter in the Sahara, which seems to us as far away as America. In one month we read all the novels pushed away indiscriminately: Paul Bourget, Colette, Agatha Christie. We discover an album of erotic photographs and an envelope containing picture postcards of bare-breasted Ouled-Naïl girls, loaded with jewels. This brother was extremely strict and before this we were in daily terror of his unpredictable temper; and now we are suddenly aware of his uncomfortable presence during those dim siesta hours. We discreetly close the bookcase as the women rise for their afternoon prayers. We feel we have trespassed into some forbidden territory; we feel we have aged.

That summer the girls let me into their secret. A strange and weighty, unexpected matter. I never spoke of it to any other woman in the family, old or young. I had given my solemn promise and I kept it scrupulously. These girls, though confined to their house, were writing; were writing letters; letters to men; to men in the four corners of the world; of the Arab world, naturally.

And letters came back from far and wide: letters from Iraq, Syria, Lebanon, Lybia, Tunisia, from Arab students in Paris or London. Letters sent by pen-pals chosen from adverts appearing in a women's magazine with a wide circulation at the time in the harems. With every number the subscriber received a pattern for a dress or a housegown that even an illiterate woman could follow.

These sisters were the only Muslim girls in their little village to have attended primary school. Their father, a robust, pious countryman, who was the most expert market-gardener in the area – could neither read nor write French. Every year he had to rely on one or other of his daughters to see that the invoices which he had to send to his accountant were correct.

The postman, the son of a local artisan, must have wondered at all these letters from such distant places landing up at his post-office, which no-one had ever heard of till then. Nevertheless, he never breathed a word: 'The three daughters of the Sheikh!' He had never set eyes on these girls who must have seemed like princesses to him! . . . The backs of the envelopes bore fancy names borrowed from Eastern film-stars, giving the impression that the senders were women. He was not deceived. He must have mused over the girls' sweethearts, 'suitors' he probably thought. He knew that the girls never left the house, except when their father drove them himself in a barouche to the smartest Turkish bath in the nearby town . . . The continual arrival of these letters, from every corner of the world, must have weighed upon his mind, feeding some secret frustration!

The only thing I can recall about these letters is their proliferation and the number of different places they came from. When the youngest sister and I spent our evenings together, we no longer discussed the novels we had read during the long afternoons, but the audacity needed to carry on this clandestine correspondence. We conjured up the terrible dangers they were exposed to. There had been numerous cases in our towns of fathers or brothers taking the law into their own hands for less than this; the blood of an unmarried daughter or sister shed for a letter slipped surreptitiously into a hand, for a word whispered behind shuttered windows, for some slanderous accusation . . . A secret spirit of subversion had now seeped into the house, and we happy-go-lucky children were casually watching it spread.

The eldest sister, who had a reputation for being very high-and-mighty and never finding any of her official suitors good enough for her, had started this correspondence as a joke. One day, while the women in the next room were starting their prayers again, she had read the following advertisement from the magazine aloud to her sisters:

' "Tunisian, aged twenty-two, blue eyes, fond of Farid el-Attrash, seeks girl pen-pal in Arab country, romantically inclined." . . . Suppose I replied to him?'

I never knew what she wrote to the first, the second or the third correspondent: did she write of her uneventful everyday life, or of her dreams, or of the books she read? Perhaps she invented adventures for herself. I never asked her. I was simply dismayed to discover how quickly she found herself saddled with a dozen distant pen-pals. The youngest sister had almost as many. But the middle one – the one who had been silently, meticulously preparing her wedding trousseau for years – the second sister, the prettiest, the gentlest, the most docile – continued to protest that she would never, ever write to a stranger. If she did so, it would indicate that she was prepared to fall in love with him. And she preferred to wait, to get on with her sewing and embroidery, ready in due course to 'love' the eventual fiancé.

And I, at thirteen – perhaps this time it was during the winter holidays – I would listen, during these evenings we spent together, to

12

the youngest of these marriageable girls describing the arguments they had had about what to write in their letters. The eldest sister sent her many pen-pals the words of Egyptian or Lebanese songs, photographs of Arab actresses or film-stars. The youngest maintained a sibyline silence about the contents of her own letters . . .

Everything is a jumble in my memories of this last visit: the novels in the brother's forbidden bookcase and the mysterious letters that arrived by the dozen. We amused ourselves imagining what the postman must be thinking – his curiosity and bewilderment. Moreover he must have felt vexed that he himself could never hope to win the hand of any of these village princesses!

The youngest sister and I continued our whispered confidences. In the periods when sleep crept over me I imagined written words whirling furtively around, about to twine invisible snares around our adolescent bodies, lying side by side across the antique family bed. The same bed in whose hollow the ancient crone used to give vent in her delirium to a corrosive litany of grievances, harping blasphemously on long-forgotten wrongs.

I was afraid and I admitted it. I was certain a light would blaze down from the ceiling and reveal our sin – for I included myself in this terrible guilty secret!

The youngest sister went on whispering spasmodically. She was in the grip of her own determined will, while the night thickened around us and all living things had long fallen asleep.

'I'll never, never let them marry me off to a stranger who, in one night, will have the right to touch me! That's why I write all those letters! One day, someone will come to this dead-and-alive hole to take me away: my father and brother won't know him, but he won't be a stranger to me!'

Every night the vehement voice would utter the same childish vow. I had the premonition that in the sleepy, unsuspecting hamlet, an unprecedented women's battle was brewing beneath the surface.

13

II

The battle of Staouéli is fought on Saturday 19 June. For five days after the landings there have been ceaseless skirmishes. More than mere skirmishes in fact: when the riflemen on both sides exchange shots, this is war to the death. The opposing ranks size each other up, judging the enemy's tactics: Arab cavalry and infantry scatter in random groups of various sizes while the French light infantry reconnoitre and advance in tight formation. In the invaders' camp there is an average of eighty dead a day.

The first French victim fell on the deck of the *Breslau* the evening before the landing when the fleet reached the Sidi-Ferruch straits outside the bay, after sailing past the Impregnable City, beyond Pointe-Pescade. An attempt to land the first troops by barge proved abortive; shells were fired from the dense undergrowth before any of the invaders could set foot on the shore of Africa. The shells burst on one of the vessels of the first line; an able-bodied seaman has his thigh shattered by shrapnel and dies instantly.

The order is given to postpone the landing until the next day. The reveille will sound to wake the men at three in the morning. Throughout the night grunts and the muffled jangle of arms are heard. The vessels are now no better than floating prisons, jammed with forty thousand soldiers and thirty thousand seamen; for days they have been enveloped in the stench of pestilence. Close around them the unspoilt nature waits silently, seeming to pose no threat, but rather offering a sort of absolution.

The next day, barely an hour after the first ten thousand men have landed on that silent, seemingly deserted shore, an Arab horseman approaches the outposts, caracoling on a hill. The howitzers are trained on him; he tries to avoid the shells, but is hit and keels over backwards. Horse and rider disappear behind a hillock; this first Arab victim is greeted with a hail of laughter and cheers.

Many more deaths follow in rapid succession. I re-read the chronicles of these first encounters and note contrasting styles. The Algerians fight like the Numidians of old, so oft described by Roman historians: they wheel capriciously in swift approach, then check their advance as if their adversary were beneath contempt, before launching their decisive, vigorous attack. Tactics that are derived from the mocking flight of an insect, rather than the glossy feline prowling through the bush, ready to pounce.

The warriors eye each other from afar, serving as mutual decoys in an attempt to synchronize the tempo of every movement that foretokens mutual slaughter. In a flash, they are locked hand to hand, then, after one brief spasm, they lie decapitated, sometimes their corpses mutilated.

First kiss of death in the opposing camps: after the overture, a change of tune. Each victory by the aggressor's fire is accompanied by discordant laughter, as if the victim were taking part in some grotesque slapstick; whereas those that face the invaders prefer to deal death by silent stealth. Abruptly this silence is rent by the distant crackle of musketry; the next moment the blade of a knife is poised above a throat and severing the jugular artery. In this hand-to-hand struggle, Turks in their flaming red and Bedouins shrouded in white fight off their assailants with a display of ferocity, accompanied by jubilant cries of defiance that culminate in a crescendo of blood-curdling shrieks.

This war will be long drawn-out, yet, from the first encounter, the Arab, galloping full tilt on his small, frisky horse, seemingly seeks to clasp his enemy to his bosom: mortal blows dealt or received at a gallop seem to be transmuted into some frozen embrace.

The face of the invader presents a grotesque parody of death's grimace. As for the bellicose natives, soon to be overcome by disaster, for the nonce they caracol exultantly, advancing to the forefront of the stage, happy to slay and be slain full in the limelight. For the time being, they are drenched in brilliant sunlight, before the final darkness falls.

There are now two chroniclers of these preliminary clashes. Amable Matterer, first officer of the *Ville de Marseille*, stands on the deck of his vessel, watching the fighting gradually penetrate further and further

15

inland; later he too will become an actor, when, on the eve of surrender, the command is issued to bombard the city from the sea. He writes time and time again, 'I am writing with my sword at my side' . . . A second eye-witness will plunge us into the heart of the battle: Baron Barchou de Penhoën, ADC to General Berthezène who is in command of the first regiments to go into action. He leaves a month after the capture of the City; in the quarantine station in Marseille, still fresh from the scene, he sets down his impressions as a combatant, as an observer and even, with unexpected insight, as one who has fallen in love with a land of which he has glimpsed the fiery fringes.

After this first encounter between the two nations, both sides watch and wait, in doubt as to their next step. Throughout this summer of 1830, both camps are haunted: are these the ghosts of the raped, flitting over the piled-up corpses? Is it the spirit of an unacknowledged love, felt only in an intuitive sense of guilt?

The fascination felt by these two writers is clear – and they both write for Paris, which this same summer is in the throes of another upheaval: the hydra-headed monster, Revolution, that must be throttled at all costs. But what if this fascination also paralysed the threatened camp?

Was it simply for the pleasure of watching the invaders closing in on him that the Aga Ibrahim, the Dey's son-in-law, with such overweening confidence, took so little heed for his own defences? Was he so sure of crushing them, as invaders offering similar threats had been crushed in former centuries? (It is true that on each previous occasion a tempest had fortuitously blown up and so contributed to the defeat of the Spaniards, English, Dutch and so many others; this time a storm blew up just two days too late to save them.) Might not Ibrahim have been prompted rather by a desire to examine the foe close at hand, to touch him, to join battle at close quarters and let their blood flow together on the same soil?

The Bedouin tribes arrive as if to participate in yet another *Fantasia*, when the less caution is shown, the more attractive the hazards. They, too, do not believe that the City can be taken, but danger spurs them on: they hope that the military might of Algiers will be shaken in the trial of strength . . .

In fact, after the capture of the City, the contingents of allied troops, who had volunteered to accompany the Beys in a well-nigh ecstatic 'holy war', will return to their own territories, their feeling of autonomy intact. The debacle will first and foremost affect the janizaries, those magnificent Turkish warriors who will always be found in the front line of every battle, blazing in brilliant colours that stand out in sharp contrast to the white burnouses of the illusive autochthons.

The day after the decisive encounter at Staouéli, the war artist Major Langlois will pause to draw dead Turks, their faces still bearing the imprint of their frenzied valour. Some of them are grasping a dagger in their right hands which they have plunged into their own breasts. At ten of the clock on Sunday 20 June, in splendid weather, Langlois executes several drawings of these proud vanquished warriors, then he does the preliminary sketches for a picture destined for the Museum. 'The public will be able to obtain lithographs,' Matterer notes on this same day.

Barchou describes the battle stage by stage. Ibrahim has made the opening gambit and decided on the plan of campaign. This becomes clear in the course of the first days' action: the Algerian marksmen are more accurate and terrifying in their skill. The range of their muskets is remarkable, due to the length of the barrel. They take their aim unhurriedly, fire and vanish.

On 18 June the Aga Ibrahim inspects the terrain: rocks, clumps of lentisks, patches of undergrowth, thorny or sandy hills, a setting in which the Arab cavalry will have no difficulty in performing their usual ballet, and the infantry will be able to fling themselves flat on the ground, like invisible reptiles. The numbers seem slightly to favour the defenders. But the Aga neglects one detail which will weigh finally on the outcome: the superiority of the Western artillery, and most of all, the unity of the French command and tactics, in the face of the discord reigning among the native chiefs.

At eight in the morning, after seven uninterrupted hours of bitter fighting, the Algerian batteries are surrounded and overpowered. And then it is the final phase: Marshal Bourmont's regiments, which till then have been cut off, succeed in routing their assailants and are able to advance. As soon as they have captured the first high ground, they come upon the camp of the Aga and the Beys; three hundred sumptuous tents have been abandoned and stand intact, as though in waiting for them.

17

On the road to Algiers there is no longer any doubt about the outcome. The Beys of Titteri, Oran and Constantine fall back on the banks of the Wadi El-Harrach. The victorious troops feel as if they were already occupying the City. They imagine themselves lying on divans and being served with coffee.

The Staouéli plateau is strewn with corpses. Two thousand prisoners are taken. In defiance of their officers, the soldiers themselves insist on shooting them all. 'One battalion's fire brought down this rabble and two thousand of them will never see the light of day again,' writes Matterer, who has remained aboard his ship during the battle.

The next day he placidly wanders among the corpses and the booty.

I only recollect one brief electrifying episode from Baron Barchou's description of his experiences, recorded in the dark night of these memories.

Barchou's tone is ice-cold, but he seems to be transfixed with revulsion by the terrible poetry of the scene before his eyes; he had caught sight of the bodies of two Algerian women, lying a little apart from one group of skirmishers.

In the case of certain tribes from the interior, whole families had come along: women, children, old men. As if fighting were a matter of sacrificing themselves as a unit, all together, without regard for sex or possessions, rather than appearing on the brow of a rise, ready to attack! The Zouaves in particular, Kabyles who were the allies of the Bey of Titteri, form a multicoloured host amid the general ebullience.

So, one month later, Barchou sets down what he recalls: 'Arab tribes are always accompanied by great numbers of women who had shown the greatest zeal in mutilating their victims. One of these women lay dead beside the corpse of a French soldier whose heart she had torn out! Another had been fleeing with a child in her arms when a shot wounded her; she seized a stone and crushed the infant's head, to prevent it falling alive into our hands; the soldiers finished her off with their bayonets.'

Thus these two Algerian women – the one in whom rigor mortis was already setting in, still holding in her bloody hands the heart of a dead Frenchman; the second, in a fit of desperate courage, splitting open the brain of her child, like a pomegranate in spring, before dying with her mind at peace – these two heroines enter into recent history.

I scrupulously record the image: two warrior women glimpsed from the back or from the side, in the midst of the tumult, by the keen eye of the ADC. A forewarning of the hallucinatory fever that will reign, punctuated with folly... An image that prefigures many a future Muslim 'mater dolorosa' who, carrion beetles of the harem, will give birth to generations of faceless orphans during Algeria's thraldom a century later.

After this prelude the fires of a black sun are fanned!... But why, above the corpses that will rot on successive battlefields, does this first Algerian campaign reverberate with the sounds of an obscene copulation?

The French Policeman's Daughter

In the little village where I spent my childhood holidays, the French policeman's wife and two daughters, Janine and Marie-Louise, used to visit the home of the three sisters. The wife, a fat white woman from Burgundy, with a loud voice and jocular manner, was quite happy to squat unceremoniously on the floor among all the Arab women, relatives from the town, widows and divorcees who were occasionally offered asylum. The slight figure of the mistress of the house trotted tirelessly to and fro from kitchen to courtyard, from courtyard to farmyard, giving her orders. She would never sit down, never had a minute to spare, except when the Frenchwoman came to visit. The latter would join in the conversation: two or three words of French, a word in Arabic with her pronunciation making one or other of the guests gurgle with mischievous, suppressed laughter.

The mother of the cloistered girls and the policeman's wife were friends: they were always pleased to see each other, and expressed their pleasure in imperceptible details of their behaviour: the serious way they looked at each other, ignoring the other women's curiosity, the cookery recipes they exchanged, and the little attentions they bestowed on each other when the Frenchwoman rose to make her departure, pink-cheeked and looking years younger. They stood facing each other, the ample form of the Burgundian confronting the spare and wiry figure of the Arabo-Berber woman ... Eventually the Frenchwoman would clumsily hold out her hand; the other would reach up on tiptoe in her loose *saroual* and, with a hop and a skip that set the frills of her blouse a-flap and the fringes of her head-dress a-dancing, ignoring the outstretched hand, would rapidly plant a kiss on each of her friend's shoulders. And every time the latter would blush with surprise, then trumpet to the assembled women, '*Au revoir, sisters!*'

As soon as the remaining visitors heard the outer door slam, they started without fail to comment on the way the two friends took leave of each other: the one with outstretched hand; the other who insisted on embracing like two peasants exchanging kisses at the market!

This subject would provide food for discussion for hours on end, while the object of their criticism went once more about her housewifely duties. She might, at a pinch, pause to mutter coldly, 'She's my friend! She's French but she's my friend!'

One relative shrieked with laughter: 'She's been your friend for years and you still can't manage to shake her hand and say *"Au revoir, Madame!"* like they do. Now, if it was a man, I couldn't do it, but in front of a woman, like myself! What would be the harm? After all, we can do things in the French way! Naturally not going out without a veil, God help us! or wearing short skirts and showing ourselves naked to all and sundry, but we can say *"Bonjour"* like them, and sit on a chair like them, why not? God created us too, didn't he? . . .'

We girls always looked forward to Janine's afternoon visits; Marie-Louise did not often come. Janine resembled her mother in build, though she was not as tall or as energetic. She had been to school with the eldest of the sisters. As soon as she arrived, the two of them shut themselves up in one of the bedrooms; their two voices could be heard in conversation, interspersed with endless bouts of giggling, a silence, then renewed confabulations. Janine could speak Arabic like a native without any accent. Before she left, she would drop by the kitchen to ask the girls' mother if there was anything she needed. The latter entrusted her with many errands: to buy needles, thread, haberdashery articles that the father wouldn't have been able to bring for her.

Throughout the week Janine was in and out of the Arab house; if it weren't for her Christian name she could have been taken for the fourth daughter of the family . . . But there was this one extraordinary difference: she was able to come and go as she liked – from bedrooms to courtyard, from courtyard to street – just like a boy! When the clatter of the knocker indicated that she had closed the heavy front door behind her, the eldest sister, her friend, paused a moment, her hand in the air. Then things resumed the normal ebb and flow of a day frozen in time in these domestic interiors, always interiors, naturally.

The youngest sister and I were fascinated by Marie-Louise. We only saw her occasionally; she must have had a job in the nearby town, or in the capital even, probably as a postal clerk or secretary in an office ... When she spent Sundays in the village, she came to visit us with Janine.

We thought her as beautiful as a model. She was dark, slim, with delicate features; she must have been quite small as I recall her perched on extremely high heels. She wore her hair in a very sophisticated arrangement of elaborate knots and twists, with a variety of combs conspicuously displayed among her dark curls and ringlets. We marvelled at her make-up: pink blush on her cheeks and crimson lipstick enhancing the cupid's bow of her lips.

With her city-dweller's style and coquettish air, we felt she had to be treated like a tourist when she deigned to accompany her mother or sister on their visits to us. She sat down on a chair; she crossed her legs in spite of her short skirt. The circle of women began quite openly to examine every last detail of her attire, and comment on everything in an undertone.

Marie-Louise let them stare. Aware of the curiosity she provoked, she waited, pretending not to understand.

'I've forgotten all my Arabic!' she would sigh casually. 'And *I* haven't got a gift for languages like you, Janine!'

This last concession in an offhand tone: to let it be understood that of course she didn't despise the Arabic language, but after all ... And we were left in doubt, behind the distance insidiously created, whether Marie-Louise was the exception, or Janine. Moreover, when their mother accompanied them, she threw such a protective sheath of awe and pride around Marie-Louise that the women present fell silent ... So, on these visits, Marie-Louise enjoyed the pleasure of acting as a foreigner.

Was it two or three years previously that Marie-Louise acquired a fiancé, an officer from the 'metropolis', as they said? It was about that time; I couldn't have been more than ten; the youngest sister, my friend, was still at primary school. She had not yet been cloistered; that summer, we walked through the village streets on various errands: carrying the tray of pastries to be baked in the baker's oven, taking some message or other to the policeman's wife ...

I still have in the forefront of my mind these to-ings and fro-ings through the narrow alleys lined with tall chestnut trees. Between the village and the distant vine-clad hills lay a eucalyptus wood; sometimes we ventured beyond the policeman's house, scampering as far as the first gum trees, and throwing ourselves down·on the carpet of leaves, savouring their acrid smell. Our daring made our hearts pound.

These escapades, in which we egged each other on, left a bitter taste; then we slowly made our way back to the policeman's house, where we remained standing in the yard, outside the open kitchen window.

'My mother wants to know if she should keep you some of the goat's milk, to put to set?' the little girl panted. 'I've come for the milk-can.'

'And I've got a message for Janine from my sister,' she added a moment later. 'Will she buy her a pair of number 1 knitting needles? My father brought some back but they're too big. We girls can't go to the drapery shop as it's right in front of the Moorish café!'

'These men!' the Burgundian woman cackled as she went on with her washing, up to her elbows in soapsuds. 'They're all the same! . . . Mine can't manage to bring home a needle!'

'My father's very good at doing the marketing!' the little girl retorted. 'He always buys the finest fruit, the best meat! My mother won't admit it openly, but we know this quite well.'

'Tell your sister not to worry. I'll let Janine know. And here's the can for the milk . . .'

While they talked I looked through the window at the passage from which other rooms opened out. In the dim light I could just make out the polished wooden furniture; my eyes were glued to the hams and sausages strung up at the back of the kitchen; the red-checked dishcloths hung there seemed as if they were simply meant for show; I stared at the picture of the Virgin above the door . . . The policeman and his family suddenly seemed like transient ghosts in this locality, whereas these images, these objects became the true inhabitants of the place! For me, these French homes gave off a different smell, a mysterious light; for me, the French are still 'The Others', and I am still hypnotized by their shores.

Throughout my childhood, just before the war which was to bring us independence, I never crossed a single French threshold, I never entered the home of a single French schoolfellow . . .

Suddenly, it's the summer of 1962: before you could say 'Jack Robinson', all the furniture that had remained hidden in the dark recesses of houses that were at once open and inaccessible –

old-fashioned bedroom suites, rococo mirrors, heterogeneous knick-knacks – all the odds and ends that furbish a home – everything spilled out on to the pavements . . . Threadbare trophies, tainted spoils of conquest, that I saw put up for auction, or piled up in the windows of the second-hand dealers, who for their part wore the proud air of Turkish pirates of yore, boasting of their booty . . . 'These are the cast-offs of a nomad people,' I thought to myself, 'the entrails drying in the sun of a society whose turn it is now to be dispossessed!'

But meanwhile I'm a little girl still standing there, leaning on the window-sill of the policeman's house. Their dining-room at the end of the passage could only be glimpsed by the light from the kitchen. For me, as for my little friend, 'our' house was unquestionably the finest, with its profusion of carpets, with its shot-silk cushions. The women of our household came from the nearby town which was celebrated for its embroidery; at a very early age they learned this art which was already fashionable at the time of the Turks. And from what remote corner of the French countryside did the Burgundian come? That was a constant theme of the afternoon conversations in the little courtyard, to which the visit of Janine and her mother had added a new life.

'French women don't all come from Paris,' asserted the busybodies. 'Most of the ones who come here, thinking they'll have such a good life in the colonies, only know how to milk a cow when they arrive! If they get more civilized later on, it's because this country offers them power and wealth. Because the laws are on their side, on the side of their menfolk!'

'You've only got to look at Janine and the way she dresses, poor girl! Just like her mother: a heart of gold, but she's never learned how to sew or embroider!'

'And Marie-Louise?'

'Marie-Louise is the exception! She possesses the innate good taste of the Parisian, combined with the refinement, the temperament of our brunettes! . . . You've noticed how jet-black her hair is, and her ivory complexion! If she were dressed up like one of our local brides, a sultan would take a fancy to her!'

One of the speakers shrieked with laughter: 'Perhaps some Arab chief, some Sheikh of the high plateaux, got the policeman's wife in the family way, when the policeman was posted in the South! . . . Any man of noble birth would have made a pass at a young, vigorous Frenchwoman, such as she must

24

have been then. Perhaps with them that's not a sin, after all!'

The eldest sister protested; she accused the relative of scandal-mongering, or of ignorance at the least. She was very fond of Janine, and she could assure them that the morals of the policeman's family were as pure as any Arabs'.

Theories went backwards and forwards, as the conversation followed its tortuous paths, always coming back to the first hypothesis: namely that, in spite of all appearances, our 'clan' though temporarily down in the world, was more refined than the foreigners with their liberated women. For they were free, and even if we did not envy them, at least we spoke of them as if they were a strange tribe, with exotic customs, with whom we had rarely come in contact until then.

Back to the youngest sister and me – once more leaning on this same window-sill of this French house – on another sunny day.

This time we are struck dumb by what we see. The mother is standing at her tub finishing her washing; the father, a short stout man, is sitting there in his shirt-sleeves (when he is out of doors his uniform disguises his rustic origins), a local newspaper open in his hand; he slowly puffs at his pipe with an expression of bland good nature. Marie-Louise is standing right in front of us, in a passage leading off the sunny kitchen, a little bit to the side; she is pressed close to a ruddy-complexioned young man with a fair moustache. This is the fiancé, the officer that everyone is talking about!

We could scarcely believe our eyes. The sight of a couple to all intents and purposes in each other's arms: Marie-Louise half-leaning on the young man who was standing stiffly upright . . . Their muffled laughter, their whispered exchanges, indicated to us an indecent intimacy. And all this time the mother carried on talking calmly to us, glancing from time to time at the couple; the father, on the other hand, had buried his nose in his newspaper.

I can remember Marie-Louise's flirtatious behaviour, as well as two of the expressions she used: sometimes 'my pet', sometimes 'darling'. I must have stared open-mouthed with stupefaction. Then she began to sway rhythmically backwards and forwards so that she brushed against the young man's chest, repeating this manoeuvre two or three times . . . accompanied by little teasing cries of 'darling' over and over again! Eventually she nearly overbalanced and put her arms round her fiancé, tightly encased in his uniform. He seemed to remain quite calm; he whispered something to her almost inaudible; he must have been asking her not to be so noisy in front of witnesses: the father who didn't raise his head, the two little girls standing flabbergasted at the window . .

An hour later, we acted out the scene in our little courtyard, for the women sipping coffee round the low table.

'And the father didn't even look up?'

'No! Marie-Louise whispered sweet nothings to the officer, she put her arms round him, then she even stood up on tiptoe.'

'You saw them kissing?' asked the second sister in amazement, not pausing in her sewing.

'Yes, indeed! . . . They both pursed their lips and kissed like birds!'

We couldn't get over the fact that the policeman, who inspired such awe in the alleyways of the village, didn't dare take his nose out of his newspaper. He must have been blushing with embarrassment; so we surmised; so went our remarks.

'Well, really! These French people!' sighed the second sister who was finishing embroidering the sheets for her trousseau.

'Marie-Louise goes a bit too far!' remarked the eldest girl, who felt it her duty to defend her friend's sister.

Then Marie-Louise came to visit us before leaving again. She had promised to bring her fiancé. This put the girls in a predicament; they were afraid of their father's reaction: for him, the presence of a man, even a Frenchman, even Marie-Louise's fiancé, would have been completely out of place . . .

Did they manage to explain to Marie-Louise, or to Janine at any rate? I can't remember the young officer actually coming to the house in fact, even for a few minutes; they must have asked him to walk slowly past the front door, so that the cloistered friends could catch a glimpse of him through the cracks in the shutters and congratulate Marie-Louise on her imposing fiancé . . .

I have a clearer memory of one of the young lady's last visits. She was standing near the margin of the well, under the vine; her hair was wound round her head to form a cone, with one soft black curl in the nape of her neck. I cannot get the image out of my mind of her delicate features, her eyes and cheeks made up, radiating happiness and her beauty enhanced by her pride in being betrothed. She simpered and tittered as she talked of her suitor, his family in France, their marriage which was to take place in a few years' time . . . Every time she pronounced the words 'darling Pilou', one or other of the onlookers, seated on the rush mat, would smile indulgently. 'Darling Pilou', Marie-Louise repeated, every time she referred to her young officer. We little girls could hardly contain our giggles and had to escape to the orchard to make fun of her. 'Pilou' was her nickname for Paul and in our minds the 'darling' that she added was a word that should be reserved for the bedchamber and secrets between married couples.

'Darling Pilou'; I have only to repeat these words to relive the whole scene: the conceited French girl with her audience of women squatting on the ground, and we excited little girls who, the following year, would be confined to the house and its orchard and who were already so strait-laced. . .

'Darling Pilou'; words followed by bursts of sarcastic laughter; what can I say of the damage done to me in the course of time by this expression? I seemed to feel, as soon as I heard it – all too soon – that a love affair, that love itself ought not to give rise to meretricious words, ostentatious demonstrations of affection, so making a spectacle of oneself and arousing envy in frustrated women . . . I decided that love must necessarily reside elsewhere and not in public words and gestures.

An innocuous scene from my childhood: but later, when I reach the time for romance, I can find no words, I cannot express my emotions. Despite the turmoil of my adolescent dreams, this 'darling Pilou' left me with one deep-rooted complex: the French language could offer me all its inexhaustible treasures, but not a single one of its terms of endearment would be destined for my use . . . One day, because all my spontaneous impulses as a woman would be stifled by this autistic state, one day the pressure would suddenly give and a reaction would set in.

III

Fort Emperor explodes on 4 July 1830, at ten in the morning. The fearsome blast fills all the inhabitants of Algiers with terror; the French army, disposed in echelon from Sidi-Ferruch as far as the citadels of the capital, rejoices. Three chroniclers now recount the events leading to the fall of the city: the third is neither a naval officer-nor an ADC on duty in the heart of the battle; he is no more or less than a man of letters, accompanying the expedition by way of secretary to the GOC. For him it is tantamount to a visit to a theatrical performance: it is true that in Paris he runs the Porte-Saint-Martin Theatre, of which his wife is the star – the celebrated actress Marie Dorval, with whom the poet Alfred de Vigny is in love.

His name is J.T. Merle; he too will publish an account of the capture of Algiers, but as a witness located in the rear of the action. He does not claim to be a 'war correspondent'; he likes to be backstage, where he feels at home. Every day he reports on his position and makes a note of everything he sees (the wounded in the field hospital, his first palm tree, an agave in flower, for want of observations of the enemy doing battle . . .) He is not tormented by any scruples that he might be shirking his duties. He observes, he notes, he makes discoveries; if he manifests impatience, it is not with the military news, but because he is waiting for a printing press, which he had asked to be purchased before leaving Toulon. When will the equipment be landed, when will he be able to compose, publish, distribute the first French newspaper on Algerian soil?

So, 'Fort Napoleon' blows up: the French soldiers who only recognize one Emperor – their own – give this name to 'Fort Emperor', also known as 'The Spanish Fort', or more exactly, *'Borj Hassan'*. This is one of the most important Turkish fortifications which date from the sixteenth century, and the key to the defence of the country to the rear of Algiers. From Sidi-Ferruch, where he has been stationed since landing, J.T. Merle notes:

'At ten in the morning of the 4th, we heard a mighty explosion, following upon ceaseless shelling since daybreak . . . At the same instant, the horizon was covered in dense black smoke, which rose to a prodigious height; the wind blowing from the East carried the smell of gunpowder, dust and scorched wool, which left us in no doubt that Fort Emperor had been blown up, either by a mine or from its powder magazines catching fire.

'There was general rejoicing, as, from this moment, we considered the campaign to be over.'

Exactly twenty-four hours later, the French army enters the city.

The battle of Staouéli, on 19 June, marked the defeat of the Aga Ibrahim and the failure of his strategy. It was the first time that the new 'Congreve' rockets were used: the French had exploded them without being really sure how accurate their aim was; their noise and unusual nature had caused panic in the Algerian camp which was already in a state of confusion . . .

The next day, however, De Bourmont maintains his position for want of logistical support. He has neither the necessary siege artillery nor pack-horses. Duperré, the naval commander, had loaded these on to the last vessel of the convoy which is still anchored off Palma. So the French army does not advance. Some of the troops grow impatient; others accuse the general staff; De Bourmont is waiting for Duperré who, for his part, has been waiting for a favourable wind ever since 22 or 23 June.

In the extended fortified camp on the Staouéli plateau, the rabble of soldiery is a prey to post-victory euphoria and indulges in unrestrained looting.

The Algerian troops have fallen back, some of them as far as the banks of El-Harrach. They challenge the leadership of the Dey Hussein's son-in-law, the generalissimo. On 24 June, fifteen thousand combatants regroup and attack a French detachment which has ventured a little too far from base; one of De Bourmont's sons, Amédée, is among those seriously wounded in this affray; he dies soon afterwards.

During the following days the Algerians intensify their harassment of the French, who realize that the enemy have a new leader: the Arab attacks are now shrewdly and systematically organized. This new leader is Mustapha Boumezrad, the Bey of Titteri; his ability assures him the unanimous support of the janizaries as well as the auxiliary forces.

According to Baron Barchou, the daily toll of French casualties from 24 to 28 June is two hundred and fifty or more. Some wonder whether the victory at Staouéli was not an illusion. Finally, after these sudden reversals, De Bourmont has the powerful artillery at his disposal; he gives the order to advance.

On 28 June, the action is nearly as fierce as at Staouéli. The Algerian offensive proves more and more effectual: a battalion of the 4th Light Horse is well nigh wiped out in a series of murderous encounters. The next day the fighting is renewed just as fiercely; the French succeed in breaking through the barrage. On 30 June, despite a mistake in direction and disagreement among his subordinate officers, after a difficult march, De Bourmont takes up his position facing Fort Emperor. Three days are needed to dig trenches and set out the huge batteries, while constantly having to disperse the Algerian attacks. Duperré twice bombards Algiers from the sea; with little result, it must be admitted. Changarnier, at that time only a company commander, notes, for his future Memoirs:

'Noisy, ridiculous shelling from the fleet which is out of range, so expending an enormous quantity of ammunition to inflict six francs' worth of damage on the city's fortifications.'

At three o'clock on the morning of 4 July, the last act begins. At Borj Hassan, an elite garrison of two thousand men – eight hundred Turks and one thousand two hundred *Kuluglis* – holds out for five hours against the fire from the French batteries. De Bourmont and his general staff survey the pounding from their position to the right of the trenches. The Dey Hussein and his dignitaries watch the deadly contest from the roof of the Spanish Consulate on the heights of the Kasbah. 'The militia, the Arabs inside the city, those who find themselves outside, all pay careful heed to the progress of the battle,' notes Baron Barchou, who has taken up his position on the slopes of Bouzaréah.

In full view of 'this enormous amphitheatre, filled with thousands of spectators,' two hours elapse, during which the Algerian guns are silenced one by one. The survivors among the militia, no longer able to resist, retreat towards the city.

A terrible explosion shakes Fort Emperor; soon afterwards it collapses in a gigantic eruption of flames and smoke. The final hope of defending the city disappears in this heap of rubble, shattered half-buried cannons and dismembered corpses – those of the last defenders. Algiers, known as the 'well-protected city', is reduced to despair.

Three noisy, ineffectual bursts of gunfire, like a final death-rattle, punctuated the Algerian retreat. They did not even touch the anticipated mass of the attackers. At Staouéli, just before the Agas and Beys evacuated their camp, a powder magazine blew up. On 25 June a small mine exploded in Sidi Khalf, in front of a brigade which halted just in time; the detonation was heard on the vessels anchored offshore; however there were very few casualties. Finally, on 4 July, this, the mightiest of forts collapses; although Fort Bab Azoun and the 'Fort des Anglais' continue to hold out, the ritual of their hopeless action reaches its climax in these final convulsions.

Was it necessary for the Turks to prove the technical inferiority of their strategy, which was so easy to discern – its navy in decline, its artillery obsolescent? Be that as it may, the unpredictability of the first commander-in-chief, the Bey's negligence or his disastrous isolation, all combined to dissipate the energy which should have been concentrated.

The Bedouin chiefs, the quasi-autonomous Beys, are stationed outside the city with the turbulent auxiliary troops. Towards the end, they await with growing concern the fall of the City – until then, anchored in its century-old irredentism.

The word which could have united these scattered forces is not heard. This word will be spoken two hundred years later, more to the West, above the Plains of Eghris, by a young man of twenty-five, with green eyes and a mystic's brow: his name, Abd al-Qadir. For the moment, the power is doubly under siege: from the invaders who trample through the ruins of Fort Emperor, but also from the over-proud vassals who watch the increasing irresolution of the Turk.

It is now ten of the clock on the morning of 4 July. Borj Hassan explodes; its destruction does not destroy the enemy. Two hours later, an emissary of the Dey Hussein slips into the invaders' camp to present the preliminary plans for the surrender.

J.T. Merle, our theatre manager who is never in the theatre of operations, conveys to us the amazement, the excitement and the pity that he has felt from the day he landed (the only time he has been in the front line) until the end of hostilities, on this 4 July.

Pity at the sight of the huddled masses of wounded who fill the field hospital; excitement over the great variety of vegetation, sometimes so exotic, sometimes so similar to French woodland. Merle's amazement is aroused by the enemy's invisibility. Up till the battle of Staouéli in fact, when the Arabs have already killed and mutilated so many imprudent or luckless soldiers, not one of theirs has been captured, dead or alive. He describes in detail, with unfeigned admiration, the manner in which every Arab skilfully handles a wooden device, to convey a wounded friend, or drag the bodies of every one of their dead through the densest undergrowth. In this, these 'decapitating savages' show a secret superiority: they mutilate the bodies of the enemy, to be sure, but they will never let one of their own be taken dead or alive . . . The land, into which the French army is gradually eating its way, is seemingly not the only thing at stake.

For this reason Merle is inspired to heights of eloquence when he portrays for us three wounded men picked up on the battlefield after Staouéli: a Turk, a Moor and a young man who was probably a Kabyle. Merle describes at length their faces, their bearing, their resignation or their courage. He devotes his whole attention to them, visits them in hospital, offers them pieces of sugar – like wounded animals at the zoo. Then, a new anecdote: the youngest of the wounded men receives a visit from an old man, his father. We are now in the midst of a real drama, like the ones that Merle is accustomed to producing on the Paris stage: 'Arab father and son, the object of French solicitude'; 'father disturbed by French humanity'; 'Arab father bitterly opposes his son's amputation which the French doctors advise'; 'Muslim fanaticism causes the son's death, despite French medical science'. This is the final tableau in the drama which Merle has thus constructed before our eyes.

Before this scene in the hospital, J.T. Merle, like Matterer and Baron Barchou, describes the unexpected arrival of an elderly native. The man has come to the French camp of his own initiative, if we are to believe him; some presume that he is a spy; others suggest that he is there out of curiosity or as the isolated bearer of a flag of truce.

In any case, Merle reports for us the curiosity aroused by the first

Arab seen at close quarters. De Bourmont, who had set up his cot on the site of Saint Sidi Fredj's catafalque, wishes to receive this unforeseen visitor, but not in this place where the Muslim sepulchre might seem to be profaned. He takes coffee with the old man a little distance away but gains no useful information. He decides to make him carry a document drawn up in Arabic, declaring his peaceful intentions.

As soon as he walks away from the French camp he is killed by his own countrymen, precisely on account of these papers which cause him to be taken for a spy working for the invaders. So, the first written words, even while promising a fallacious peace, condemn their bearer to death. Any document written by 'The Other' proves fatal, since it is a sign of compromise. 'These proclamations were not even read,' states Merle, who alleges that religious 'fanaticism' is the cause of an unnecessary death.

The Frenchman relates the other significant event: at the hospital a wounded man has not been amputated because his father withholds his permission! But our author does not tell what we are given to understand from other sources: namely that the host of military interpreters, brought along by the French army from the Middle East, prove incapable of translating these first exchanges – could the local Arab dialect be so unintelligible?

Outside of the battlefield, speech is at a standstill and a wilderness of ambiguity sets in.

J.T. Merle starts up his printing press, which he has triumphantly landed on 25 June; he writes:

'Gutenberg's infernal machine, this formidable arm of civilization, was set up on African soil in a few hours. Universal cries of "Long live France! Long live the King!" greeted the accounts of our landing and first victories, as soon as they were distributed.'

Whatever occasional writers may succeed him, J.T. Merle was the first to print his stories in this way between one battle and the next, fresh from the shock of this preliminary action. What he sets down in black and white seems to anticipate the victory by a split second . . .

However, this publicist – nowadays he would be called 'a front-line reporter' – is only interested in describing his own ridiculous rôle. He lags permanently behind any decisive battle; he never witnesses any actual events. He is like the marine artist Gudin who was arrested the day after the battle of Staouéli by a zealous officer who mistook him for a looter, because he had dressed up for a joke in clothing abandoned in an Arab tent.

When the professional scribe ventures inopportunely into terrain where death is lurking, he suddenly realizes the limitations of his fate: he is not destined to be either a warrior launched into the turmoil of battle, nor the vulture pouncing on the remaining booty . . . The war correspondent or war artist wanders in a twilight zone, a prey to a malaise which separates him from the greatest suffering, and which does not prevent him trembling with abject fear . . .

And J.T. Merle trembles, all the way from the Sidi-Ferruch to Algiers, although he travels this road two full days after the surrender of the city! For him, death lurks in every smallest thicket; it might spring out at him without the benefit of a stage setting, without the threat of a sudden impalement.

My Father Writes to My Mother

Whenever my mother spoke of my father, she, in common with all the women in her town, simply used the personal pronoun in Arabic corresponding to 'him'. Thus, every time she used a verb in the third person singular which didn't have a noun subject, she was naturally referring to her husband. This form of speech was characteristic of every married woman, from fifteen to sixty, with the proviso that in later years, if the husband had undertaken the pilgrimage to Mecca, he could be given the title of 'Hajj'.

Everybody, children and adults, especially girls and women, since all important conversations took place among the womenfolk, learnt very quickly to adapt to this rule whereby a husband and wife must never be referred to by name.

After she had been married for a few years, my mother gradually learnt a little French. She was able to exchange a few halting words with the wives of my father's colleagues who had, for the most part, come from France and, like us, lived with their families in the little block of flats set aside for the village teachers.

I don't know exactly when my mother began to say, '*My husband* has come, *my husband* has gone out . . . I'll ask *my husband*,' etc. Although my mother did make rapid progress in the language, in spite of taking it up fairly late in life, I can still hear the evident awkwardness in her voice betrayed by her laboured phraseology, her slow and deliberate enunciation at that time. Nevertheless, I can sense how much it cost her modesty to refer to my father directly in this way.

It was as if a flood-gate had opened within her, perhaps in her relationship with her husband. Years later, during the summers we spent in her native town, when chatting in Arabic with her sisters or cousins, my mother would refer to him quite naturally by his first name, even with a touch of superiority. What a daring innovation! Yes,

35

quite unhesitatingly – I was going to say, unequivocally – in any case, without any of the usual euphemisms and verbal circumlocutions. When her aunts and elderly female relations were present, she would once more use the traditional formalities, out of respect for them; such freedom of language would have appeared insolent and incongruous to the ears of the pious old ladies.

Years went by. As my mother's ability to speak French improved, while I was still a child of no more than twelve, I came to realize an irrefutable fact: namely that, in the face of all these womenfolk, my parents formed a couple. One thing was an even greater source of pride in me: when my mother referred to any of the day-to-day incidents of our village life – which in our city relatives' eyes was very backward – the tall figure of my father – my childhood hero, seemed to pop up in the midst of all these women engaged in idle chit-chat on the age-old patios to which they were confined.

My father, no-one except my father; none of the other women ever saw fit to refer to their menfolk, their masters who spent the day outside the house and returned home in the evening, taciturn, with eyes on the ground. These nameless uncles, cousins, relatives by marriage, were for us an unidentifiable collection of individuals to all of whom their spouses alluded impartially in the masculine gender.

With the exception of my father . . . My mother, with lowered eyes, would calmly pronounce his name 'Tahar' – which, I learned very early, meant 'The Pure', and even when a suspicion of a smile flickered across the other women's faces or they looked half ill at ease, half indulgent, I thought that a rare distinction lit up my mother's face.

These harem conversations ran their imperceptible course: my ears only caught those phrases which singled my mother out above the rest. Because she always made a point of bringing my father's name into these exchanges, he became for me still purer than his given name betokened.

One day something occurred which was a portent that their relationship would never be the same again – a commonplace enough event in any other society, but which was unusual to say the least with us: in the course of an exceptionally long journey away from home (to a neighbouring province, I think), my father wrote to my mother – yes, to my mother!

He sent her a postcard, with a short greeting written diagonally across it in his large, legible handwriting, something like 'Best wishes from this distant region' or possibly, 'I am having a good journey and getting to know an unfamiliar region' etc. and he signed it simply with his first name. I am sure that, at the time, he himself would not have dared add any more intimate formula above his signature, such as 'I am thinking of you', or even less, 'Yours affectionately'. But, on the half of the card reserved for the address of the recipient, he had written 'Madame' followed by his own surname, with the possible addition – but here I'm not sure – of 'and children', that is to say we three, of whom I, then about ten years old, was the eldest . . .

The radical change in customs was apparent for all to see: my father had quite brazenly written his wife's name, in his own handwriting, on a postcard which was going to travel from one town to another, which was going to be exposed to so many masculine eyes, including eventually our village postman – a Muslim postman to boot – and, what is more, he had dared to refer to her in the Western manner as 'Madame So-and-So . . .', whereas, no local man, poor or rich, ever referred to his wife and children in any other way than by the vague periphrasis: 'the household'.

So, my father had 'written' to my mother. When she visited her family she mentioned this postcard, in the simplest possible words and tone of voice, to be sure. She was about to describe her husband's four or five days' absence from the village, explaining the practical problems this had posed: my father having to order the provisions just before he left, so that the shopkeepers could deliver them every morning; she was going to explain how hard it was for a city woman to be isolated in a village with very young children and cut off in this way . . . But the other women had interrupted, exclaiming, in the face of this new reality, this almost incredible detail:

'He wrote to you, *to you?*'

'He wrote his wife's name and the postman must have read it? Shame! . . .'

'He could at least have addressed the card to his son, for the principle of the thing, even if his son is only seven or eight!'

My mother did not reply. She was probably pleased, flattered even, but she said nothing. Perhaps she was suddenly ill at ease, or blushing from embarrassment; yes, her husband had written to her, in person! . . . The eldest child, the only one who might have been able to read the card, was her daughter: so, daughter or wife, where was the difference as far as the addressee was concerned?

'I must remind you that I've learned to read French now!'

This postcard was, in fact, a most daring manifestation of affection. Her modesty suffered at that very moment that she spoke of it. Yet, it came second to her pride as a wife, which was secretly flattered.

The murmured exchanges of these segregated women struck a faint chord with me, as a little girl with observing eyes. And so, for the first time, I seem to have some intuition of the possible happiness, the mystery in the union of a man and a woman.

My father had dared 'to write' to my mother. Both of them referred to each other by name, which was tantamount to declaring openly their love for each other, my father by writing to her, my mother by quoting my father henceforward without false shame in all her conversations.

IV

The City, not so much 'captured' as declared an 'Open City'. The Capital is sold: the price – its legendary treasure. The gold of Algiers, shipped by the crateful to France, where a new king inaugurates his reign by accepting the Republican flag and acquiring the Barbary ingots.

Algiers, stripped of its past and its pride, Algiers, named after the foremost of its two islands – 'El-Djezaïr'. Barbarossa had freed these islands from the grip of Spain and made them a hideout for the corsairs who had scoured the Mediterranean for three centuries or more . . .

An Open City, its ramparts destroyed, its battlements and earthworks demolished; its ignominy casts a shadow over the immediate future.

A fourth man chronicles the defeat, adding his spadeful of words to help fill the paupers' grave of oblivion. I choose him from among the natives of the city: Hajj Ahmed Effendi, the Hanefite Mufti of Algiers, is the most eminent spiritual personality after the Dey. As the fall of the city becomes imminent, many of the inhabitants of Algiers turn to him. More than twenty years later, he reports the siege for us in the Turkish language, writing his reminiscences of the events of 4 July from his exile in foreign parts, after the Ottoman Sultan had appointed him Governor of a city in Anatolia.

'The explosion shook the city and filled all the inhabitants with terror. Then Hussein Pasha summoned a council of the city elders. There was an outcry from the entire population . . .'

Then he briefly mentions the mediators who conducted the first parleys, and whom the French chroniclers, for their part, describe at great length.

39

The French have installed their batteries in the ruins of Fort Emperor, to bombard the Kasbah, the fortress, the seat of power, and the discussions open to the sound of shelling from both sides. There is a pause in this harassing fire when a Turk, 'whose costume, combining elegance and simplicity, announced a person of distinction', arrives by a secret path, carrying a white flag. He is in fact the Dey's secretary. He hopes to prevent the French from entering the city by proposing to pay tribute-money on behalf of the army who are probably prepared to disavow their Pasha. As he does not offer capitulation, there is no point in further talks.

The digging of trenches continues; the French and Algerian batteries, the latter set up on Fort Bab Azoun, continue to exchange fire, rending the air with their noisy duel. Two Moors, Hamdane and Bouderba, now turn up, but still without any official status. After a preamble, the discussions begin: Hamdane has travelled in Europe and speaks French fluently. During a pause in the firing they leave, with the realization that the foreign penetration can no longer be avoided, except at the price of desperate resistance.

But in his council chamber on the Kasbah, Hussein is more confident than the army chiefs – the three Beys outside the city are not even consulted when the final decision is taken – and for one moment seems determined to fight to the death . . . Eventually it is decided that two official emissaries should be sent, together with the sole European diplomat remaining in Algiers since the landing – the British Consul, accompanied by his deputy.

This delegation is received by the complete French general staff, 'in a little shady meadow'; they take their seats on three or four tree trunks that have been freshly felled. According to Barchou, who is present at the negotiations, the Englishman, in his quality as mediator and friend of the Dey, speaks 'of Hussein's haughty, fearless character, which can drive him to extremes'.

So the interchange begins: De Bourmont dictates the precise terms of the capitulation demanded by the French: their troops must have access to the city 'unconditionally', including the Kasbah and all strongholds; the Dey and the janizaries must leave the country, but their personal possessions will be guaranteed; the inhabitants will be permitted to practise their religion and all property and womenfolk will be respected.

'The terms of this agreement were dictated by the GOC to General

Desprez and Deumier, the senior administrative officer of the Quartermaster General's staff. It was decreed that the Dey should put his seal to the accord as a sign of his approval and that the exchange of documents should take place in the course of the evening,' so another ADC, E. d'Ault-Dumesnil, reports two years later.

It is approximately two o'clock on this Sunday afternoon in summer. In the west of the city the first groups of refugees are already leaving Algiers, making for Bab el-Oued.

So the dialogue is opened with the two Moors, Bouderba and Hamdane: after some verbal exchanges, the text drafted during the conference to arrange the abdication is now finalized. But the words prove an obstacle, I mean the French words.

An hour later, Dey Hussein sends back the document: he does not understand what underlies the expression 'to surrender unconditionally' used by the aristocratic De Bourmont and recorded in the draft made by his ADC.

It is suggested that an interpreter go to explain the text to the Dey, and thereby vouch for the integrity of the French. An old man by name of Brasewitz is designated – the identical person whom Bonaparte had sent to Murad Bey in Egypt. Thus Brasewitz was the first to enter the city.

We have both his written account (a letter to the minister Polignac) and a verbal report (as told to J.T. Merle a few days later) of his experiences during this hazardous expedition. On the afternoon of this fourth day of July, he follows the Turkish secretary through the New Gate into the city: he is the object of threats all along his path from the inhabitants of Algiers who wish to continue the fight. And now they see the symbol of their forthcoming enslavement riding through the street before their eyes.

Finally he comes face to face with the Dey who is seated on his divan, surrounded by his dignitaries. Brasewitz turns his back on the assembled janizaries. As he translates each of the clauses aloud, there is mounting anger behind him. The young officers oppose any terms of surrender, preferring certain death. 'Death! Death!' they shout . . . More than once the interpreter believes himself in danger. Having explained the details of the accord (which must be signed before ten the following morning), he drinks the lemonade which the Dey has first tasted, observant to the last of the rules of etiquette, even on the eve of his humiliation. Brasewitz then departs, unharmed.

But J.T. Merle, who meets the interpreter on 7 or 8 July, adds that he contracts a nervous illness from the risks he has run and because of his advanced age, and dies a few days later. As if the explanation of this arbitrary expression 'surrender unconditionally', which the French general had used unthinkingly, was destined to claim at least one victim: the bearer himself of the communication!

It seemed that Brasewitz had to pay with his own life for ensuring that this expression is correctly translated into the enemy's language (I am not sure whether this was the Turkish of the unseated Ottoman rule or the Arabic of the Moorish city).

For the moment, he is on his way back at nightfall to the French stations, his mission accomplished. The Dey signs his letter of abdication the next morning.

Algiers prepares to live through her last night as a free city.

Others will tell of these last moments: a *bach-kateb*, general secretary to the Bey Ahmed of Constantine (who continues for another twenty years or so to regroup the insurgents in the East) writes his account in Arabic. A German prisoner, who is freed the next day, describes this same night in his own language; two prisoners, who had escaped from drowning when their ships were wrecked a few months before, give a report of it in French. To these, we must add the British Consul who makes a note in his diary of this turning-point in history . . . I, for my part, am thinking of those who sleep through this night in the city . . . Who will sing in days to come of the death throes of their liberty? What poet, in whose breast hope springs eternal, will see the promised port after drifting in stormy seas? . . .

Many decades later, the Mufti Hajj Ahmed Effendi describes his fellow citizens' revolt with great wealth of words:

'For myself, not being able to bring myself to a final decision, I assembled the pious Muslims . . . I made them pledge to follow me against the enemy. And so, in point of fact, they did penance and after having said their last farewells to one and all, they set off behind me, chanting "Tekbir!" as they marched. At this same moment the women rushed out in our path, hurling their children at our feet, and crying, "It will be well if you are victorious, but if you are not, know that the Infidels will come to dishonour us! Go then, but before you leave, put us to the sword!" '

42

If the scene is overburdened with lofty language, it does at least suggest the chaos of this transitional stage. Thousands of refugees clog the road to Constantine in the exodus. Others rush down to the shore by the light of the summer moon and fling themselves into the boats which take them to Cape-Matifou. Whole families, loaded with their bundles. I imagine there are more humble folk leaving than the well-to-do or merchants. Which worthies will remain, hoping to save their fortunes and their homes? Which citizens will prefer to pack up their last remaining effects, their few jewels, and lifting their children and womenfolk on to mules, hasten to catch up with the Bey of Constantine's army or that of the Bey of Titteri, returning to the Mitidja plain?

The city loses in one night nearly two thirds of its population. Two thousand five hundred of the soldiers who reject the abdication, considering it dishonourable, regroup around the Bey Ahmed, who is still bearing arms.

When the Mufti, Ahmed Effendi, receives an assurance from the Dey that the French have promised not to enter any mosques and to respect the lives of civilians, he is able to calm the people's agitation.

'The entire population,' he writes, 'men and women, thronged around the threshold of my house, with the heart-rending cry: "Since we must perish, it is better to perish before the door of an *alim*!" '

The victorious army prepares the scene for the following day's events: De Bourmont orchestrates the triumphal entry for 5 July – the artillery and the sappers will have the honour of heading the procession. He is anxious for the Sixth Regiment to precede him into the city with its drummers.

Certain appointments must be made to come into force simultaneously with the occupation of the Capital: the Chief of Police, the Head of the Navy, the men in charge of the finances . . . A place is designated to be occupied by each of the divisions commanded respectively by the three major-generals.

The French enter the city the next morning, two hours later than scheduled, but to the sound of the drums of the Sixth Regiment as arranged. Hussein waits in the Kasbah, concerned to preserve his dignity to the last, and only two hours after their arrival does he deign to receive Colonel Bartillat who is in command of the first contingent. Bartillat is also to publish his description of the scene. Through his eyes we see the first courtyard of the palace with its lemon tree, the same lemonade offered as a sign of hospitality. Then the Dey and his suite disappear, while a Turkish official stands stoically in the palace entrance, awaiting the arrival of the French general.

This Turk is the *khasnaji* – the Minister of Finance. It is he who was in charge of Fort Emperor's resistance the day before. He carries out the transfer of duties according to protocol, in the presence of De Bourmont and his staff: he accompanies the French to the Algerian State Treasury. This is the very heart of the spoils: an accumulation of gold sufficient to repay all the expenses of the gigantic expedition, and also help to enrich the French treasury and even line some individual purses.

Thirty-seven witnesses, possibly more, will relate the events of this month of July 1830, some fresh from their experiences, some shortly afterwards. Thirty-seven descriptions will be published, of which only three are from the viewpoint of the besieged: the account by the Mufti, the future Governor of Anatolia; that by Bey Ahmed's secretary who will stay on under colonial rule; the third being that of the German prisoner.

If we exclude the British Consul's diary from all this mass of literature (and he is the only one in a genuinely neutral position – however his diplomatic status delays the publication of his testimony), if we eliminate the account given by an Austrian prince who came as an observer to De Bourmont, there still remain thirty-two chronicles in French of this first act of the occupation drama.

The senior officers in particular are infected by a veritable scribblomania. They start to publish their memoirs the following year; the chief of general staff is the first, followed shortly afterwards by others. By 1835 or thereabouts, nineteen army officers, with four or five from the navy, have contributed to this literary output. After the 'principals', the 'extras' are infected by this same haste to rush into print: a priest serving as army chaplain, three doctors including one senior surgeon and one assistant medical officer! Even down to the artist Gudin (who composes his memoirs much later), not forgetting our publicist J.T. Merle, Alfred de Vigny's rival in love.

Such an itch to put pen to paper reminds me of the letter-writing mania which afflicted the cloistered girls of my childhood: sending those endless epistles out into the unknown brought them a breath of fresh air and a temporary escape from their confinement . . .

But what is the significance behind the urge of so many fighting men to relive in print this month of July 1830? Did their writings allow them to savour the seducer's triumph, the rapist's intoxication? These texts are distributed in the Paris of Louis-Philippe, far from Algerian soil, where the capitulation has fairly quickly legitimized all manner of expropriations: physical and symbolic usurpations! Their words thrown up by such a cataclysm are for me like a comet's tail, flashing across the sky and leaving it forever riven.

For this conquest is no longer seen as the discovery of a strange new world, not even as a new crusade by a West aspiring to relive its past as if it were an opera. The invasion has become an enterprise of rapine: after the army come the merchants and soon their employees are hard at work; their machinery for liquidation and execution is already in place.

And words themselves become a decoration, flaunted by officers like the carnations they wear in their buttonholes; words will become their most effective weapons. Hordes of interpreters, geographers, ethnographers, linguists, botanists, diverse scholars and professional scribblers will swoop down on this new prey. The supererogatory protuberances of their publications will form a pyramid to hide the initial violence from view.

The girls who were my friends and accomplices during my village holidays wrote in the same futile, cryptic language because they were confined, because they were prisoners; they mark their marasmus with their own identity in an attempt to rise above their pathetic plight. The accounts of this past invasion reveal *a contrario* an identical nature: invaders who imagine they are taking the Impregnable City, but who wander aimlessly in the undergrowth of their own disquiet.

Deletion

The conquest of the Unconquerable . . . Faint images flake off from the rock of Time. The flickering flames of successive fires form letters of French words, curiously elongated or expanded, against cave walls, tattooing vanished faces with a lurid mottling . . .

And for a fleeting moment I glimpse the mirror-image of the foreign inscription, reflected in Arabic letters, writ from right to left in the mirror of suffering; then the letters fade into pictures of the mountainous Hoggar in prehistoric times . . .

To read this writing, I must lean over backwards, plunge my face into the shadows, closely examine the vaulted roof of rock or chalk, lend an ear to the whispers that rise up from time out of mind, study this geology stained red with blood. What magma of sounds lies rotting there? What stench of putrefaction seeps out? I grope about, my sense of smell aroused, my ears alert, in this rising tide of ancient pain. Alone, stripped bare, unveiled, I face these images of darkness . . .

How are the sounds of the past to be met as they emerge from the well of bygone centuries? . . . What love must still be sought, what future be planned, despite the call of the dead? And my body reverberates with sounds from the endless landslide of generations of my lineage.

PART TWO

THE CRIES OF THE *FANTASIA*

I myself had to lead an expedition into the mountainous region of Béjaia, where the Berber tribes had been refusing to pay taxes for some years . . . After I had penetrated into their country and overcome their resistance, I took hostages to ensure their obedience . . .

Ibn Khaldun
Ta'rif – (Autobiography)

Captain Bosquet Leaves Oran
to Take Part in a *Razzia*

Oran, October 1840: the war against the Amir was resumed the previous year, since when the French garrison has remained on the defensive.

The fortified position between the two camps of Misserghin and Le Figuier is controlled for a distance of two to three leagues, covering an area containing a few gardens for the canteen-keepers and a couple of wretched taverns, just enough to support the outposts isolated in the midst of a deserted countryside and offer some distraction for the troops. To the east, near the seashore, stretches the farm belonging to the sole French settler, one Dandrieu who arrived during the truce of 1837. To the west, begins the territory of the Douaïr and Smela tribes who are allies of France – as they were of the previous Turkish rulers, for whom they served as police and tax-collectors.

The rest of the country forms a vast plain, overrun by factions recognizing the authority of Abd al-Qadir, who has just made one more appeal for a sacred union against the occupying army. The final phase of the war is beginning: it will last a further eight years.

From time to time closely escorted French convoys pass along the roads to Tlemcen, Mostaganem, Azru. No European would venture off the roads into the footpaths in the vicinity.

In the spring of that year Franco-Algerian hostilities had flared up again in the interior: the Atlas tribesmen had a firm grip on the region from Cherchel to Blida and Midia, which Field-Marshal Valée, accompanied by the royal princes, the Dukes of Orleans and Aumale, was doing his best to contain. These tribesmen had brought thousands of auxiliaries to supplement Abd al-Qadir's regular troops and those of his lieutenants. Valée thought he was simply organizing a route march; in fact he had to wage war again in the Chiffa gorges; then he returned to Algiers, continuing to send off an endless stream of despatches and pompously worded communiqués on the situation. The Mitidja plain was freed of insurgents but the unrest persisted.

On 20 August Lamoricière, a young general of only thirty-three, formerly in command of the Zouaves, is appointed to command Oran in the west. He chafes at the bit for two whole months: how is he to pass as quickly as possible from the defensive to the offensive? Has not Bou Hamedi, the Amir's lieutenant, just attacked the Douaïrs on their own territory? By so doing is he not preventing the French from replenishing their supplies?

Lamoricière, whom the Arabs call 'The-man-with-the-fez', makes full use of Daumas's intelligence service and Martimprey's maps and land surveys; for some weeks this information has been based on reconnoitres carried out by the spies of Mustapha ben Ismaël, the Chief of the Douaïrs.

There are indications that the Gharabas and Beni Ali tribes are on the move beyond Tlelat, a wadi that flows into the vast salt lake south of Oran. Their chiefs are known to be die-hard supporters of the Amir. Twelve leagues – some forty miles – separates the limit of their positions from the first French stations: the distance seems too great for a possible attack . . .

Nevertheless, Lamoricière is tempted: if he could succeed in seizing the wealthy enemies' flocks and possibly even their silos, it would improve the atmosphere in the garrison and lift the troops' morale. Moreover, such a victory would ensure a not inconsiderable benefit, the replenishment of supplies for the winter.

The young general frets and fumes impatiently but Oran is riddled with spies. The operation, the first foray to leave Oran since the resumption of hostilities, must be prepared in the utmost secrecy, but it seems difficult to deceive the enemy scouts. Nevertheless the attack is fixed for 20 October.

Two men will chronicle this expedition: Captain Bosquet, whom Lamoricière has sent for from Algiers to become his ADC, and Captain Montagnac, whom the defeat at Sidi Brahim, five years later, will transform into a martyr. The latter's regiment had recently sailed from Cherchel and landed at Oran on the 14th of this same month. The two officers, unbeknown to each other, correspond with their respective families, and thereby allow us to accompany them as eye-witnesses and actors in this operation. We relive the military advances of this autumn of 1840 in the letters received by the future Field-Marshal Bosquet's mother (he is to be a hero of the Crimean War twenty years later) and the epistles addressed to Montagnac's uncle or sister. The posthumous publication of these documents ensures the continuing reputation of their authors as they describe the ballet of the conquest of our territory.

What territory? That evoked by our seething memory? What ghosts rise up behind these officers, as they resume their correspondence every evening after they have removed their boots and tossed them into the barrack-room?

At noon on 21 October, the order is given to the infantry, Yusuf's Spahis and the cavalry of Mustapha ben Ismaël, the *Kulugli*, to assemble at the Figuier camp, on the road leading south-east. At six in the evening the general and his staff review the astonished officers and men: two thousand five hundred infantrymen, seven hundred cavalry, in addition to an equal number of native cavalrymen (three hundred Spahis and as many Douaïrs) as well as two companies of sappers and six howitzers.

Despite Mustapha ben Ismaël's scepticism, Lamoricière gives the order to set off: these troops, who have only recently landed and so are unfamiliar with the terrain, have to cover at least thirty miles by night to be able to take the enemy by surprise at dawn.

The convoy of mules moves off, laden with baggage and litters for bringing back the wounded. The infantry marches on either side of them. Over the last few months they have been issued with lighter equipment in preparation for the new tactics founded on rapid attack, like those of the natives.

The company makes good speed from the Tlelat wadi to the vantage point selected, a ravine just before the region of Makedra. The cavalry covers the men on the left, without overtaking the van of the silent column. Mustapha ben Ismaël's scouts regularly go ahead to verify that beacons are not being lit on the neighbouring hills to warn the Gharabas and Ouled Ali tribesmen. These scouts – bandits and, for the most part, horse-thieves – are known as *Sahab ez-Zerda* or 'booty-sharers' since they receive a large proportion of the booty in return for their information which is worth its weight in gold.

On arrival at the Makedra ravine, three 'booty-sharers' go ahead. An hour later they have not reappeared. Bosquet, who rides up and down between the head and the rear of the column, to see that there are no stragglers, guesses the general's anxiety. Have their spies been surprised and killed? A fourth Douaïr scout, the Aga Mustapha's deputy, disappears into the night.

The march slows down; the cavalry falls back to the rear. Finally the Douaïr returns on his steaming horse, a white patch in the darkness that is slowly growing lighter.

'The Gharabas are there,' he reports. 'The alarm has not been given! They have not struck camp. They are all asleep in their tents!'

Hurried whispers are exchanged around the Aga and the general. The latter gives his final orders. They are only two hours' march from their destination and with dawn still to break, the effect of surprise is assured. The *razzia* promises to be profitable: they have hopes of abductions, pillage, and perhaps even a massacre – as the enemy will be half-asleep they will be unable to fight. 'The night is ours,' muses one or other of these captains . . . Bosquet notes the colours of the sunrise.

At a signal from Lamoricière the cavalry gallops ahead: the *chasseurs* in their black tunics are massed together in the middle; on their right the Aga Mustapha leads the *goum* of Douaïrs who ride with standards flying. This sturdy, thick-set septuagenarian stands up in his gold stirrups, his white beard streaming before him, bursting with eagerness to do battle that belies his years.

'*Etlag el-Goum!* Forward!' he shouts, in a voice that is almost boyish.

'There were jeers and bloodthirsty yells, promising death to the victims they were about to despoil,' Bosquet relates, with admiration for the momentum with which this *Fantasia* is launched. On the left, the scarlet-uniformed Spahis, led by the 'renegade' Yusuf, reach the summit of the crest. In the dawn light they are silhouetted 'like some sinister, supernatural horde' . . .

A couple of miles further on, a vast circle of tents comes into view; the finest, of white embroidered wool, are situated in the middle. Old Mustapha gallops forward to lead the attack, quivering with impatience to surprise his enemy Ben Yacoub, the Aga of the Gharabas: but in vain. As dawn breaks over a scene of pandemonium in the camp, the attackers find only women, half-naked warriors who leap on their unsaddled horses and youngsters who, yataghan in hand, are killed defending their mothers and sisters. Ben Yacoub had left the previous day with the bulk of his contingent to join the Amir in Mascara. Bodies are piled up in inextricable heaps; they lie crumpled in pools of blood; they collapse among torn, bloodstained hangings. I hear the echo of muffled groans, more poignant than lamentations, yells of triumph or shrieks of terror. Tongues of flame lick at half-open chests, spilling jewels and copper ornaments among the corpses of the first victims. Women fall fainting. Yussuf's Spahis join in the looting that begins before the fighting has even ended.

The *chasseurs*, for their part, lay about unremittingly with their swords, cutting a diagonal swathe through this immense horde which scatters in confusion. The panic now reaches the flocks illumined by the flickering light of torches planted in the ground and the luminous cloud of smoke from the conflagration: the bleating of sheep rises up from the fold like a rumble of thunder from the still dark horizon.

When the *chasseurs* reach the second encampment two leagues further on, they find that all the Ouled Ali warriors have disappeared, together with the notables' women-folk. The only living creatures are the flocks which they bring back in droves to the middle of the valley. The Douaïrs and the Spahis now arrive and poke about under these abandoned tents, finding only negligible booty.

Rumours circulate. Lamoricière's officers order the troops to fall in: witnesses speak of one of the Douaïr scouts who is reported to have ridden through the camp with the Aga's wife on his horse. He is said to have let her escape, probably in exchange for the jewels she was wearing; he will certainly never be seen again.

Without a word, Lamoricière is led to the most magnificent of the tents: a fifteen-year-old youth is lying on his back, his face turned towards the ground with his eyes wide open; there is a gaping wound in his chest and rigor mortis has already set in.

'He defended his sister against five soldiers!' a voice at the back explains.

Yusuf rides up to the general, his triumphant shadow lengthening before him. Women prisoners crouch on piles of velvet; they wait in outward calm. The oldest one, with uncovered face, stares haughtily at the watching Frenchmen. Bosquet guesses that at the slightest word from them she is prepared to hurl insults. He examines the silent women as he draws near to his commanding officer.

'One is the Aga's daughter, the others are two daughters-in-law and some of his relatives!' explains Daumas, who must have questioned the

53

serving-women who are standing round in the background.

'The girl's a real beauty! She refused to weep for her brother, she's proud of him!' an admiring voice whispers in Bosquet's ear.

Lamoricière curtly asks why some women have nevertheless been slain a little distance away.

'Seven in all were executed by our soldiers,' someone explains. 'They greeted us with insults!'

'They shouted, "Dogs! Sons of dogs!" the termagents!' exclaims one of the Spahis, at Yusuf's side. The latter maintains a calm silence, betraying a hint of irony in the face of Lamoricière's scruples. For they are all aware that their general is a follower of Saint-Simon and his strict ideals of social justice.

Holding his cane in his trembling hand, Lamoricière turns his mount and rides off tight-faced, followed by his impassive ADC.

Now the only sounds are the murmurs which accompany the widespread looting. A few fires die down. As the last traces of the night mists fade, a ragged ribbon of cries drifts upward from the plain. Dawn claws at the sky, scarring it with pink and mauve striations; then ephemeral hues and flickering flashes have suddenly vanished. The soldiers moving about on the plain are silhouetted in the clear clean light.

'Our little army is celebrating with feasts,' Bosquet writes on 1 November 1840. 'Over the whole town there floats the delicious aroma of roast lamb and fricasseed chickens . . .'

And he adds, in the same letter, 'I'll tell you all about it: there's a bit of everything in this *razzia*; a route march, wise planning, admirable energy on the part of the infantrymen who marched non-stop in spite of their fatigue, perfect co-ordination on the part of our magnificent cavalry, and then every possible touch of poetry in the setting which formed the backcloth to the foray.'

Thirteen days later, back in Oran, Montagnac also writes to his uncle, 'This little fray offered a charming spectacle. Clouds of horsemen, light as birds, criss-crossing, flitting in every direction, and from time to time the majestic voice of the cannon rising above the shouts of triumph and the rifle-shots – all this combined to present a delightful panorama and an exhilarating scene . . .'

Joseph Bosquet, who normally writes to his mother in Pau, this time addresses his letter to a friend, his 'dear Gagneur'. His description of the attack is spiced with reflections, the admiration he feels in retrospect for Lamoricière, this inspired leader who has the knack of infecting his men with his own enthusiasm, and so multiplying their spirit tenfold and increasing the frenzy of Mustapha ben Ismaël's 'brigands'.

Finally the wind of conquest rises for our Bearnese author and he sees himself at the helm . . . The enemy? For the moment, he does not mention any enemy – neither the Amir nor any of his celebrated red horsemen, not one of his dare-devil lieutenants, not one of his 'fanaticized' allies. The setting that he sets forth for us emphasizes the victims' surprise and terror. The long march hour after weary hour through changing landscapes, the riders wheeling their horses round for the dawn raid, this is later fixed for all time in the telling. The orchestrated attack gaining momentum: *animando, accelerando*; spurring on the stampeding horses; trampling the dying under their hooves; overturned tents bespattered with blood. And Bosquet lingers musing over the violence of the colours, fascinated by the patterns traced by the falling bullets; but the intoxication of a war thus seen in retrospect has lost its quickened tempo.

Our captain indulges in the illusion of a manly sport: to be at one with insurgent Africa, and how better than in the intoxication of rape and the murderous *razzia?* . . .

Bosquet, like Montagnac, will never marry; no need of a spouse, no dreams of settling down as long as the joy of battle remains alive, galvanized by words. To relive, in memory, the quickened pulse in the face of danger; a bitterness, unsuspected by the women-folk of his family who dream and wait, clings to the well-turned phrases of his epistles.

Among these febrile accounts, some passages stand out, a blot on the rest: for example the description of a woman's foot that had been hacked off to appropriate the anklet of gold or silver. Bosquet mentions this 'detail' almost casually. Another example: the description of the corpses of the seven women (why *did* they choose to hurl insults when caught by surprise?) who become, in spite of the author, scrofulous excrescences on his elegant prose style.

As if love of warfare and love in wartime gave off a persistent stench, which our Bearnese officer deplores! Might it not be that the barbarity of the natural scene contaminates these noble attackers? . . .

With the impossibility of confronting the elusive enemy in the battlefield, the only hold is on mutilated women, the tally of cattle and sheep, or the glint of looted gold. The only confirmation that the Other, the Invisible Enemy has got away, slipped through the net and fled.

But the enemy slips back in the rear. *His* war is mute, un-documented, leaving no leisure for writing. The women's shrill ululation improvises for the fighting men a threnody of war in some alien idiom: our chroniclers are haunted by the distant sound of half-human cries, cacophony of keening, ear-splitting hieroglyphs of a wild, collective voice. Bosquet muses over the youth killed defending his sister in the luxurious tent; he recalls the anonymous woman whose foot had been hacked off, *'cut off for the sake of the khalkhal...'* Suddenly as he inserts these words, they prevent the ink of the whole letter from drying: because of the obscenity of the torn flesh that he could not suppress in his description.

Does the writer of the war in Africa – like Caesar in former times, the elegance of whose style anaesthetized one *a posteriori* to his brutality as a general – does he aspire by this means to repopulate a deserted theatre?

The woman prisoners can be neither audience nor actors in the pseudo-triumph. What is more serious, they refuse even to look. The Count of Castellane – who had taken part in similar cavalcades and now writes for the *Revue des Deux Mondes* in Paris – notes contemptuously: these Algerian women smear their faces with mud and excrement when they are paraded in front of the conqueror. The elegant chronicler is not mistaken: this is not merely to protect themselves from the enemy, but also from the Christian, who is not just the conqueror, but also alien and taboo! They use the only mask at their disposal; they would use their own blood if the need arose ...

Even when the native seems submissive, he is not vanquished. Does not raise his eyes to gaze on his vanquisher. Does not 'recognize' him. Does not name him. What is a victory if it is not named?

Words protect. Words erect a pedestal in readiness for the triumph that lies in store for every Rome.

This correspondence, despatched from day to day from the encamp-ments, offers an analogy with love-letters: the recipient suddenly becomes the excuse for taking a good clear look at oneself in the muted

light of one's own emotions . . . War and love leave similar impressions: the hesitant courtship dance before the image of the one who
takes flight. And this flight gives rise to fear: and one writes to suppress
this fear.

The letters of these forgotten captains who write about worries over
problems of supplies and prospects of promotion and who sometimes
reveal their personal philosophies – between the lines these letters
speak of Algeria as a woman whom it is impossible to tame. A tamed
Algeria is a pipe-dream; every battle drives further and further away
the time when the insurgency will burn itself out.

It is as if these parading warriors, around whom cries rise up which
the elegance of their style cannot diminish, are mourning their
unrequited love for my Algeria. I should first and foremost be moved
by the rape or suffering of the anonymous victims, which their writings
resurrect; but I am strangely haunted by the agitation of the killers, by
their obsessional unease.

Their words, lodged in volumes now gathering dust on library
shelves, present the warp and woof of a 'monstrous' reality, that is
made manifest in all its unambiguous detail. This alien world, which
they penetrated as they would a woman, this world sent up a cry that
did not cease for two score years or more after the capture of the
Impregnable City . . . And these modern officers, these noble horsemen, riding with their powerful arms at the head of their motley corps
of infantry, these new crusaders of the colonial era, overwhelmed by
such a clamour of voices, wallow in the depths of concentrated sound.
Penetrated and deflowered; Africa is taken, in spite of the protesting
cries that she cannot stifle.

Useless to go back to the death of Saint Louis outside Tunis, or to
Charles V's defeat at Algiers, for which reparation is now made; no
need to invoke the ancestors united by Crusades and Jihads . . . When
the French women glance through the letters from their victorious
correspondents, they join their hands as if in prayer; and this devotion
from their families casts a halo round the seducers in the act of
ravishing the opposite Mediterranean shore.

I

First love-letters, written in my teens. The journal of my cloistered day-dreams. I thought these pages told of love, since their recipient was a secret lover; but they spelled out danger.

I tell of time that passes, the summer heat in the closed apartment, siestas which offer me an escape. The silence of my solitary confinement feeds this monologue which is disguised as a forbidden conversation. I write to get a grip on these beleaguered days . . . These summer months spent as a prisoner do not prompt me to rebel. I feel this time spent behind closed doors is simply a holiday interlude. Soon the new school year will begin and lessons will bring the promise of a quasi-freedom.

Meanwhile my epistles written in French fly far away in an attempt to widen the boundaries of my confinement. These so-called 'love-letters' – though this belies their nature – are like the slats of blinds through which the sun's glare is filtered.

Ripple of words, sweet words that the hand sets down, that the voice would whisper against the wrought-iron bars. What longings can be admitted to this distant friend, with such apparent freedom, simply because we are so far apart? . . .

My words betray no inner turmoil. More than twenty years later I realize that the letters do not so much express love as disguise it, and it is as if I were glad of the constraint: for the father's shadow looms. The half-emancipated girl imagines she is calling on his presence to bear witness: 'You see, I'm writing, and there's no harm in it, no impropriety! It's simply a way of saying I exist, pulsating with life! Is not writing a way of telling what "I" am?'

I read the young man's replies in an alcove or on a terrace; but always with pounding heart and hands trembling with excitement. The sensation of transgressing washes over me like vertigo. I feel my body instinctively poised ready to run away, yielding to the slightest call. The message from 'The Other' is sometimes pregnant with desire, but has lost any power of contamination by the time it reaches me. Once passion has been expressed in writing, it cannot touch me.

One day when I was about eighteen and had long since ceased attending the Quranic school, I received a letter containing the text of a long poem by Amr El-Qais. The sender insisted that I learn the verses off by heart. I deciphered the Arabic script; I made an effort to memorize the first few lines of this 'muallakat' – what is known as 'suspended poetry'. Neither the music nor the pre-Islamic poet's passion awoke any echo in me. At most the brilliance of the masterpiece caused me to close my eyes for a second: an abstract melancholy!

Since then, what intimate outpourings are to be encountered in this ante-room of my youth? I did not write to lay bare my soul, not even for any thrill, even less to express my ecstasies; but rather to turn my back on them in a denial of my body – with an arrogance and naïve sublimation of which I am only now aware.

The fever which assails me finds no outlet in these barren phrases. My hesitating voice seeks for words to express a latent tenderness. And I grope with outstretched hands and closed eyes for some possible way of unveiling . . . My unseeing secret takes refuge deep in the dark cavern; it lifts up its voice in song, which will force a way out through the smallest needle's eye.

Two or three years later, I receive an impassioned letter from my lover, during a period of separation. We are quite newly married, I think. He has written in an agony of suffering, like a sleep-walker; he recalls, one by one, each aspect of my body.

I read this moonstruck letter once only. I feel a sudden chill come over me. I can scarcely persuade myself that this document concerns me; I put it away in my wallet, without re-reading it. Will this intensified love find an echo in me? The letter bides its time, an obscure talisman. Desire uttered in excoriating terms, from a distant place, and without the caressing inflections of the voice.

Suddenly these pages begin to emit a strange power. They start to act like a mediator: I tell myself that this cluster of strangled cries is addressed – why not? – to all the other women whom no word has ever reached. Those of past generations who bequeathed me the places of their confinement, those women who never received a letter: no word taut with desire, stretched like a bow, no message run through with supplication. Their only path to freedom was by intoning their obsessional chants.

The letter that I put away became a first for me: the first expression of what those anonymous women who preceded me were waiting for and of which I was the unwitting bearer.

The episode has other repercussions. The period of separation is prolonged. I go to stay in the Normandy countryside with some friends. I quarrel with a man whose attentions are unwelcome; at first I smile indulgently: he'll get over his passing fancy, I am unmoved by his passionate eloquence, I cut short his outpourings, suggesting we go back to being friends, sharing our reading, exploring this new countryside together. The only thing I need is friendship from a man and the possibility of dialogue . . . But when I silence him, in his impatience he steals into my room while I am out. He admits this soon afterwards. In my anger I burst out, 'Let's put an end to this friendship since there's no future in it!'

The stranger sniggers, like a child getting his own back, 'I went through your handbag!'

'So what?'

'I read a letter, written by the man you're throwing me over for!'

'So what?'

My coldness is a pretence: I am upset by the man's indiscretion. I grow hard, I withdraw. He adds thoughtfully, 'What words! I never imagined he loved you so much!'

'What business is it of yours?'

Did I really receive those written words? Are they not now tainted and debased? . . . I had kept that letter in my wallet, as if it were a relic of some lost faith.

During the ensuing weeks I do not re-read it. The peeping-tom's eyes have upset me. This man's fascination with the other man's unguarded words, which speak so frankly of my body, makes him a thief in my eyes; worse, an enemy. Have I not behaved foolishly, been grievously negligent? I am haunted by a feeling of guilt: could this be the evil eye? The eye of the peeping-tom? . . .

A month later, I am in the market of a Moroccan city. A wide-eyed beggarwoman has followed me, carrying a sleeping baby whose head lolls on her shoulder. She asks me for money and I give her a coin and excuse myself. She goes off and soon afterwards I notice that she has stolen my wallet out of my handbag that I had left open . . .

I realize immediately she's taken the letter.

I don't feel at all distressed; but I begin to wonder vaguely what this might symbolize: were not these words perhaps intended for her – words which she will be unable to read? She has become in fact the very object of that desire expressed in syllables that she cannot decipher!

A few days later I was caught up in one of those casual street conversations with another beggarwoman who commented gaily to me, 'O sister, you at least know where you will be lunching presently! As far as I'm concerned, every day's a new experience!'

She laughed, but there was bitterness in her voice. I thought once more of the letter which the first stranger had stolen, not without some justice.

Words of love received, that a stranger's eyes had sullied. I did not deserve them, I thought, since I had not kept their secret. Those words had found their true home. They had fallen into the hands of that illiterate woman who disappeared. She will have crumpled up the letter or torn it up and thrown it in the gutter . . .

So I recall the travels of that love-letter – and its shipwreck. The memory of the beggarwoman is linked unexpectedly to the image of my father tearing up that first note – oh, such a banal invitation – in front of me, and my rescuing the fragments from the waste-paper basket and obstinately piecing the message together in defiance. As if from then on I would always have to set myself to make good everything that my father's hands might destroy . . .

Every expression of love that would ever be addressed to me would have to meet my father's approval. I could assume that he had had his watchful eye on every letter, even the most innocent, before it reached me. By keeping up a dialogue with this presence that haunted me, my writing became an attempt – or a temptation – to set the limits on my own silence . . . But the memory surfaces of the harem executioners; I am reminded that every page written in the dim light will stir up a hue and cry, leading to the usual cross-examination!

After the episode with the beggarwoman, the author of the letter and I resumed our so-called 'conjugal' life together. But with our happiness in each other now made public, our story hastened to its doom, its death-knell rung by the intruder who first cast eyes on the intimate wording of the letter and then by the beggar who stole it while her child slept on her shoulder.

To write *confronting* love. Shedding light on one's body to help lift the taboo, to lift the veil . . . To lift the veil and at the same time keep secret that which must remain secret, until the lightning flash of revelation.

The word is a torch; to be held up in front of the wall of separation or withdrawal . . . To describe 'The Other' 's face, to fix his image; to continue to believe in his presence, in the miracle he performs. To reject a photograph, or any other visual image. Armed solely with the written word, our serious attention can never be distracted.

From now on, anything written becomes a litmus test for the logic of the silence maintained in the loved one's presence. When we stand face to face and modesty prevents our bodies yielding, then the word seeks all the more to strip us bare. Natural reserve slows down a gesture or a look, exacerbates the touch of a hand; and if we proudly insist on unadorned austerity of dress to affirm a deliberate neutrality – then our voices are simultaneously stripped of grace notes and utter only plain, precise, pure words. Point-blank speech offers surrender, a rash of lilies in a dark alleyway . . .

As a preliminary to seduction, love-letters do not demand any outpourings of the heart or soul, but the precision of a look. When writing, I have but one concern: that I should say enough, or rather that I should express myself clearly enough. Rejecting all lyricism, turning my back on high-flown language; every metaphor seems a wretched ruse, an approximation and a weakness. In former times, my ancestors, women like myself, spending their evenings sitting on the terraces open to the sky, amused themselves with riddles or proverbs, or adding line to line to complete a love quatrain . . .

And now I too seek out the rich vocabulary of love of my mother tongue – milk of which I had been previously deprived. In contrast to the segregation I inherited, words expressing love-in-the-present become for me like one token swallow heralding summer.

When the adolescent girl addresses her father, her language is coated with prudishness . . . Is that why she cannot express any passion on paper? As if the foreign word became a cataract on the eye, avid for discovery!

Love, if I managed to write it down, would approach a critical point: there where lies the risk of exhuming buried cries, those of yesterday and as well as those of a hundred years ago. But my sole ambition in writing is constantly to travel to fresh pastures and replenish my water skins with an inexhaustible silence.

Women, Children, Oxen Dying in Caves

In the spring of 1845 insurrection begins to flare up again among all the Berber tribes in the western regions of the hinterland.

The Amir Abd al-Qadir regroups his forces on the Moroccan frontier. After five years of hot pursuit, his enemies – Lamoricière and Cavaignac to the west, Saint-Arnaud and Yusuf in the centre and Bugeaud in Algiers – think he has been finally routed. They begin to hope: could this be the end of the Algerian resistance? On the contrary, the fuse is being laid for a new explosion.

A new young leader now makes his appearance: Bu Maza, 'the Man-with-the-goat', to whom an aura of prophecy and miraculous legends clings. Inspired by his preaching the tribes from the mountains and the plains rise up in answer to his call. War resumes in the region of the Dahra from Tenes to Mostaganem on the coast, from Miliana to Orleansville in the interior.

In April, the Sharif Bu Maza scores victories over both the armies that advanced from Mostaganem and Orleansville respectively. When they try to surround him in the centre of the massif, he despatches one of his lieutenants to attack Tenes. Saint-Arnaud no sooner hurries to save Tenes, than Bu Maza suddenly appears and seems about to capture Orleansville. Help is urgently summoned to protect this city. The Sharif then threatens Mostaganem. The Amir himself has never demonstrated such promptness in attack . . . Will this new prophet, Bu Maza, turn out to be merely Abd al-Qadir's lieutenant or, surrounded as he is by a hierarchy of disciples, will he set himself up as an independent leader, owing allegiance to no-one? Nothing is certain, except for his style of attack, swift as lightning.

As he travels through the Dahra, with his banners waving, bands playing before him, the people acclaim him as 'the master of the hour'.

He takes every opportunity of wreaking ruthless retribution on those Caïds and Agas appointed by the French.

In May, three French armies scour the countryside; they put down every insurrection, burn the rebels' villages and property, force tribe after tribe to beg for mercy. Saint-Arnaud goes one better – as he boasts in his correspondence: he compels the Beni-Hindjes tribesmen to hand over their rifles. Never, in fifteen years, has anyone achieved such a result.

Bosquet, promoted head of the Arab bureau in Mostaganem, has an inventory drawn up. Saint-Arnaud's seconds in command, Canrobert and Richard, supervise operations; even very ancient weapons are recovered, dating from the Andalusian exodus in the sixteenth century . . . More and more Irredentists are taken hostage and stagnate in the prison in Mostaganem, known as 'The Storks' Tower', as well as in the Roman reservoirs in Tenes which have been transformed into jails.

It is now the beginning of June. Field-Marshal Bugeaud (ennobled with the title of Duke of Isly in honour of his victory the previous year) inspects the results of the repression: leaving Miliana with more than five thousand infantrymen, five hundred cavalry and a thousand pack-mules, he criss-crosses the Dahra. On 12 June he sails from Tenes for Algiers. He leaves his chief of staff, Colonel Pélissier, to complete the task: the tribes of the interior who have not yet surrendered must be forced into submission.

Columns set out again from Mostaganem and Orleansville in a pincer movement; in spite of their co-ordinated efforts, they do not succeed in surrounding the elusive Sharif. They leave only scorched earth behind them, hoping to force the rebel leader to quit or dig himself in.

On 11 June, before embarking, Bugeaud sends a written order to Pélissier, who is advancing towards the Ouled Riah territory. Cassaigne, the Colonel's ADC, is later to remember the exact wording:

'If the scoundrels retreat into their caves,' Bugeaud orders, 'do what Cavaignac did to the Sbeah, smoke them out mercilessly, like foxes!'

Pélissier's army consists of half the Marshal's strength: four infantry battalions, including one of foot *chasseurs*, to which are added the cavalry, one artillery section and one Arab *goum* from

65

the Makhzen tribe who have thrown in their lot with the French.

During the first four days Pélissier concentrates his action against the Beni-Zeroual and Ouled Kelouf tribes, and rapidly forces them to surrender. There remain the Ouled Riah tribesmen from the highlands, who retreat along the banks of the River Shaliff, so enabling the French column, two thousand five hundred men strong, to continue its advance.

On 16 June Pélissier pitches camp at the place known as Ouled el-Amria, where one of the Sharif's lieutenants holds sway. Orchards and homes are totally destroyed, houses belonging to the militant leaders are razed to the ground and their flocks raided.

The next day the Ouled Riah on the right bank of the river initiate negotiations. They might be prepared to surrender. Pélissier makes known the exact figure of the reparations exacted: the number of horses and rifles to be handed over.

The Ouled Riah waver; they deliberate all day, at the end of which they are still reluctant to hand over their weapons. The other Ouled Riah tribesmen, who have only bound themselves to take part in a few skirmishes, withdraw to the area in their rear where there are caves that are reckoned to be impossible to storm. These are situated on an abutment on the Nacmaria Jebel, in a promontory between two valleys, at an altitude of over 1,200 feet. Since the time of the Turkish rulers tribes have taken refuge with their women and children, flocks and munitions in these subterranean depths which run for more than 600 feet and open out on to almost inaccessible gorges. Their silos permit them to hold out for long periods and so defy the enemy.

The night of 17 to 18 June is far from peaceful. Although Pélissier has had the orchards cut down around the encampment, native warriors crawl very close; there are many nocturnal alarms. The Orleans *chasseurs* are on the alert and beat off the intruders every time.

At daybreak on 18 June, Pélissier decides to make a move: he leaves part of the camp under the command of Colonel Renaud and despatches two battalions of infantry up the mountainside without their knapsacks; they are accompanied by the cavalry and the Makhzen *goum*, together with one piece of artillery and some mule-litters for bringing back any wounded.

El-Hajj el-Kaim's Arab horsemen caracole in the forefront of this final march: they cannot resist performing their *Fantasia*. Is this not perhaps to disguise their anxiety in the face of these menacing heights which they know to be inhabited? Some of the Arab troops have deserted during the hours of darkness (may they not have had some foreboding of the tragedy that is about to ensue?). Pélissier is determined to act swiftly.

The leader of the Arab *goum* remains impassive. These last few days he has faithfully performed his rôle as guide, untiringly indicating every location and property.

'There are the El-Frachich caves!' he cries to Pélissier, who is accompanied by young Cassaign and Goetz, the interpreter; he points to an overhanging plateau in the foreground of the barren countryside.

'If they've gone to earth in their caves, we'll soon be walking over their heads!' he adds with a sudden burst of humour.

For Colonel Pélissier the approaching dawn makes a solemn backdrop, befitting the overture to a drama. The curtain is about to go up on the tragic action; Fate has decreed that he, as the leader, must make the first entrance on the stage set out before them in this austere chalk landscape.

'Everything fled at my approach,' he writes in his detailed report. 'The direction taken by a part of the native population was sufficient to indicate the site of the caves to which El-Hajj el-Kaim was guiding me.'

Pélissier is a master of strategy. After taking part in the Algiers landing he had published a text-book of military theory based on the observations he had made there. He then left Algeria, only returning in 1841, when he is stationed first in Oran. His reputation has preceded him; now he must live up to it.

As soon as he reaches the El-Kantara plateau overlooking the caves, Pélissier sends a reconnoitring party of officers to try to find an entrance opening on to the ravine: the main one is uphill. A howitzer is set up in front of it. A smaller entrance is discovered lower down. Each one is placed under the guard of a captain and a few carbineers; the cavalry is disposed under cover to charge any possible fugitives, the 6th Light Horse in the van, the Orleans *chasseurs* close to the colonel.

These manoeuvres are not carried out without difficulty: some of the Ouled Riah are posted in the trees and hidden among the rocks to cover the entrance to the caves or take diversionary action. Their shots cost the French six wounded, including three non-commissioned officers; the seventh man to be hit dies instantly: he is one of the Makhzen horsemen who dismounted to try to get nearer to the ravine ready to issue the challenge.

Pélissier replies with a few shells. The men on the lookout vanish. The vice is closing on the refugees. The colonel orders faggots of dry brushwood and bundles of grass to be rolled down from the escarpment and set alight outside the upper entrance. But the cave slopes away inside, so that the task at which the soldiers labour all day turns out to be ineffectual. As soon as the heat of the burning mass lessens, the defenders nearest to the entrance open fire, shooting at random.

By nightfall the besiegers are joined by those who had been left behind in the camp . . . Pélissier's position may well become critical: the Ouled Riah, with cattle and provisions, can hold out for a long time; the French, on the other hand, have only enough supplies for three or four days . . . If the neighbouring tribes, which have already been subdued, get wind of Pélissier's increasing impotence, may they not suddenly resume hostilities? How will they manage to retreat in this precipitous terrain? Already some of the Arab auxiliaries are smiling and whispering among themselves that they must be the laughing-stock of the Ouled Riah, who they imagine making themselves quite at home in the vast interior chambers.

During the night – a bright moonlit night – 'an Arab carrying a *guerba* emerged from an exit which up till then had been hidden from us by a clump of thuyas; he was wounded as he tried to reach the water supply . . .' They conclude that the refugees are short of water. Pélissier takes heart: on the morning of 19 June he opens negotiations in the hope of reaching a settlement. At the same time he makes it quite clear that he is prepared to adopt strong measures if that is the only solution.

Another exit has been discovered: it leads to the cave which opens on to the lower entrance. So this can be used for another fire. Bigger fires will be lit in both openings and this time the smoke will penetrate into the caves.

Pélissier puts more and more men to cutting wood, felling the trees around about and collecting brushwood and straw, but he still does not ignite the fires; he prefers to get the final phase of the negotiations going.

The refugees seem disposed to surrender: at nine o'clock they send a first emissary; after they have held a council of notables, a second messenger arrives; a third finally asks for *aman*. They agree to pay the reparations demanded and to leave the caves; their only fear is that they will be taken hostage and kept in the infamous 'Storks' Prison' in Mostaganem. Pélissier is surprised (coming from the general command in Algiers, he is unaware of the wretched reputation of these jails); he promises to see that this fate does not befall them; in vain. The Ouled Riah are resolved to pay up to 75,000 francs indemnity but are reluctant to trust him on this last score.

Goetz, the interpreter, is sent to translate Pélissier's message. He again assures them they will be allowed to go free. The deliberations last another three hours. The besieged are unwilling to surrender unarmed; they insist on the French withdrawing some distance away from the caves. Pélissier, concerned about his prestige, will not accede to this condition.

Goetz now delivers the ultimatum: 'You have just a quarter of an hour to leave! No man, woman or child will be taken prisoner to Mostaganem! . . . In a quarter of an hour, we shall resume the work that was going on above your heads; then it will be too late!'

In his report, Pélissier stresses the fact that the period of respite was extended; he emphasizes the shilly-shallying on the part of the besieged; he writes, 'I had reached the limit of my forebearance.'

It is one o'clock. Throughout the morning, while the negotiations were continuing, wood was still being collected. Pélissier also has the foresight to have platforms erected at the top of the El-Kantara spur, so that the brushwood can be thrown down more easily. So the fire is rekindled and the blaze fed throughout this day and the following night. To begin with, the fire burns up slowly, as on the previous day; the inflammable material had been thrown down in the wrong place. An hour after the resumption of operations, the soldiers hurl the faggots 'correctly'. What is more, the wind rises and fans the flames; almost all the smoke enters the caves.

The men are happy, they have plenty to occupy themselves with. They continue to stoke the fire until six o'clock on the morning of 20 June, that is for eighteen hours non-stop. To quote the words of a French witness:

'Words cannot describe the violence of the blaze. At the summit of El-Kantara the flames rose to a height of more than two hundred feet and dense columns of smoke billowed up in front of the entrance to the cave.'

In the middle of the night, some explosions were heard coming from inside the caves, quite distinct explosions. Then nothing. The silence continued until morning. Then the fire died down.

On his return to Algiers, Bugeaud's thoughts are mainly dictated by political considerations. The resumption of the insurgency is not a bad thing after all; the ministers in Paris will need him, 'the saviour' – had he not declared the previous year that Abd al-Qadir had definitely been routed? But several Abd al-Qadirs are springing up. From every region they appear, a second one, a third, each one more 'fanatical' than the last, certainly more shabby and bedraggled, less and less like leaders with whom the French authorities can envisage signing treaties.

'Smoke them out like foxes!'

That is what Bugeaud had written; Pélissier had obeyed, but when the scandal breaks in Paris, he does not divulge the order. He is a true officer; a model of *esprit du corps*, with a sense of duty; he respects the law of silence.

But he gives his account of the incident. 'I was forced to resume the collection of brushwood,' he writes when he methodically composes his routine report three days later. He describes the operation in detail: the many stages of the negotiations, the experienced nature of each of his envoys, the resumption of parleys for the last time, outside the lower entrance to the caves. He did not just grant them a quarter of an hour's respite, he states, but 'five times a quarter of an hour' . . . Those wily, suspicious, hard-bargaining Muslims didn't trust a Frenchman's word. They preferred to rely on the security of their subterranean hideout.

The order had been carried out: 'Every exit was blocked.' As Pélissier draws up his report, his words bring back that night of 19 June, lit up by flames two hundred feet high which devour the cliff-face of Mount Nacmaria.

I, in turn, piece together a picture of that night: 'a cannibalistic scene', writes a certain P. Christian, a doctor who had roved between the French and Algerian camps during the 1837 to 1839 truce. But I prefer to turn to two eye-witnesses: first, a Spanish officer, fighting with the French army, and who formed part of the vanguard; he publishes his account in the Spanish newspaper the *Heraldo*. The second, an anonymous member of the company, describes the tragedy in a letter to his family that Dr Christian publishes.

The Spaniard describes the flames – two hundred feet high – enveloping the El-Kantara promontory. The soldiers, he states, shove wood into the cave – 'like into an oven' – to keep the furnaces stoked throughout the night. The nameless soldier shares his vision with us, writing with even more violent emotion:

'What pen could do justice to this scene? To see, in the middle of the night, by moonlight, a body of French soldiers, busy keeping that hellfire alight! To hear the muffled groans of men, women, children, beasts, and the cracking of burnt rocks as they crumbled, and the continual gunfire!'

The silence had in fact been broken from time to time by the sound of shots; Pélissier and his entourage had interpreted these as signs of internal dissension. But this inferno, which the French army gazes at in admiration as if it were a living, necrophagous sculpture, cuts off fifteen hundred people and their cattle. Is this Spanish witness the only one to put his ear against the rock, and overhear the paroxysms of death on the march? . . .

I imagine the details of this nocturnal tableau: 2,500 soldiers keeping vigil, watching the progress of their victory over the mountain-dwellers . . . Some of these spectators no doubt feel avenged for so many other vigils! Oh, those African nights! The cold, the landscape congealed by the darkness, the sudden shrill yelp of a jackal! The invisible enemy never seems to sleep; horse-thieves daub their bodies with oil and slip into the camp, unhobble the animals, sow sudden panic, in the course of which sleepers and sentinels of the same camp kill each other. The alarm is sounded so many times in the night! In the local language, the alarm is called 'the lion lashing its tail' – and in this way the natives admit their fear of the royal beast, 'The Nameless One'.

The flames are still licking the side of the El-Kantara promontory. The gunshots are followed by silence; a ripple of sound, then a distant hammering that eats into the heart of the mountain. The soldiers gaze upwards, waiting for the mountain to divulge the violent secret hidden in the rocks.

Nacmaria, on the morning of 20 June, 1845.

In the light of dawn, an unsteady figure – man or woman – emerges from the last glowing embers of the fire. It totters forward, pauses after a few steps, then collapses to die in the sun.

Over the next few hours, three or four survivors stagger out to gulp down a mouthful of fresh air, before they too succumb . . . During the whole morning it is impossible to get near the caves which are surrounded by smoke and a quasi-religious silence. Each man wonders what drama was enacted behind these chalk cliff-faces which have been barely blackened by the lingering smoke: 'The problem,' the Spaniard adds in his account, 'was solved.'

Pélissier orders an emissary to be despatched; according to his report, 'he returns with several breathless men who give us some indication of the extent of the damage'.

These messengers inform Pélissier as to the situation: the fumigation has wiped out the entire Ouled Riah tribe – 1,500 men, some of them elderly, women, children, flocks by the hundred and all their horses . . .

The day after the fatal outcome, before he enters the caves himself, Pélissier sends in a detachment of about fifty sappers and an equal number from the artillery with their equipment, accompanied by two officers from the Engineers and two from the artillery. The Spanish officer is one of them.

The carcasses of the animals, already in a state of putrefaction, lay near the entrance, surrounded by woollen blankets; the refugees' personal effects and clothing are still smouldering . . . From there the men, lanterns in hand, followed a trail of ashes and dust to arrive at the first cave. 'An appalling sight,' writes the Spaniard. 'All the corpses are naked, in attitudes which indicated the convulsions they must have experienced before they expired. Blood was flowing from their mouths; but the most horrifying sight was that of infants at the breast, lying amid the remains of dead sheep, sacks of beans etc.'

These 'spelaeologists' go from cave to cave. An identical sight awaits them everywhere. The refugees in these hidden depths have been totally exterminated. 'This is a terrible tragedy,' the Spaniard concludes, 'and never at Sagonte or at Numance has more barbaric courage been displayed!'

Now, in spite of the officers' efforts, some of the soldiers start looting there and then: stripping corpses, making off with jewellery, burnouses, yataghans. Then the reconnaissance party returns to the colonel who is unwilling to believe the extent of the catastrophe.

More soldiers are despatched – it is now the afternoon of 21 June, the first day of summer 1845! Among them is the anonymous writer of the letter published by P. Christian: 'I visited the three caves,' he begins, 'and this is what I saw.' He, too, discovers the carcasses of oxen, donkeys, sheep, lying in the entrance; their instinct had driven them in search of the last breath of air that could penetrate from the outside. Amidst the animals, sometimes even beneath them, lie the bodies of women and children; some of them had been crushed by the panic-stricken beasts . . . The nameless writer lingers particularly over one detail:

'I saw a dead man, with one knee on the ground, grasping the horn of an ox in one hand. In front of him lay a woman with her child in her arms. It was easy to see that this man had been asphyxiated, together with the woman, the child and the ox, while he was struggling to protect his family from the enraged animal.'

This second witness arrives at the same estimate: more than a thousand dead, not counting all those who are heaped one on top of the other, forming an indistinguishable mass; not counting the infants at the breast, nearly all of them wrapped in their mothers' tunics . . .

Some sixty moribund prisoners creep out of this subterranean tomb. About two score of them will survive; some of them are cared for in the field hospital . . . Ten of them are even set free!

Pélissier explains that 'by a providential chance, the most obdurate among the Sharif's party succumbed'. Among the survivors are the wife, the son and daughter of Ben Nakah, one of Bu Maza's caliphs for this region. These are the only prisoners that Pélissier boasts of!

By the afternoon of 21 June 1845, the smoke over the promontory has dispersed. I ponder over Pélissier's next order:

'Bring them out into the sun! Count them!'

Perhaps, carried away by his determination to see the matter through, he may have added roughly, 'Bring the savages out! Let's see them all stark and stiff! Bring out their rotting corpses! Then we shall have won, we shall have made an end to it!' . . . I can't say for sure what the military policy was; this is just a surmise; I am telling the story in my own way and is it so purposeless to imagine what motives these butchers had?

What fascinates me most – more even than the progress through the dark caves, holding lanterns aloft to reveal the asphyxiated victims – is the moment when they bring out the carcasses and put them on display:

'Approximately six hundred are brought out of the cave,' the Spanish officer notes, and he emphasizes the distress of the colonel and his staff who all seem stunned, in a cold stupor.

Six hundred members of the Ouled Riah tribe, laid out in the fresh air side by side, without distinction of sex or rank; notables with the poorest, fatherless orphans, widows, repudiated wives, swaddled babes at their mothers' breasts or clinging to their shoulders . . . Corpses with smoke-blackened faces sleep, stripped of their jewellery and burnouses, but even more denuded by the silence which enfolds them. They will be neither washed nor wrapped in winding-sheet; there will be no wake held for one day or even for one hour . . .

The Arabs of El-Kaim's *goum* – who three days before had performed an incongruous *Fantasia*, all unaware of the tragedy to which it will be an overture – move warily away: the corpses lined up in wretched heaps seem to stare at them, to nail them to the mountainside, and they cannot escape from this curse as long as the corpses are not buried.

The main body of the French company has remained at a distance. Except for the stretcher-bearers and the reconnaissance unit, the soldiers only glimpse this shambles from far off . . . The looted objects circulate, sold among themselves. Then words are exchanged: those who have been into the caves describe the tangled mass of corpses which could not be brought out. These Frenchmen begin to realize what a scene of carnage, what a necropolis lies beneath their feet . . .

Did Pélissier himself enter the caves personally? some ask. The third day of the tragedy is 22 June, the day when the colonel makes his report. He is supposed to have said, as he emerged, 'It's horrible!'

Others report that he sighed, 'It's terrible!'

Be that as it may, he states, in the prescribed report:

'These operations, Field-Marshal, are such as one undertakes when obliged to do so, but one prays to God that one will never again have to carry them out!'

So, Pélissier suffers, probably turning to pray to God . . . The troops comment on the outcome. On this twenty-second day of June, they enjoy the tangible results of the operation: numerous neighbouring tribes, including those members of the Ouled Riah who had withdrawn to the other bank of the Shaliff, the Beni Zeltouns, the Tazgarts,

74

Madiounas and Achachs, all send their delegates. They hand over their rifles and present the *gada* horse, the symbol of submission. Some of the soldiers are only too happy to forget the six hundred corpses exposed on the hillside (which the Makhzen loyalists eventually bury in a communal grave). They boast of their success in taking these caves which in three hundred years of Turkish domination had never been captured!

Victory had apparently been won on this hillside. But the next day, 23 June, Nature has her revenge: the stench of death is so strong (ravens and vultures fly ceaselessly over the ravine, and the soldiers even see them carrying off the remains of human corpses!) that Pélissier gives the order, that same day, to move the camp half a league further away . . .

As if the sun, the summer bearing down its incalescent burden, and all nature join forces to expel the French army.

It is time to depart, the stench is too great. How can one get rid of the memory? The corpses exposed in the hot sun have been transmuted into words. Words can travel. The words, for example, of Pélissier's verbose report, which arrive in Paris, are read at a parliamentary session, unleash a uproar of controversy: insults from the opposition, embarassment on the part of the government, fury of the warmongers, shame throughout Paris in which the seeds of the 1848 Revolution are germinating . . .

Lieutenant-Colonel Canrobert, when posted to the garrison in this same Dahra region, will later deliver his judgement:

'Pélissier made only one mistake: as he had a talent for writing, and was aware of this, he gave in his report an eloquent and realistic – much too realistic – description of the Arabs' suffering . . .'

Let us leave the controversy there: could the outcry in Paris over the report be nothing more than a political reaction? Thanks to his 'too realistic' description, Pélissier suddenly resurrects, before my eyes, those Ouled Riah who died in their caves on the night of 19 to 20 June 1845.

The dead woman found lying beneath the body of the man who was protecting her from the bellowing ox. Because of his remorse, Pélissier keeps this corpse from drying in the sun, and these Islamic dead, deprived of the ritual ceremonies, are preserved from oblivion by the words of his routine report. A century of silence has frozen them.

The asphyxiated victims of the Dahra, that words expose, that memory disinters. Pélissier's report, the Spanish officer's denunciation, the nameless soldier's troubled letter, all this writing is engraved in letters of iron and steel on the precipitous crags of Nacmaria.

Less than two months later, twenty leagues away, it is Colonel Saint-Arnaud's turn to smoke out the Sbeah tribe. He blocks up all the exits and 'when the job is done' he makes no effort to bring out a single one of the rebels. Enter not the caves! Let no man keep the tally! No auditing. No conclusions.

A confidential report is sent to Bugeaud who this time takes care not to forward it to Paris. The report will be destroyed in Algiers . . . In 1913, sixty-eight years later, a respectable academic named Gauthier looks for it, finds no trace of it, wonders even if Saint-Arnaud had not made up the whole story in order to have something to boast about. Might he not have 'imagined' this new fumigation, to be Pélissier's equal and to score one over him! . . . No! the researcher finds the record of this incident in accounts given by the descendants of the tribe.

Less than two months after Pélissier, Saint-Arnaud well and truly asphyxiated at least eight hundred Sbeahs. He simply kept silent about this ruthless triumph. This is death indeed. To be interred in Saint-Arnaud's caves and never exhumed!

But, even he, this fine man, this prudent man, this man who makes a success of everything, this man who will be chosen from among all the leaders of the African campaign to organize the future coup d'état of 2 December 1851, the man who in action keeps firm check on his own words and thereby his fears, even he cannot help writing to his brother:

'I have all the exits hermetically sealed and create a vast cemetery. The bodies of these fanatics will be buried in the earth for ever! . . . No-one has been down into the cave! . . . I sent a confidential report to the Field-Marshal, stating everything simply, without any terrible poetry, nor any imagery.'

Then he concludes emotionally on what is intended to be a poignant note:

'Brother, no-one is more prone to goodness by nature and disposition than I! . . . From 8 to 12 August I have been ill, but my conscience does not trouble me. I have done my duty as a leader and tomorrow I shall do the same again, but I have developed a distaste for Africa!'

One of Bu Maza's lieutenants, El-Gobbi, also wrote of these events – whether in Arabic or French I cannot say, as his account has not been found. However, twenty years later the contents of this document were noted by others, who in turn wrote of them.

When Saint-Arnaud has completed his macabre task, he withdraws to a distance from Ain Merian, and stations his army there for some ten days. The natives dare not make a final attempt to rescue their entombed compatriots. However, one of Bu Maza's disciples, who has a reputation in this region for amorous as well as military exploits, one 'Aïssa ben Jinn' (a nickname that can be translated as 'Jesus, Son of the Devil'), this same Aïssa arrives on the scene and addresses the other Sbeah tribesmen as follows:

'Down below, there is a woman much beloved of me! Let us try to discover whether she is alive or dead!'

At his command the other fractions of the tribe clear the opening. Some ten or more victims stagger out alive. They had been in the upper galleries of the caves, 'which', Gauthier notes when he inspects the scene, 'make up a precipitous vertical maze'.

In the other galleries, where the poisonous gases from the fumigation had lingered, they walked on corpses, so El-Gobbi tells us, 'as on straw litter'. These they left entombed.

On the site of the former Ain Merian encampment a settlers' village was created, known as 'Rabelais'. In 1913 Gauthier found a survivor of the fumigation there, an octogenarian who had been a boy of under ten at the time, and who had been one of those who had survived because Aïssa the 'Son of the Devil' wanted to free 'a woman he had much loved'.

And the university professor, carrying out his researches in peaceful colonial Algeria – where men sleep, work, get rich on the turf fertilized with corpses – this academic can write when he has finished his research:

'There are few things as distant from current experience as a fumigation . . . I am aware of my impartiality – I may say my dispassion – I don't in fact see how a spelaeologist can be otherwise.'

Nearly one and a half centuries after Pélissier and Saint-Arnaud, I am practising a very special kind of spelaeology, since in my descent into those dark caverns my only hand-holds are words in the French language – reports, accounts, evidence from the past. Could my exploration – contrary to E.F. Gauthier's 'scientific' activities, be obstructed by a belated 'partiality'?

I am obsessed by the memories exhumed from this double necropolis, which spur me on, even if I feel I am opening a register of the dead, in the region of the forgotten caves, for those who will never have eyes to read.

Yes, I am moved by an impulse that nags me like an earache: the impulse to thank Pélissier for his report which unleashed a political storm in Paris, but which allows me to reach out today to our own dead and weave a pattern of French words around them. And Saint-Arnaud, too, whose letter to his brother, while breaking an agreed silence, lets me know the site of the cave-sepulchres. And even if it seems too late to open them now, so long after the 'Son of the Devil' sought for the woman he loved, those cinnabar-red words still have the power to cut like a plough-share into my flesh.

I venture to express my gratitude – however incongruous. Not to the first fumigator, Cavaignac, who was forced by Republican opposition to settle matters quietly; and not to Saint-Arnaud, the only real fanatic; but to Pélissier. After the spectacular, brutal killing carried out in all naïveté, he is overcome with remorse and describes the slaughter he has organized. I venture to thank him for having faced the corpses, for having indulged a whim to immortalize them in a description of their rigid carcasses, their paralysed embraces, their final paroxysms. For having looked on the enemy otherwise than as a horde of zealots or a host of ubiquitous shadows.

Pélissier, the barbarian, the military leader subsequently discredited, is for me the foremost chronicler of the first Algerian War! For he approaches the victims when they have barely ceased their final twitches – not of hatred – but of a frenzied death-wish . . . Pélissier, butcher-and-recorder, brandishes the torch of death which illuminates these martyrs. These men, these women, these children, for whom no mourners could ever officiate (no lacerated faces, no measured keening) for the mourning women too perished in the same holocaust . . . An entire tribe! The survivors, groping their way towards the shores of dawn, are not even resurrected; they remain empty shadows rather, for whom the sole light, even at high noon, is that of the scalding-house.

Pélissier, composing his report on 22 June 1845, must have had some inkling that in writing of the war he is brushing the skirts of death with its need of ceremonial, lighting on the footprints left by the dance of death . . . The whole countryside, the Dahra mountains, the chalk cliffs, the valleys with their charred orchards find their inverted mirror-image in the funeral caves. The petrified victims are meta-morphosed into mountains and valleys. The women, lying among the cattle in their lyrical embraces, reveal their aspirations to be the sister-spouses of their men who do not surrender.

When Pélissier walks, a silent witness, through these caves which will be forever inhabited, he must have been guided by a palaeog-rapher's instinct: in which strata of the amorphous mass of corpses and cries would he find victors and vanquished inextricably fused?

After Pélissier emerges from this promiscuous contact with the fumigated victims clad in their ashy rags, he makes his report which he intends to compose in official terms. But he is unable to do so; he has become for all time the sinister, the moving surveyor of these subterranean *medinas*, the quasi-fraternal embalmer of this tribe which would never bend the knee . . .

Pélissier, speaking on behalf of this long drawn-out agony, on behalf of fifteen hundred corpses buried beneath El-Kantara, with their flocks unceasingly bleating at death, hands me his report and I accept this palimpsest on which I now inscribe the charred passion of my ancestors.

II

I could well have been my brother's confidante when he first took to the hills to join the maquis, but he was neither my friend nor ally when I needed him. I was far away, isolated and absorbed in my own dreams of romance – dreams that consumed me with an irrational fire – more incongruous than those fires blazing in the mountains. My brother, not yet a grown man and ever on the move . . . Ear cocked in the dark for those on his trail, shunted from prison to prison – after the feverish tempo of these odysseys, we met again one day and in a sudden burst of confidence he let fall a single word, '*hannouni*'.

My brother, with his crooked boyish smile, reminds me – half-jokingly, to disguise his affection – of the local dialect spoken in the mountains where we spent our childhood. The expressions of endearment, the diminutives peculiar to the speech of our tribe – half-way between the Berber language of the highlands and the Arabic of the nearby city (the former capital which had fallen into ruins and then been repopulated by the Andalusian exodus):

'If a friend uses one word to you, when she's off her guard . . .'

I wait; he hesitates, then adds softly, 'She only has to murmur the word "*hannouni*", then you know for sure: "So! she's from my region!" '

I interrupt him with a laugh, 'That brings back fond memories! . . . For instance, that sweet auntie! . . .'

Changing the subject, recalling the gushing aunts and cousins of the tribe, the one who fondles the babies, saying over and over again, 'My little liver . . . *hannouni*!', the old granny who only says it to little boys because she doesn't care for girls (they cause too many worries), who . . .

How can you translate this *hannouni* by a word like 'tender-hearted' or '*tendrelou*'? Or by 'my darling' or 'my precious heart'. Instead of saying 'precious heart', we women prefer the expression 'my little liver', or 'the apple of my eye' . . . This word '*tendrelou*' seems like the hidden heart of a fresh lettuce, a sound embedded deep in our childhood, which flourishes among us and which, so to speak, we swallow . . .

We were walking, I think, in a deserted street of the capital. We had run into each other unexpectedly one summer afternoon, and we had laughed, like two strangers who meet like this and realize they are both equally at a loose end. With this only brother – slender, tall, some two years younger than me – I often adopted a mischievous flirtatious manner, introducing him as 'my elder brother', because his hair was prematurely greying, despite his youthful figure . . . This was the only insight he ever gave me into his private life: one word revealing his loves. I felt a somewhat bitter-sweet embarrassment.

I turned away. I began to reminisce about the past and the old aunts, elderly relatives, cousins. This one word could have filled my nights when I was in love . . . To the brother who was never my ally, to the friend who never joined me in my labyrinth. This word – a lotus-blossom opening out in the bright August sunlight, when languid conversation drifts to a halt, this diminutive, making a gap through which dammed-up speech can flow again . . . I could have . . .

Said that a succession of a thousand nights borne up on the crest of pleasure, breasting its nocturnal waters, a thousand times each time, and on the snow-capped peaks of paroxysm the word of a phantom-childhood appears – sometimes my lips form it silently, awakening it; sometimes it is exhumed by a caress along one of my limbs and the sculpted syllables rise to the surface, I am about to spell it out, just once, whisper it to be free of it, but I refrain.

Because of the other – what other face faintly suggested or conjured up will receive this unvoiced word of love?

I desist. Every night. Every tenebrous night through which my body swims to scale the heights of ecstasy.

So, in a dusty avenue of our capital, my big brother has given me back this tormented term, fretted with mystery or melancholy. Does he breach the dyke? A flash of lightning, in which I glimpse women's profiles leaning over his shoulder, lips murmuring, another voice or my own voice calling. The shadow of a wing, this salt-lake-word.

My brother's tall figure involuntarily erects the barrier of incest and conjures up dark thickets of memory, from which only this sound of lips emerges, only a breeze from the scorched hillsides of the past where I bury myself. Where those who waited are asphyxiated and their flesh left to rot, while they still waited for love – that might prove cruel or tender, but love that cried aloud.

The Naked Bride of Mazuna

For fifteen years El-Djezaïr had been in the hands of the infidel. Its fall had been followed by that of Oran, betrayed by its own Bey. Blida, too close to the foot of the Atlas, had not been able to hold out against the enemy attacks and twice its Moorish inhabitants fled before the French army; Midia, likewise, higher in the massif, where the Amir had many a time been besieged with his lieutenants and had had to summon the chiefs of the nearby mountain tribes to his aid. In the distance, Constantine had twice been attacked and had defended itself house by house until the Bey Ahmed was finally forced to withdraw to the Auras mountains to continue his resistance, leaving the 'City of Passions' to fall finally into the hands of frenzied plunderers.

Bône, on the Eastern coast, had long since capitulated; Bougie, likewise, after many vicissitudes, although the independent Kabyle chiefs continued to swoop down beneath its ramparts, fighting on, with their women riding in their midst, deliberately defying death out of bravado or in the exhilaration of a holy war. On the Western shore, Mostaganem had surrendered, since the proud city of Tlemsen in the interior had not been able to hold out, nor Mascara, Abd al-Qadir's unruly capital; moreover the Amir himself had just lost his whole retinue; shortly before this. Cherchel – the ancient city of Caesarea – had fallen, but when the French entered its ruins they found no-one in the abandoned city except a madman and a paralytic woman.

There remained the cities and towns high in the massifs, where the invaders made only a few rapid incursions to reach the plateaux overlooking the desert and its many oases . . . They never penetrated the mountain peaks to the North: Kabylia, long to remain impregnable, together with the Bahors heights in the extreme East and the Atlas range itself, whose jagged barrier formed a backcloth to the clashes between the French columns and Ben Allal's regulars and those of old Berkani.

In the heart of the Dahra mountains, on a northern spur, a secret city stood in isolation: the venerable city of Mazuna, huddled behind its ramparts, twenty leagues from Mostaganem and Miliana, not far from Tenes, where for the past year settlers had been moving into wooden hutments, and near to Cherchel, whose inhabitants had drifted back into bondage. It had once been the headquarters of the Turkish Beylik for the West; for fifty years at least it had slumbered in twilight dust. It had retained its autonomy, like the centres in the extreme South, preserved from occupation . . .

Fifteen years had passed since the fall of El-Djezaïr.

In the year when Algiers fell, an only daughter was born to the *Kulugli* Caïd of Mazuna, Si Mohamed Ben Kadruma. She was called Badra, meaning 'full moon'. For the people of Mazuna, Badra's beauty – her green eyes, milky complexion, rounded bosom, her figure, slender as a young palm tree, her jet-black hair that fell below her waist – all attested to their city's past splendour.

Badra's mother was the daughter of the *Khasnaji* of the proud city of Tlemcen from whence she had travelled to wed the Caïd with a bridal retinue whose splendour was inscribed in legend. She had died giving birth to Badra and shortly afterwards, the *Khasnaji* had himself been killed in battle when the Mechouar's janizaries declared themselves in opposition to the Amir, and the latter avenged himself by deporting all Turkish families.

No-one had ever spoken in front of little Badra of her maternal family's misfortunes: however, is it not said that fortune will not favour the child over whose cradle no maternal uncles smile! Nevertheless Badra had kept her nurse, a half-caste from the West, a freed slave who had fed the child's imagination with obscure legends, tales of magic . . . She was said to have come from the interior of Morocco; the Caïd's two wives, both daughters of local chiefs – as good as saying, peasants – both mistrusted and feared her.

Badra – a princess, isolated in the heart of a city fallen from its ancient glory. For the last year, the town which still maintains its past proud inflexible customs, has been seething with scheming and unrest. The Caïd Ben Kadruma, although barely sixty, is ageing. At twenty, under the Turkish rule – the elders of the city still speak of it – he distinguished himself in the troubles which marked the terrible uprising against the Bey of Oran. That was well before 1830! He gave proof of courage as well as intelligence! . . . On his way back from Mazuna to Oran, the Bey had been ambushed in a narrow gorge; he managed to escape himself, but his entire corps of guards was massacred by the redoubtable Sbeah and the Ouled Jounes tribesmen. The Bey returned the following spring with twice the number of troops – of whom the majority, newly converted, spoke neither Turkish nor Arabic – and carried out merciless reprisals. The young Caïd, who had only recently inherited his title, led the delegation which tried to temper the Ottoman cruelty.

In April 1845, the Caïd Ben Kadruma found himself in a similar situation, heading a delegation of Mazuni notables who greeted a French column which rode up to the gate of the city – the same gate that they had refused to open to Abd al-Qadir two years before, in spite of his red-uniformed horsemen and artillery. The French had recently clashed in bitter fighting with the zealots of the Sharif Bu Maza, the new hero of the mountains, whom the tribesmen were greeting with joy that boded ill for their enemies. During the day news had reached Mazuna of a battle that had been fought on the plain of Ghris: the French had charged, but had lost twenty of their men! The Sharif had vanished like the wind on his swift charger.

When the French arrived, in a state of exhaustion, the Caïd presented himself to their commander, made his speech, followed by that of his *hadri* colleague and listened impassively to the threats made by the Colonel, a certain Saint-Arnaud, who had come from Miliana . . .

Without dismounting, red-faced, shrill with anger, Saint-Arnaud declared that Mazuna would soon be reduced to a heap of ruins because of the duplicity of its population; he shouted that France was not deceived; he knew that theft and banditry were the city's most flourishing business, or at least the receipt and sale of stolen goods; far too many flocks of sheep could be heard bleating in the gardens and these must belong to refugees and rebellious tribes . . . Throughout this diatribe, the official in charge of the Arab Bureau, a man named Richard, whose skull was bandaged due to a wound received in the recent battle, slowly translated for the dozen notables who stood with bent heads, draped in their ample robes.

When he had finished, the Caïd replied curtly, stony-faced, 'God's will be done! Mazuna is a neutral city, a free city! . . . It is the only city to resist the Amir and we did not open our gates to him; we shall hold out alone against any masters, just as we resist all bandits!'

'The Sharif was here less than forty-eight hours ago! He recruited three hundred foot soldiers from among you, and two *khojas*! We know this; we've got proofs!' the Colonel angrily retorted, and Richard impassively translated the vehement words.

'I have never met him face to face!' the Caïd replied in French.

Wrapping his head in a fold of his brown burnous, he stepped back out of sight among the massed delegation.

Saint-Arnaud's information was correct, but the Caïd has spoken the truth. Bu Maza had simply taken up his position under the ramparts a few days previously; there he had received his adepts and his new disciples, but the Caïd himself never made a move: he would not even go to meet the Amir, and even less any local chief. 'A ruse,' his enemies said; 'the pride of his *Kulugli* ancestors,' his disciples retorted.

Nevertheless, the Caïd was feeling his age. The day that Saint-Arnaud proffered his insults and threats, a *goum* encircled the city, led by Si M'hamed, the Aga of Ouarsenis. As soon as the French left, he came to pay his respects to Ben Kadruma. He stood on the threshold and bowed.

The two men faced each other for a moment in silence: the ruler of the city, in his morning finery, but grim-faced, despite the temporary peace of mind gained from his attendance at public prayers at the principal mosque; the Berber with his eagle profile, in his new russet robe of office, the uniform of his enfeoffment by the French. With what ulterior motive did this man – well-known to be redoubtable – come, ostensibly to assure the Caïd of his friendship?

'I shall pursue the Sharif without respite,' he now declared. 'If he had not tortured and killed my friend, the Aga Bel Kassem, I might have believed in his divine mission! The sons of the city and the neighbouring mountains rush recklessly to join him . . . Despite his youth, and his apparent asceticism – of which I have my doubts – for me he is a trickster and a charlatan!'

'How can we detect trickery nowadays?' replied the Caïd. 'Our liberty has vanished, the days of misery have barely begun!'

The Aga of Ouarsenis abruptly changed the subject; he spoke of his eldest son.

'After leaving the *zaouia* of Mazuna, where he was the best student, he has studied in Tunis and Kairouan!'

He boasted of his knowledge and bravery; he dreamt of the boy's succeeding him in his office. The Caïd did not reply. 'I will never give him my daughter,' he thought, sensing what was coming. They bade each other farewell and the Aga took his leave. That same day his *goum* left the ruined, despoiled city which closed its gates upon them.

It was then the middle of April; the spring was spent in skirmishes, numerous brief clashes, interminable hot pursuits. On market days the young Sharif's name was on everybody's lips: they said how handsome he was; they told of the sign on his brow, of how he was invulnerable to bullets, they spoke of his fleet charger, of his prophetic words and his lieutenants; one day, the most prestigious of all these, Aïssa ben Djinn, appeared in person in a market-place.

Badra's nurse had gone out that day to fetch fresh herbs and phials of rare perfumes and came back puzzled. She described him to Badra: 'The "Son of the Devil", as they call him, serves the beloved Sharif! He has a scar on his chin, but his bony face, all angles, appears so handsome: a veritable hero of liberty! In the early days of Islam, Sidi Ali must have looked like that to Fatima, our beloved Prophet's daughter! . . .'

'So what if Aïssa ben Djinn was cruel!' the nurse mused. 'He was a poet,' she added. 'They say that in every tribe, perhaps even in every old house in Mazuna, all the beautiful women dream about him. For he must rejoice the heart of every one in spite of all the dangers, since he loves love, just as he loves Liberty! . . .'

Badra sat and listened to the nurse describe the hero.

'If the Sharif,' she replied, 'came to ask my father for my hand, such as I am now, I would reply that I am ready to marry him on the spot!!'

And it befell that very evening that the Caïd's two wives entered the room with the blue ceramic tiles.

'Your father bids us tell you . . .' the first one began, 'that the Aga of Ouarsenis, Si M'hamed, has today asked for your hand for his eldest son!'

'Your father has given his consent. They will come next Friday for the *fatiha* and to take you away the following day!'

Badra was stunned. 'My poor darling!' sighed the nurse, taking her in her arms.

It was impossible to tell which of the two women was shedding more tears on the silken couch perfumed with musk ... The two stepmothers left together, their coloured taffeta robes rustling in the silence.

Thus, early in July, the Aga of Ouarsenis made his triumphant entry into Mazuna at the head of an imposing escort, followed by carriages bearing the most beautiful women of his tribe. As the porter opened the heavy gates to him, he looked down on him from his mount and offered him his copper cup, saying, 'I give this to you, so that you will always remember this day!'

The porter took the carved *setla*. So, it was true: Bu Maza had been put to flight and the Aga had killed many of his disciples and dispersed the rest; he had even laid hands on his treasure and his banners.

He dared not bring them here, to this city which he knew to be loud with admiration for the exploits of the Sharif and his lieutenants. If he had ventured to show a single one of the stolen banners, the porter himself would doubtless have spat at him: 'You are nothing but jackals while he is a lion, hiding temporarily in his lair!'

'He gives me the copper cup,' the Mazuni thinks, 'to emphasize that he is henceforward doubly rich: with the spoils from our hero and now to carry off tomorrow the most beautiful of our daughters in his retinue!'

The Aga of Ouarsenis rode through the heart of the old city, under hostile eyes – some of the notables nevertheless nodding their heads in cautious greeting. The procession of more than one hundred horsemen paraded along the green edges of the ravine that cut diagonally through the city. The ride lasted two long hours, while in the Caïd's home in the West, against a century-old olive grove, the women's shrill ululations rose in the air.

The Berber horsemen began their *Fantasia* in the market-place; it went on far into the warm summer night. Badra was seated like an idol in the midst of the guests and the women of the city; her face was hidden, only her hands and feet were visible beneath her shot-silk draperies. Prayers, interspersed with blessings, rose up in sheaves, while the Mulattress, her face bathed in tears, tendered to her mistress the henna paste, mixed in a cup from Medina.

The city shook with the sound of galloping hooves and volleys of shots; the chorus of women called on the Prophet and local saints to bless the wedding which was to take place the following day . . . Mazuna was living through its last night as a free city and the virgin, under the gaze of the guests in all their finery, finally let her tears flow.

The bridal procession left Mazuna at the first light of dawn with the palanquin bearing the bride in the lead, preceded by five or six horsemen, chosen from among the youngest first cousins of the absent bridegroom.

Standing in front of her dwelling, the Caïd Ben Kadruma was the only one to glimpse Badra's face. Some claimed later that he spoke to her of her dead mother and then, in cryptic terms, abruptly asked her forgiveness.

The hundred or so horsemen who had arrived the preceding day again paraded with the same haughty air. The carriages bearing the women-folk related to the Aga were now joined by others in which were seated the bride's stepmothers, her two paternal aunts and a dozen ladies from the city. They were going on to Miliana where, it was said, a seven-day feast was being prepared.

In the raised palanquin, facing the gilded and painted bride, the Mulattress sat in a blue gown glittering with sequins, a scarlet silk kerchief covering her frizzy hair. Next to her sat the Aga's daughter, not much younger than Badra, scarcely less beautiful.

The Aga Si M'hamed rode at the head of the imposing procession, never taking his eyes off the palanquin. The next festivities, he thought, would be for the marriage of his own daughter, perhaps to the son of his new colleague, the Aga of the Sbeah, Si Mohamed, who had succeeded Bel Kassem who had been killed by Bu Maza.

One of the young men in the vanguard suddenly broke rank and galloped up to the Aga.

'A group of horsemen in red robes has appeared in the West, beyond the first valleys!'

'The red robes of the Spahis!' exclaimed the Aga.

He reined in his horse, stared in the direction indicated: he could see nothing but a distant speck, scarcely moving. He waved his arm, signalling to the procession to halt. The four horses drawing the palanquin reared suddenly, so that the *attatich* pitched over to the left for a moment . . . A woman gave a faint scream, but the palanquin righted itself.

'It's my friend the Aga Mohamed's escort!' Si M'hamed exclaimed in his stentorian voice. 'He promised me he would meet us with his guards and horsemen. He has arrived for the *Fantasia*! Let us give him a worthy welcome!'

The horsemen who had ridden ahead gradually returned; the procession re-formed and awaited orders.

'Form two rows!' the Aga commanded.

While the men took up their new positions, with only the guards around the palanquin retaining their original places, the Aga of Ouarsenis rode around, smiling, proud of this encounter which reminded him of the festivities of his youth, perhaps of his own wedding.

'They are approaching!' someone observed.

A cloud of dust growing ever thicker covered the horizon. As the dust haze spread, tall figures could be clearly distinguished bending low over their sturdy mounts, with flecks of scarlet, their unmistake-able Spahi capes, swirling behind them in the wind raised as they raced. Suddenly the regular, staccato thud of galloping hooves was upon them like the syncopated chugging of some invisible machine . . . Only a few of those present, more observant than the rest, were surprised at the number approaching: twenty, thirty horsemen or more, a vanguard probably. Shortly afterwards they could identify the crouching figures more distinctly, making out their bent legs, their long-barrelled rifles slung across their chests.

'I can't descry my colleague!' the Aga murmured, erect in the midst of his companions who had come to a halt over a distance of some hundred yards.

The invisible women watching in the barouches grew agitated. Since there was talk of an imminent *Fantasia*, they gave voice in chorus to one preliminary prolonged cry, an echoing ululation, by way of prologue to the festivities. Almost simultaneously a rifle shot rang out in the forest striated with shrieks. Someone shouted that a whole host was approaching from the rear. The Aga M'hamed, still isolated, instinctively drew nearer to the palanquin. He was still looking for the Aga of the Sbeah; even if he could not be distinguished from his Spahis, he was now within hailing distance of his colleague. Si M'hamed was suddenly anxious, both for his daughter and his daughter-in-law.

Shots; an impenetrable dust-screen; flashes of light piercing the haze. A man groaned, then gave vent to a cry of rage: 'Treachery! Treachery!'

The wave of riders swept down with a dull roar which split tenfold into piercing howls, then a tremor rippled through the horde like a field of corn laid low by a storm:

'Mohamed ben Abdallah!'

'Mohamed ben Abdallah!'

Light finally dawned on the Aga Si M'hamed: now the carbines were chattering uninterruptedly and already one man, then a second man had fallen near him under the volley of shots.

'Treachery! Treachery!' panic-stricken voices repeated, amid the hubbub and confusion.

It was, alas, the Sharif Bu Maza, with his men! As they approached, some of them, laughing wildly, cast off in a dramatic gesture the Spahis' cloaks which they had donned as camouflage.

'They've killed my friend, the Aga Mohamed and his guards!' the Aga thought. 'Then they must have stripped off their uniforms to disguise themselves so as to approach us with impunity. With Bel Kassem and Mohamed now dead, I am the only one left of the three of us, and I too shall soon be dead!'

He alone had kept his rifle loaded. All his men had their weapons loaded with blanks. Around him all was turmoil; in the rear, his men were in flight. More than a dozen fell at the first encounter; a few others had time to use their daggers . . . The Aga himself engaged in a hand-to-hand struggle with one of the Sharif's men – he recognized him, by his physique, as a Sbeah from the nearby locality. At the same time, his mind was filled with conflicting thoughts: to stay near the palanquin and defend the two girls; to defend himself till the bitter end, and kill as many as possible of the enemy; he felt no hatred, but he seemed to be enveloped in a white veil of bewilderment. His first assailant fell back wounded; then he found himself facing two, three combined against him. Only their gleaming eyes were visible.

'How could that devil of a Sharif have managed to return so quickly and so secretly from fighting against the Flittas?'

These thoughts passed mechanically through his mind while he defended himself with an agility which he knew in the long run to be useless . . . His first wound, in the right side under his armpit, jerked him upright in the saddle and, for the first time, he caught sight of his rival clearly outlined on a hilltop, a new scarlet banner held high above him. Bu Maza was surveying the joust, like an eagle poised above his prey.

At the second wound, the Aga knew he would not survive this mêlée. Now he was beset by four assailants; one of them stood back to gaze at the open wound. The Aga killed one, wounded the second who recoiled but came back to the charge; the third one hesitated.

'Allah is great!' Si M'hamed shrieked towards the palanquin. The black face of the nurse could be seen peeping at this terrible encounter through a gap in the silken hangings.

The greater part of the *goum*, now leaderless, were drifting to the rear. Some of the wounded fled, pursued by Aïssa ben Djinn and his soldiers. Bodies of men and horses were already piling up around the bleeding Aga, reeling in the saddle.

It would still have been possible for him to leap to the ground and attempt to escape. The thought did not even cross his mind. 'My daughter! My daughter-in-law!' he kept repeating. As from a great distance he could hear women's hysterical screams, interspersed with men's shrieks from both sides. The Mulattress was leaning half out of the gaping hangings of the palanquin moaning, 'O Allah! O Allah! O Sidi Yahia, Sidi Abd al-Qadir!'

As his adversaries closed in on him for the third time, planting a dagger in his midriff, the Aga felt a chill penetrate him. 'It is the end!' he thought without regrets, as drowsiness overcame him and the sky seemed to shroud him in a vast blue-grey canopy, stretching far into the distance.

He had the impression that the motionless figure of the Sharif on the hillside, although still some way off, was quite close by. Bu Maza was laughing.

The Aga was finally unseated and fell headlong towards the palanquin with the renewed cry, 'Allah is great!' The curtains opened and the Aga's daughter leapt down on to the victim's body, screaming 'My father! My father!'

The girl threw herself on the ground, draped in her green silk finery, thinking to protect her father in his death-throes: four of the Sharif's horsemen watched her with fascination. Apart from the rest, Aïssa ben Djinn raised his arm in a grandiloquent gesture.

'The bride of Mazuna is free!' he cried in a note of parody.

Having stood long overlooking the field of battle, Bu Maza now approached, his face expressionless. Before even glancing at the women, he softly asked Aïssa, 'How many of these dogs are dead?'

'Twenty to thirty of their men are left lying here. The women are in our hands; the rest of the soldiers have fled!' someone close by replied.

'That traitor of an Aga fought to the bitter end! He certainly showed courage!' declared Aïssa, pointing with his foot towards the body.

He made as if to approach the daughter who was clinging to the corpse, sobbing, her hair in disarray. The Sharif stopped him with a sign.

'This one will be for me!' he was about to say.

Then he looked up: Badra, dazzling in her wedding attire, was alighting majestically from the palanquin.

Mohamed ben Abdallah, known as Bu Maza, also called 'Moul es-Saa' or 'The Master of the Hour' by the Achaba, Mediuna, Beni Hadjes, Sbeah and other equally bellicose tribes of the Dahra, Bu Maza, the new idol of these mountains, but also the terror of the citizens of Mazuna, sat erect on his chestnut mount which the Flittas in the West had presented to him. This proud steed had belonged to old Mustapha himself, the celebrated chief of the Douaïrs whom they had ambushed in a narrow defile and killed, two years before. Bu Maza gazed admiringly at Badra, without admitting that this prey dazzled him.

She slowly alighted as the velvet hangings of the litter were raised by the Mulattress who stood frozen behind her, her eyes nearly out of their sockets. Only a little of the colour has drained from Badra's face; her diadem is poised on her head-dress of violet shot-silk; her hair in two braided strands interlaced with silken cords hangs about her bare neck and falls over the opening of her corsage which is adorned with two rows of sequins . . . She calmly takes two, three steps forward, bringing her close to the corpses: she barely lowers her eyes, the better to let the Sharif gaze into her face.

Her embroidered mules, her gown of emerald velvet, the gold belt encircling her high waist, the veil of silvery gauze floating about her arms and falling down to her knees, every detail of her costume made her an unreal apparition: the horsemen behind Bu Maza seemed to hold their breath.

Aïssa ben Djinn, on one side, near to the Aga's daughter who still clung to her father's body, murmured ironically to himself, 'After the hyena, here now is the young lioness!'

His chief, silent, his white cleric's hand poised on the damascened

93

leather pommel, pretended not to hear. A moment passed; a horse whinnied in the distance; another reared. The men seemed to grow impatient, but they all remained silent and respectful. Aïssa ben Djinn approached Bu Maza and this time said aloud, 'We'll bring the two girls with their servant to your tent presently, my lord!'

The Sharif's narrow gleaming eyes never left Badra's silhouette. He finally half turned his head to his lieutenant. He did not smile. He simply gave a slight nod of acquiescence.

With one abrupt movement he wheeled his horse and rode off to ascertain the result of the other ambush two leagues away: the soldiers of the *goum*, who had fled through the gorges of the wadi, had been waylaid by Sbeah foot soldiers . . . Volley after volley of shots had greeted them. A messenger had just announced that the Aga's men had been decimated in this second ambush.

One hour later Bu Maza retired to his tent which had been pitched for the night.

No-one knew, the next day, if the two virgins had scorned the Sharif when he came to take his place before them, or if it was he who was reluctant to use force when faced by his victims – were they repelled or fascinated by him?

The dead Aga's daughter, whether out of loathing or vengeance, kept her father's dagger in her hand the whole of the day and throughout the following night. 'I'll kill myself, or I'll kill you!' she kept on repeating in her frenzy and did not cease her wild cries even when Bu Maza made as if to approach. The young leader seemed at a loss for words: only a slight narrowing of his eyes betrayed what surprise he might have felt in the face of these females who, despite or because of his brilliant victory, would not yield.

The servant was ordered to take the daughter, still convulsed with hate, out of the tent. They spent the rest of the night outside: it was the beginning of July, a few days after the full moon. A fire of olive branches warmed them with its bluish flames.

Thus Badra remained alone with the Sharif, on this night which should have been her wedding night. From time to time a jackal howled in the nearby valleys. Behind the thuyas a scout started. The guard was then reinforced. But the torches all remained alight in the chief's tent. Clasping the Aga's sleeping daughter in her arms, the Mulattress listened. Not a voice, not a sound from nearby! 'How can a man resist the dazzling beauty of my little Badra? . . .' Mechanically, she recited fragments from the Quran. 'Is the Sharif a man?'

At dawn the flap of the white tent was raised. Bu Maza emerged into the pale early-morning light, but inside the tent the flame of the candle still cast its pool of light . . . The Sharif blinked. Before she was aware of his approach, the Mulattress found him near her. He nodded and withdrew. The servant entered.

Badra looked as if she had not stirred since the preceding evening. She sat like a statue, her eyes closed, her eyelids still painted blue, fine beads of perspiration on her brow, in the moist air . . . 'The weight of the diadem,' thought the servant, falling to her knees.

And only then, overcome with tenderness and emotion, she began to remove the bejewelled ornaments from the bride's head, ears and neck: the *açaba* with its pendants, the triangular *chengals* for the ears, the numerous *bessita* necklaces from Fez, the heavy brooches set with emeralds, the rosy *trembleuses* of the head-dress. 'All these jewels,' she thought, 'protected her from the covetousness of all too human desire. The Sharif – may Allah preserve him – did not deign to touch the gold to touch the girl, and the girl . . .'

Badra, relieved of the weight on her head and shoulders, huddled in her nurse's arms.

'I am dead!' she sighed. 'I am dead!'

After her attendant had laid Badra down to rest, she thought how the mortified girl must have wept; she said to herself . . . 'He disdained the rarest pearl of Mazuna!'

In the course of the morning, a relative of the 'Son of the Devil' came to tell him that a delegation of Mazunis had arrived, led by the *Kulugli* Caïd himself, and been received by the Sharif.

'How much did that dog, son of a dog and lackey of the Christians give you as dowry for your daughter, you who have served more glorious masters?'

The Caïd Ben Kadruma, his head bowed humbly as befitted a suppliant, was forced to divulge the amount.

'You will pay twice that to get your daughter back and regain your honour!'

Each of the leading citizens then discussed the ransom for each of the women who were waiting a little way off. The Sharif had scornfully left these parleys to his lieutenants.

'These men are perfidious and tomorrow, at our first setback, they will return to attack us and throw themselves on the mercy of the French colonel!'

'But what can you expect of these Moors!' someone remarked. 'For generations, from father to son, the sole reason for their actions has always been fear!'

All the women prisoners, except Badra and the Aga's daughter, were clustered round the marabout Sidi Ben Daoud, where the Sharif's scarlet banner had been flying since the previous evening; now they learned that the ransom would be paid within the hour and they would soon be free . . .

Some of them bore bleeding scratches on their faces and necks where they had lacerated themselves as signs of mourning for husbands and sons who remained without sepulture on the field of battle. Others, relatives of the bride, showed neither fear nor sorrow. They waited patiently, impassive, at the most merely heaving languid sighs. From time to time there was a whisper from one of them; they were breathless with curiosity: how could they discover whether the Sharif, or one of his redoubtable lieutenants, was going to keep the two virgins, or at least Badra, the more beautiful?

Soon the amount of ransom demanded of the Caïd circulated among these city ladies. And, reinforced by the meal of couscous with chicken prepared for them by the marabout's *wali*, they were able to forget their fatigue in smug pleasure at the sum, as if the value of a virtuous and beautiful woman – more priceless than the jewels – could be calculated in gold pieces!

The tents remained pitched for a second night. The Sharif decided that they would leave the encampment the following dawn. His scouts had returned just before dusk: they reported that the garrisons at El-Asnam, Miliana and Tenes had been filled with consternation at the news of his victory . . . The colonel had already sent messengers to General de Bourjolly and to the leader of the Tenes column. The French would move the next day or in two days at the latest.

'We shall cross the Beni Hindjes,' declared Bu Maza; 'from there we shall return to the Flittas' country.'

The gold from the citizens of Mazuna had arrived. The burghers had been forced to spend the night cooling their heels before being made to hand over their treasure.

'We are neither looters nor highway robbers, and God's justice can wait!'

The Sharif's lieutenant Ben Henni, chief of the tribes around the ancient city of Tenes, came to confirm that its Moorish population, like that of Mazuna, spoke of nothing but the Sharif's reappearance. The two important mosques had resounded with heartfelt prayers! In their defeat, these cities were moved partly by fear, partly by newfound zeal for the faith.

'Saint Sid Ahmad ben Yusuf was right to make them the butt of his famous axioms!' someone murmured near to the Sharif, who did not smile.

Aïssa ben Djinn whispered in his ear, '*Seigneur*, it is time to hand over the women. My men have counted the *duros* of the ransom. The tally is correct! . . . You have enough to raise double the number of troops from all the loyal tribes as far as Mostaganem; perhaps you could even join forces with the Amir!'

The Sharif interrupted in an undertone: 'I hear that his messenger is in fact approaching, bearing a letter! . . . You see to the women!' Then, after a pause, 'Let us keep the Aga's daughter! She persists in her insults: let the blood of the maid follow that of the father! . . . I give her to you!'

Aïssa bowed his head as sole acknowledgement of the gift that had just been made to him. Then he began, 'I have a suggestion: send back the Mazunis' wives and daughters without their jewels! . . . They are worth as much again as all the ransom money!'

And he burst out laughing.

'They rightly call you "Son of the Devil",' the Sharif retorted with a smile. 'Do as you like with them. This extra booty is yours!'

The women filed one by one out of the tent, some in coloured veils, some in faded white. They stood before Aïssa ben Djinn who was surrounded by four of his men. An unarmed *chaouch* waited in ceremonial attire.

'You must each remove every item of jewellery and hand it to the *chaouch*! If anyone hesitates or shows reluctance, then I'll tear off her jewels with my own hands and her clothes as well!' Aïssa announced in his sonorous voice.

A cacophony of chatter and squeals broke out among the women, unable to control their agitation. Then one of Aïssa ben Djinn's men raised his rifle and fired several shots into the air and silence fell.

The *chaouch* sat down cross-legged and waited; his scarlet turban slid down over his brow; his venerable mustachios framed a smile; his pose seemed to caricature that of a *cadi*.

'Brigands! Highway robbers!' hissed one of the women.

And the others immediately protested: 'Hold your tongue, wretch! Do you want to get us all assassinated?'

One by one the ladies came forward, slowly, solemnly, with faces and bodies completely shrouded. One by one hands emerged from folds in the coloured veil, dropped a jewelled fillet, brooches, a pair of *khalkhals*, three, four or five rings . . . The inventory was taken by a *khoja* who inscribed on a tablet the number of items and their description.

It took over an hour for the women to hand over all their precious ornaments. Meanwhile the Sharif rode to and fro on his chestnut, a little way off . . .

Suddenly there was an unexpected pause, a moment of suspense: from the chief's tent the bride emerged, her face uncovered; she walked stiffly under the weight of her adornment, bearing her rich diadem before her in both hands. She was the last. She seemed to be wearing all the jewels of the entire city. 'She's the cause of all our misfortunes!' exclaimed one of her stepmothers.

Badra approached with lowered eyes, as if she knew the way instinctively. Her nurse followed her, weeping: would there never be a wedding for the girl? The Sharif, who was riding away, halted, looking down on the colourful scene, while behind the cactus hedge the sky was growing lighter.

Badra paused in front of Aïssa ben Djinn, who ventured no comment: he too looked calmly on with admiring eyes.

With an ample gesture, as if she were in her bridal chamber, she laid down her tiara, then her heavy earrings, then the four, five, six pearl necklaces, then the brooches – ten at least – then . . . 'Allah! Allah!' sighed the *chaouch* and asked for another casket. The scribe, his eyes dazzled as much by the splendour of the precious stones as by the beauty of the bride herself, forgot to write down the inventory.

The girl now wore nothing but her light gown with its loose folds and her waistcoat with full gauze sleeves. With one rapid movement she took off her conical cap embroidered with gold, and placed it with the other jewels – and her thick black tresses streamed down her back. Then, stooping quickly, she removed her green velvet mules, also embroidered with gold. With a dancer's lithe twist of her hips, she wriggled out of her heavy sequined girdle. Then she stooped down once more, removed her ankle bracelets and presented them, almost stealthily, to the stupified *chaouch*. Then the sound of horses' hooves was heard. Bu Maza was galloping away.

'Enough!' screamed a woman's voice from the midst of the group of prisoners.

'Will she strip herself naked?' added another, from the front. Then a collective babble of hostile voices arose.

In two strides the nurse was at her side. She wrapped her arms around the frail adolescent, clothed only in her emerald gown, her hair streaming in the wind, her face raised to the sky, and repeating softly, 'I am naked! Praise be to God, I am naked! Praise . . .'

The Mulattress gently fondled her exhausted child, cradling her like a mother and gradually persuaded her to join the murmuring group of prisoners.

No-one asked what had become of the other maiden, the dead Aga's daughter. The Sharif's tent had been struck. His column was the first to leave, his banner flying in the lead, the band of flutes and drums playing a shrill melody. Aïssa ben Djinn's men brought up the rear, their mules laden with jewels and the gold from the ransom.

Two weeks later, after smoking out the Sbeah fraction not far from the Nacmaria caves, Colonel Saint-Arnaud finally caught up with Bu Maza who had been trying to avoid doing battle for a time.

Treasure and *smala* were seized and Canrobert, Saint-Arnaud's adjutant, dispersed the partisans . . . The Aga's daughter, the Sharif's prisoner, disappeared in the confusion of the encounter (did she share his tent and persist in mocking him with her insults? – no-one knew). Two days later, as her brother, who was acting as guide to Canrobert's Spahis, rode under an oak tree, he heard a frightened voice whisper, 'Brother! Ali, my brother!'

The Aga's son halted under a branch of the tree. A slender figure jumped down and landed right in the astonished young man's saddle.

'I've been hiding there for two days!' the girl murmured, after they had embraced.

On their return to Tenes the French column reported how the brother and sister had been miraculously united . . . But in the Mazuna market-place the *meddahs* recounted to the people how the Sultan, whose coming had been prophesied, had stripped the wives and daughters of the traitors and their allies, handing them over 'naked'. Mohamed ben Kadruma sold everything he owned, and after repudiating his two wives decided to undertake the pilgrimage to Mecca, accompanied by his daughter.

'On my return,' he announced to some of his family, 'I shall not come back to live in this city which will no longer be free! I shall go into exile, like so many others, to Tunis, to Damascus or even to Istambul.'

The year before these events took place, a farmer, who had been a lieutenant in Napoleon's army, and had been ruined about 1840 when the Rhone twice overflowed its banks, emigrated to Algeria. Bérard – that was his name – chose to settle in Tenes, the new town which Bugeaud's army built with wooden houses, later replaced by stones from the imposing Roman ruins.

Bérard soon abandons farming. He sets himself up as a stationer, selling paper, pencils, exercise-books; he even opens a reading-room. The insurrection breaks out in the Dahra, with all changing fortunes, including the Mazuna wedding which Bu Maza transformed into an ambush.

The bookseller Bérard, thanks to his experience as a veteran of the Emperor's army, but also thanks to his education and his greying hair, has become one of the leading citizens of European Tenes, alarmed by the nearby disturbances. He is in command of one of the newly-established militia . . . Twenty years later, he writes his account of the uprising: but he never went to Mazuna. No European was yet to venture there; the neutrality of the ancient city was frozen in eternal slumber.

One of Bu Maza's lieutenants, El-Gobbi, also wrote his account of the events. Did he take part in the attack on the wedding procession? Was he one of those who, standing beside his leader, admired Badra's 'naked' figure? It is reasonable to imagine that he did.

When Bérard composes his memoirs, he declares that he had knowledge of El-Gobbi's account. Could he perhaps have read a translation of the Arabic text, or might he have had a copy of the original in his hands? For the moment, this is lost.

Finally everything lies dormant: the bodies of the women, crushed beneath the weight of their jewels; cities weighed down by the burden of their past; and so too the epigraphs left by long-forgotten witnesses.

III

The couple moved into a little flat in Paris, in which a bookseller carried on his business, and where they were to celebrate their wedding.

Preparations for the ceremony progressed in an atmosphere of unreality as if catastrophe were waiting round the corner: might there not be some hitch at the last minute preventing the guests and even the bridal couple themselves from attending? . . .

The bride-to-be prowled around the dark rooms with their many bookcases. Her mother, a slender woman of under forty, with a heavy braid of black hair down her back, arrived on the night flight, accompanied by her youngest daughter, barely more than a child. The three of them spring-cleaned the flat, then the mother and fiancée went to buy a makeshift trousseau at the Grands Magasins: underclothes, a silk suit in sky-blue checks, a pair of shoes.

The wedding date had been fixed a month ago by the fiancé who was on the run and constantly had to move from one lodging to another; the girl was staying in a students' hostel and kept in touch with each new address. They had been living in this precarious way for the past year but were safe for the time being.

One of the previous hide-outs had been opposite an institution for deaf-mutes. It had had to be abandoned in a hurry. The caretaker was a dumpy, dishevelled little woman; every evening, in her frustration over her husband's daily drunken bouts, she would let fly a stream of obscenities in the courtyard. One day, she saw off two policemen who came to enquire about the young student. 'Oh, that bird's flown ages ago!' she snorted.

As soon as the police had gone, she hurried upstairs to warn the couple, declaring, 'I just can't abide cops! It's in my blood!'

The police had originally begun their enquiry about the young man

101

for a fairly innocuous reason: as a student his military service had previously been deferred but he was now due for call-up. His old parents, in their mountain village, alarmed by frequent guerrilla attacks and the subsequent round-ups of all suspects, warned their son that they had been forced to give his address in Paris, which they hoped was no longer valid.

'He doesn't write to me any more!' his father told the investigators. 'He must be working in France to pay for his studies. We are poor. I can't send him any money!'

Then he had dictated a letter to his twelve-year-old daughter, 'Write: "They'll find you! You must move house!" '

The son didn't wait to be told twice. Hence the panic before the wedding. That summer, a rival Nationalist faction was increasingly threatening a vendetta. They objected to former militants (workers who used to meet before the war in North African cafés) joining the unified organization. The first clash between rival underground networks had resulted in five or six deaths in a restaurant in the centre of Paris. The main dailies had reported this incident as a matter of gangsters taking the law into their own hands to settle old scores.

The couple continued to roam the streets, chatting together, momentarily free of the others and the 'Revolution'; nevertheless, even if their embraces in a doorway could not claim that they were making history, still their happiness was part of the collective fever; and they were always on the look-out to see if they were being shadowed and to throw the police off their trail. But the police were not seen to be the greatest danger.

Sometimes they noticed one persistent figure following them or one who, on the contrary, vanished too conspicuously, then they had to give their pursuer the slip, spot the person on the watch and outwit him: the couple knew that the secret fratricidal struggle was all around them. The rival networks posted threatening letters to each other, couched in hysterical terms, announcing imminent retribution in the name of some imaginary rights, such as a woman scorned in love might write in desperation to her rival.

As they strolled through the Paris streets together, at every crossroads the girl's eyes instinctively avoided the tricolour flag whose red reminded her of the blood of her compatriots recently guillotined in a Lyons prison; and she dreamed of them both suddenly becoming invisible in the early spring sunshine that streamed

102

down over them, and disappearing to sail the high seas together.

They ought to leave: they talked of nothing else. To leave together! To return to their own country and join the maquisards in the mountains, people careless of danger like themselves. However, the young man raised objections: 'We're not being realistic; you're living in a dream world! You're only imagining there'll be other women students! We shan't be able to fight side by side . . . The only women in the resistance are peasants, used to the forests and brambles! Perhaps, at the best, a few nurses!' She couldn't understand why he refused her access to this dream-garden of adventure where they would share the hazards cheerfully together like twins . . . The previous evening hadn't they easily given two policemen the slip in the corridors of the Métro, as if it had been a game, after which they had collapsed with helpless laughter? . . .

They continued to be at loggerheads (she thought they were really only in disagreement over tactics) until they finally arrived at a compromise: as it was impossible to leave for home immediately they might as well slip over the border as soon as possible, separately if necessary (only the young man figured on a list of suspects). They would meet in Tunisia, joining other refugees; from there there must be crowds of volunteers leaving to join the underground. She persisted in believing that girls were being accepted as volunteers; were not the Nationalist leaders anxious to make it known that all were equal in the struggle?

They argued endlessly as they walked, filling in the detail of their plans; and as they outlined their future, the young man decided they must get married as soon as possible, and then leave . . .

The previous spring, the representatives of the two families had met back home, without the couple, to celebrate their official betrothal. They learned afterwards that this ceremony had provided the occasion for drawing up the marriage certificate 'in advance'. The groom's uncle had signed by proxy; as for the bride, even if she had been present, her father would have had to act for her, as her guardian. The marriage was legalized, in spite of their absence far away: they had laughed at this formality, which seemed like something out of a comedy.

'Write to your family,' the fiancé suddenly demanded, overcome by desire or subconscious anxiety. 'Tell them we're getting married here a month today! After all, by law we are already married!'

The flat – belonging to a bookseller, a Frenchman who had been detained for the past month for having helped a Nationalist network – had been empty since the owner's arrest, and for that reason the police were no longer watching it. A friend let them know about it on his discharge from prison.

They decided to move in temporarily. The bride-to-be spent the days before the wedding buried in the rare books with their luxurious bindings, after doing her best to light the ancient coke stove: these winter mornings the rooms were filled with smoke which gave off no warmth.

When the bride's mother and young sister arrived, they were not completely out of their element. The brother, still an adolescent, had been arrested in Lorraine as an 'agitator', and began his term of detention by being constantly shunted from prison to prison; the mother had learned to travel by train, by plane, by boat, just like any Western tourist, and every three months she visited her only son in whatever city in France or Navarre he had been dumped.

The women set about putting the Parisian flat in order: waxing the floor, cleaning up the kitchen, ordering new bed-linen which was delivered at the last minute for the newly-weds, finally giving some thought to the traditional meal for the day after the wedding – the mother considered this an essential institution and invited their dozen or so friends and cousins, immigrant students and workers in Paris . . .

Watching her youthful mother bustling cheerfully about, the bride felt like a minor character in some arcane play. She mused aloud about the conventions that would have had to be observed back home, but to these exiles their homeland seemed no more real than a sunken city or a desolate ruin. As the fiancé spent more and more time running off to political meetings, and disaster waited to pounce, so their doubts grew about the ceremony due to take place forthwith. What sort of ceremony would that be?

The girl realized that she was upset by her father's absence – though, to be sure, if the wedding had been celebrated in the customary manner, it would have been an exclusively feminine affair.

But tradition demanded that when the women in the bridal retinue are ready to escort the bride, the father wraps his burnous around her and leads her over the threshold in his arms. At this moment of separation, the mother weeps copiously, sometimes noisily – you'd think it was a wake without the liturgy. By adding her lamentations to the din made by singers and neighbours, every mother expresses her distress at the loss of the daughter who should be her support when the fatigues of age befall her. But she is also overcome with sad memories of her own dreams as a woman . . .

My mother, for her part, found herself in a wintry Paris and had no cause to weep. Even if the wedding had taken place back home, in the dead grandmother's house with its many terraces, even if the Andalusian tenor had sung his sentimental songs accompanied by the sound of the rebec one whole night through, the night of the deflowering and its mounting exhilaration – my father would not have borrowed any burnous of pure wool, woven by the women of the tribe, to wrap around me and lead me over the threshold. He would not have made any concessions to protocol: he claimed to be a 'modernist', scorning recent fashions as the stranglehold of city customs. However much the old women may have insisted that he ought to be concerned about divine protection, he would have . . . But what's the use of imagining . . . would he even have faced my fiancé, who he felt, throughout our long secret engagement which eventually became official, was robbing him of his eldest daughter?

It was true: the marriage took place far from my father's protection, not that he withheld this in the form wished for by the elders of the family. It was true: these two men could not have faced each other in this ambiguous situation, neither of them prepared to give way to the other, probably subconsciously hating each other.

As we prepared to celebrate the wedding in our temporary Paris abode, which the Nationalist uprising brushed with its fringes, thoughts of my father filled my mind: I decided to send him a telegram, assuring him formally of my love. I've forgotten the exact wording of the message, possibly: 'Thinking of you on this auspicious day. I love you . . .'

Perhaps I needed to make this public gratuitous declaration: 'I-love-you-in-French', before making bold to voice it in the dark (in what language?) during the hours prior to the nuptial rites of passage?

One by one, the ritual accompaniments of wedding ceremonial were discarded: the shrill female voices, the clamouring crowd of veiled women, the smell of over-abundant victuals – the din kept up so that the bride could be left alone and naked in the midst of the throng to grieve on the threshold of a new life . . .

Marriage for me meant first and foremost departures: hasty crossing of frontiers, new conspirators to be met on new soil. The arrival of my mother and young sister were links with my gradual memories of the past. They brought with them the inherent, underlying gravity of our lives: in the hollow of each shared silence each one of the three of us was constantly thinking of the adolescent transferred from prison to prison, my brother.

And I tiptoe up to the cry uttered on deflowering, the purlieus of childhood recalled as I make my way through these symbols. More than twenty years later, I seem to hear this cry as if it rang out yesterday: expression of neither pain nor wonder . . . Voice of infinite range in aerial flight, presence of solemn eyes opening on to a vertiginous void and only gradually growing aware.

A cry which might ring out at every wedding, without the *Fantasia*, even in the absence of caparisoned horses and riders in flaming crimson. The sharp cry of relief and sudden liberation then abruptly checked. Long, infinite, first cry of the live body.

The young man had always known it: when he crossed the threshold of the room − the shell enclosing transcendental love − he would feel himself in the grip of silent solemnity and before approaching the girl lying there motionless, he should give time to his devotions.

Before a man approaches the couch which will be stained with blood, man, every man, should turn his thoughts submissively to God; he should fall on his knees, prostrate himself, lie prone, fill his heart with Allah, the Prophet and the most familiar saint of his region or his tribe, appeasing his hunger first with the sacred words.

The maiden's calm eyes smile. How can this blood be transformed into a ray of hope, without the two bodies being soiled? A well nigh mystical approach. In this Parisian wedding permeated with nostalgia for the native soil, no sooner has the bridegroom set foot in the room with its brand-new bed, and pink-shaded lamp placed on the floor, than he hurries to the waiting woman, he gazes down at her and forgets all else.

Hours later, lying beside her trembling form, he remembers the neglected ceremonial. He who had never prayed, he had decided to do so just this once, prior to consummating his marriage. He is tormented by a sense of foreboding:

'Our union will not be preserved,' he murmurs.

The bride, amused by this superstitious melancholy, reassures him.

She confidently paints the future of their love: he had promised that the initiation would take as many nights as need be. And yet, at the beginning of their first hurried night, she had already been penetrated. The cry, pure pain, secretes an inner core of wonderment. It soars in a swelling curve. Wake of thrusting dart, it rises in the air; falling, at its nadir, in multi-layered sediment, lurks an unspoken 'No!'

Did I manage one day to ride the surging tide to reach this crest? Did I feel this refusal tremble on my lips? On these banks, the body stiffens in denial, pouring its passion into the current of the nearby river. What matter then if the soul's cry pour forth without restraint?

And I must tell also of my victory, its taste of lost sweetness as the wave swept over me. Victory over modesty, over reserve. Blushing, but insistent, I managed to say to my young mother and sister who gave me so much affectionate support, 'Please leave me alone in the house tonight! . . . "He" will find you a room for the night at the hotel!'

I expressed this wish in a formal tone of voice . . . Since I was not destined to enjoy a noisy crowded wedding with food in abundance, let me be offered a deserted place in which the night could stretch out immense enough, empty enough for me to face 'Him' – I suddenly found myself thinking of the man in the traditional way.

That cry, in the house of our clandestine existence. I enjoyed my victory, since the house did not fill with women, peeping curiously, and in the brief absence of a woman and a little girl, that cry unfurled its spiral of refusal and reached up to the timbers of the ceiling.

The lamp is still alight . . . The bridegroom, wanted by the police, is trapped in the mire of broken promises: he had vowed to say his prayers before.

'Before what?' I wonder as I lurch along the passage, avoiding the mirrors, a wounded gazelle.

Before that cry, of course. 'No!' I think, 'neither God nor any magic formula will protect this love which the man hopes will last "till death do us part".' Travelling in the Métro during the next few days, I stare closely at all the women I see around me. I am devoured with curiosity as if I were some primitive creature: 'Why do they not say, why will not one of them say, why does each one hide this fact: love is the cry, the persistent pain which feeds upon itself, while only a glimpse is vouchsafed of the horizon of happiness? Once the blood has flowed, silence sets in and objects are drained of colour.'

There were no peeping women, dreaming of repeated ravishment. There was no matchmaker draped in the bloodstained sheet, performing her lewd dance with grunts and shrieks of laughter, gesticulating like a fairground Karagoz – the indications of death frozen in the act of love, a body left lying there on stacks of mattresses . . . Normally the bride neither cries out nor weeps: she lies an open-eyed victim on the couch, after the male has departed, fleeing from the smell of sperm and the idol's perfume; and the closed thighs prevent any cry from escaping.

There was no bloodstained sheet on display the following days.

Sistrum

*[Sistrum, n. (pl. -tra). Jingling in-
strument or rattle used by ancient
Egyptians esp. in rites of Isis. OED]*

*Long silence, night rides, coils curling in the throat. Rhonchial râles, streams
of abyssal sounds, springs from which issue interlacing echoes, cataracts of
murmurs, susurrus in braided brushwood, tendrils soughing under the tongue,
hushed hisses, and the flexured voice hauls up sullied sighs of past satiety from
memory's subterranean store-house.*

*Cacophany of recalcitrant cymbal, thistle or scissors rending this tessitura,
shards of shipwrecked sighs, water lapping against the valanced bed, scattered
laughter striating claustral darkness, plaints pacified then diffused behind
closed eyelids whose dream strays through some cypress grove, and the ship of
desire drops astern, before the raven of sexual ecstasy croaks its contentment.*

*Molten words, splintered firestones, diorites expelled from gaping lips,
fire-brand caresses when the harsh leaden silence crumbles, and the body seeks
for its voice, like a fish swimming upstream.*

*Renewed râles, watery stairways to the larynx, splashes, lustral sprinkling,
the plaintive moan escapes then the prolonged song, the drawn-out song of the
rich female voice closes round the copulation, follows its tempo and its figures,
is exhaled as oxygen, in the bedchamber and the darkness, a tumescent twisted
coil of forte notes hanging in the air.*

*Suffering or solemn gasps of act of love, sulphur-mine of anticipation, fever
of staccato notes.*

*Silence, pleasure's defensive rampart, protecting the final reckoning – in
what language written, Arabic or French?*

Creation every night. Brocaded gold of silence.

PART THREE

VOICES FROM THE PAST

And I come to the fields and spreading courts of memory,
where are treaures of unnumbered impressions of things
of every kind, stored by the senses.

Saint Augustin
Confessions, X.8

Quasi una fantasia . . .
Ludwig van Beethoven
opus 27
Sonatas 1 and 2

First Movement:

The Two Strangers

Two men, two strangers intruded so intimately into my life as to seem for a few brief moments to be of my own flesh and blood: we engaged in neither philosophical discourse nor in polite or friendly conversation. Two complete strangers crossed my path, each close encounter accompanied by a cry, a scream – it is of little significance from whom it came, from one or other of those strangers or indeed from myself.

I am seventeen. The morning sun shines on the murmurous city. I come suddenly upon a street that tumbles downhill as far as the eye can see; at the end of every thoroughfare, at the end of every little alleyway, the sea watches, waiting patiently. On I hurry.

We have had a trivial lovers' tiff, which I make into an issue; I hurl a defiant ultimatum at him; an invisible breach occurs and spreads – it is the first . . . I scan the distant horizon; I am spurred on by some strange impulse, a conviction that I must abandon everything; I race along, wishing I had wings. The sun is shining on the murmurous city, other people's city . . .

Frenzy, impetuosity, exhilaration of the all-or-nothing; I rush headlong down the street. Even though I have put nothing into words, probably planned nothing, except to let myself be borne along by this pure spontaneous impulse, my body hurls itself under a tram as it turns a sharp corner of the avenue.

Am I in the vicinity of the port? One final image emerges as I sink into oblivion, seeking annihilation in this flight towards the sea: the glimpse of a ship's masts, piercing the blue sky, like some vast water-colour. Just before all goes dark, I feel the double ridge of the tramlines under me.

113

When, a few minutes later, they lifted me up and I slowly emerged out of the shadow of the tragedy, I caught one isolated voice raised above the commotion made by the crowd of idle onlookers; that of the tram-driver who had just managed to brake in time. In the pallid void of my return to life, I was struck by one detail which assumed a curious importance: the 'Poor White' accent of the man who was so upset that he cried over and over again, 'My hand's still trembling. Look!'

And he repeated the words, almost protesting, and his voice struck me again. I opened my eyes wide. As I lay in the middle of the road, I became aware of the man's burly figure, then his face as he bent over me: the crowd must have made way for him so that he could be reassured. He probably stared hard at the girl who lay still as death, but who was nevertheless alive.

Since then, I've forgotten everything about this stranger; but I can still recall the timbre of his voice, above the swell of sounds that surged around me. Betraying the agitation that would not leave him, making him cry over and over again: 'My hand's still trembling. Look!'

He must have held up his hand to show the crowd of witnesses what had saved me by controlling the speed of the tram.

They lifted her up from underneath the vehicle; an ambulance took her to the nearest hospital; she had only sustained minor bruises. But what she really felt was wonder, to find that, as in a trance, she had gone (so she thought self-importantly) 'to the end' – to the end of what? At the most to the end of the zigzag path of adolescence. So she woke up to the sound of the tram-driver's voice, then sank back to stagnate again in uncertain days and finally let the love story run its course. Never spoke to anyone of her fall – a romantic gesture or expression of rebellion without a cause. Did she even discover the real nature of despair?

The only thing that clung so closely to her was that accent from the poor European districts of the city, that way of speaking which had made her most aware of the tram-driver's voice: Death briefly trails a wing along the ground leaving this jewel behind.

A long history of convulsive love; too long. Fifteen years pass, what happened is of little account. A rapid succession of surfeited years, a happy life is compact, uneventful. Satiety lasts long; too long.

Two, three years elapsed; an unhappy life is compact, uneventful; brief breathing spells in the tedium of time, days streaked with silence.

A woman walks alone one night in Paris. Walking for walking's sake, to try to understand . . . Searching for words and so dream no more, wait no longer.

Rue Richelieu, ten, eleven o'clock at night; the autumn air is damp. To understand . . . Where will this tunnel of interior silence lead? Just the act of walking, just to put one foot energetically in front of the other, feeling my hips swinging, sensing my body lightly moving, makes my life seem brighter and the walls, all the walls vanish . . .

Someone, a stranger, has been walking behind me for a while. I can hear his footsteps. What matter? I am alone, I feel quite alone, I see myself as whole, intact, how can I express it? 'At the beginning', but of what? At least of this new journey. The space is blank, the long empty road is mine alone, I walk at ease, letting my footsteps beat out my own rhythmic accompaniment while the surrounding stones look on.

While the solitude of these recent months dissolves in the fresh cool tints of the nocturnal landscape, suddenly the voice bursts forth. It drains off all the scoriae of the past. What voice? Is it my own voice, scarcely recognizable?

At first this residue, these dregs, this coal-slack cakes and clogs my palate, then the mixture of impurities is flushed from my mouth in a harsh deep-throated cry which seems to go before me.

One single, prolonged, interminable, amorphous tear-drop, a precipitate congealed in the very body of my former voice, in my frozen larynx; this nameless coagulate is washed away in a trail of unidentifiable rubble . . . This nauseating network of sound seems scarcely to concern me; viscous syrup of rasping gasps, guano of old hiccups and choking sobs, smelling of some strangled corpse rotting within me. The voice, my voice (or rather the voice that issues from my open mouth, gaping as if to vomit, or chant some dirge) cannot be suppressed. Perhaps I ought to raise my hand in front of my face to staunch this invisible blood?

At least lessen the intensity of the flow! Behind their walls strangers gather their thoughts, while I am only a wandering exile, in flight from other shores where women are white walking wraiths, shrouded figures buried upright, precisely to prevent what I am doing now, to prevent them uttering such a constant howl: such a wild, barbaric cry, macabre residue of a former century! . . . Lower a little the volume of this death-gasp, turn it into some ill-timed measured chant. Incantation in an interminable exile.

115

Rue Richelieu stretches out long and narrow in front of me; not a soul in sight. Stop when I reach the end; simultaneously switch off this outlandish voice, this *lamento* which I involuntarily sing.

I've forgotten the unknown person behind me who's still following me; he slows down when I do, and just when I'm about to lower my anguished voice or silence it completely, he protests, 'Please, Madame, please don't cry out like that!'

The wailing stops short. In the pool of light shed by a street-lamp, I turn round, expressionless: what is this intruder thinking? That I'm in pain?

'Please go away!'

I speak almost gently, astonished that this stranger should be so upset. I cannot recall his face, I scarcely remember his build, but I can still hear his voice, warm and vibrant, quavering slightly from the urgency of his request. He is upset because 'I cry out', he says. Is this where my attempted revolt will lead, after rumbling underground? . . . This unknown man's reaction is a sudden revelation, I can use it to protect me. No eavesdropper can hurt me any more.

'Please!' I repeat more softly.

Instinctively I draw back. The lamp-light falls on the tall figure, reflected in the glint of the man's eyes as he stares at me. I lower my gaze. He goes away. Two bodies in momentary proximity, scarcely meeting, sharing a brief instant of distress. A fantasy embrace.

Hearing the man implore me, like a friend, like a lover, I regained soon afterwards my zest for life. I threw off the shackles of love, ridding myself of the canker that consumed me. Spending every day laughing, dancing, walking. The only thing I long for is the sun.

So two messengers stand at the entrance and the exit of an obscure love story. No stranger will have come so close to me.

Voice

My elder brother Abdelkader had taken to the hills to join the maquis, some time ago. 'France' came right up to our doorsteps; we were living at the Sidi M'hamed Aberkane *zaouia* . . . 'France' came and burnt us out. We went on living there, just the same, among the blackened stones . . .

Then it was the turn of my second brother, Ahmed, to leave. I was thirteen. The soldiers came again; again they burnt our house down. The other people helped us rebuild it. Time went by; a year perhaps.

Then the soldiers had a skirmish with the partisans on the road through the nearby forest. They raided us the same day. They were looking for 'proof' and they found it: we were in fact looking after some of the Brothers' clothes, and even storing some ammunition. They took my mother and my brother's wife away. They burnt our house down for the third time.

Then the Brothers came that same evening. They took us higher up into the hills, towards Sidi bou Amrane. We reached the *douar* before dawn. The partisans tried to find a place where we could all stay: the women, my old father, my little brothers; we all followed them.

At first the people there wouldn't let us stay: 'The soldiers'll come and burn down our houses too! These people can't stay here! The *zaouia* has been burnt and our *douar* will be burnt down too!'

They kept up their protests for a long time. But Si Slimane and Si Hamid (Si Boualem had been arrested) wouldn't give in.

'These people are going to live here!' they insisted. 'You'll just have to make the best of it! . . . Are some of you afraid of the consequences? Let them go and give themselves up to the enemy, if they prefer . . . These people are staying here!'

So we made ourselves at home there. We kept in contact with the

117

Brothers. We all worked. Once again 'France' arrived and burnt the whole place down. And that was when Hamoud's son gave himself up.

'France' decided to move the whole population down into the plain. But our family stayed where we were, with my mother, who'd been set free. My brother Ahmed, may the Lord have mercy on his soul, left by night to try to find us another shelter.

He didn't have time to return and show us the way. Shortly before dawn the enemy surrounded us. They shouted, 'We'll force you down, like the others!'

When some men tried to force me to my feet, I shouted, 'I won't go!'

A soldier grabbed my one arm, a second one seized the other; I kept on shouting. They pulled me like this out of the house.

So they took us away. On the way they had to cross a wadi. However, it had rained the previous day. The water rushed down in a torrent. One man picked up my young sister to carry her across. She struggled with all her might, shouting, 'Put me down!'

The man was a *goumier*.

'We're only trying to help you!' he exclaimed.

I intervened: 'She told you not to touch her! So don't touch her!'

So then we stayed in the village at Marceau. They put us in a sort of shed: all concrete, grey walls, grey floor . . . We had to spend the night there, in the cold and the children's urine.

In the morning an old woman who seemed to be living nearby came up to the door and whispered, 'I'm going to work in the fields! Ask them to let you go outside, don't stay here!'

We went out. They divided us into new groups, women and children on one side, the few old men on the other. They took us to the outskirts of the village where they put us in tents. They thought they'd be able to keep a closer eye on us there.

A few days passed. We watched the guards' movements and kept a check on the intervals between their rounds. We had to slip in and out to find bits of work to do, so that we had something to live on. Some of the women went gleaning, but only on the edges of the fields. The babies cried all the time. The few cattle and hens were soon slaughtered.

The men in the mountains got a message to me: 'Come back here with one of your sisters; we need you up here!' I nearly danced for joy; I clenched my teeth to hold back my ululations.

For I'd also heard that my younger brother was hiding nearby. I managed to slip out; for a whole day I looked for some landmarks but I couldn't find which way we'd come. In the evening I was forced to return, exhausted, but determined to try another time . . . Two days later I left again, but it was still no use. When I got back my mother was crying: she quietly dried her tear-stained face and didn't ask any questions.

The third time, I finally made contact. My sister, who was one year younger than me, started out with me. But I had second thoughts and told her, 'You must go back!'

It suddenly occurred to me that my mother would be all alone with the little ones. Who would help her? I only realized that when I was actually on my way. My sister did what I asked, but rather grudgingly. Perhaps she held it against me subsequently.

After walking for several hours with the guide I reached the partisans' hiding-place. My brother Ahmed was with them. He embraced me and these are the exact words he said: 'Oh, sister, since I see you, my sister, here, it's as if I were seeing my mother!'

I burst into tears, I don't know why. I touched him, happy to find him in good spirits, but I cried . . .

From that time, Ahmed and I stayed together. There were a few other girls in this group of partisans, a bit older than me; two from Cherchel, Nacera and Malika, and others from the surrounding region.

Some time after this one of the maquisards gave himself up. He led the enemy to us. Not on the first night, but the second. The soldiers surrounded us at dawn.

Alas! the men who were supposed to be keeping watch had fallen asleep, I don't know how. That same night my brother Ahmed and another man had gone out to fetch food. On their way back they realized the enemy were approaching. They ran back as fast as they could, shouting, 'Get out! Get out quickly!'

We were just outside the shelter when they started firing. That morning I felt very tired; I couldn't start running straight away; it was as if my legs were paralysed, perhaps because this was the first time I'd been in an attack . . .

'Run, for God's sake, run!' my brother urged me from behind, almost pushing me.

'I can't! You run on in front! You go first!'

'Run, sister!' he implored me as he went, and I can still hear his voice ringing in my ears. 'If they catch you, they'll torture you!'

He was running in front of me when he fell: a bullet hit him behind the ear. He fell right in front of me . . . He fell forward on his face and as he fell he even knocked down a boy who cut himself on a rock. But the boy picked himself up.

The boy and I went on running: I followed the youngster, I was unfamiliar with the region. Bullets were flying around us, our flight lasted a long time, I saw nothing but the child in front of me . . . Then I found myself alone; I continued along a wadi, as far as a wood, beyond the hills. Then I realized that everything was quiet all around: I stopped.

I tried to find my bearings. From where I was standing I could see a few huts. I thought, 'That must be Trekech.' I knew the men in that *douar* were in with 'France'. I went the other way, across a field. I sheltered in a clump of trees. I could hear an aeroplane in the distance. I crouched down and didn't move out of my hiding-place.

A little way off two roads met. I spotted some uniforms for a moment; they disappeared. I suddenly had an urge to cough. I was afraid they'd catch me. I picked some oak leaves (they are said to be good for a cough) and chewed them silently. I still didn't move, I must even have dozed off.

Night fell. I was wide awake and when I heard a jackal howl my heart was in my mouth . . . I came out from under the trees and made my way very stealthily towards one of the two roads. In the distance I caught a glimpse of burning, then I noticed two or three cows that had been left in an empty field. I leaned up against them for a moment to get warm, then I was frightened someone would come for the animals and denounce me. I thought I'd better go on along the road . . . Other animals, further on, seemed to have fled from another fire . . . I was so cold! It was a winter night: it wasn't raining, but there were still odd patches of snow in the ditches, on the stones.

What was I to do? Sleep on the ground, in spite of the cold? But I would be at the mercy of wild boars and jackals. Climb a tree? I was afraid I'd drop asleep and fall out . . . Finally I found a sturdy oak with a huge trunk. I climbed up and made myself as comfortable as I could, holding on to a branch. I managed to spend the night there, drowsing off a little. I put my trust in God's protection!

The next day I stayed in hiding till it was dark. The fighting was going on not far away. I felt like a ghost, I could hear people moving about as if they were in another world!

I was afraid the helicopters would fly over and catch sight of me. Then everything gradually went quiet; the war vanished, like a dream. I must have suddenly fallen asleep from exhaustion. Before the night was over, a little before dawn, I saw a herd of goats filing past, with a shepherd walking peacefully behind them as if nothing were amiss, as if I'd dreamed of running away and being followed. 'My brother, my brother Ahmed!' I thought in distress.

I jumped down from my tree. The shepherd stopped, beckoned to someone behind him. Four men who looked like partisans appeared in the distance; a fifth one, behind them, was waving to me. 'I've wasted enough time!' I thought. 'I'm going to see where my brother fell!'

'It's your brother, your brother Abdelkader!' someone shouted to me.

I realized it was my other brother, but I wanted to find my younger brother, the one who'd been killed . . . I made a dash, running as fast as I could. With God's help I found my way immediately and was the first to reach the spot.

Ahmed was lying there: the enemy had emptied his pockets of all his papers, all the photographs he'd had on him. They'd taken his best clothes. The only thing left of his partisan's uniform was the trousers. His old woollen shirt was all torn and bloodstained.

I saw the wadi nearby. I tried to carry him; I managed to drag him, his bare feet scraped along the ground behind me . . . I wanted to wash him, at least to moisten his face. I took water in the palms of my hands; I started to sprinkle it over him, as one does for one's ablutions, without realizing that I was crying, sobbing all the time . . .

My elder brother Abdelkader came up behind me and suddenly said angrily to the others, 'Why did you show her the body? Can't you see she's only a child?'

'I saw him fall!' I said, turning round suddenly. 'Right in front of me!' And my voice gave way.

Clamour

The girl's long yellowish hair must at one time have suddenly turned flaming red. The suspicious-minded old busy-bodies had said her green eyes were like those of a 'prowling cat'. Wide green eyes whose irises were flecked with gold . . . How proud the mother had been of the daughter born after three boys!

She's the one, the thirteen-year-old shepherd-girl, the Amrounes' eldest daughter, the one the cousins, neighbours, relations by marriage, paternal uncles, all accuse of behaving as if she were the fourth son in the family, running away like that from the douar *and the French soldiers, instead of staying put with the other females! So she wandered about, so she hid in trees during that interminable pursuit.*

And now she grieves for her dead brother, in this dawn of a still summer day; a new Antigone, mourning for the adolescent lying on the grass, stroking the half-naked corpse with henna-stained hands.

The wadi is not quite dry; the rustle of water can be heard flowing far down between steep banks covered with brambles and sweet-scented moss. A few feet away four men stand watching in an irregular circle; they turn towards a fourth man, stockier, seeming awkward in his uniform: the second Amroune brother. He's out of breath from running; he points vaguely in the girl's direction.

The dead man sleeps, face down . . . The girl – little more than a child – has dragged the corpse herself, shortly before the men arrive. She tried to drag it down to the stream but could not get further than the first rough ground . . . She splashes water on the faces, but he does not wake: she rests it sideways again a rock.

Then she turns round, to protest, or to make sure . . .

'But I saw him fall! Right in front of me!'

She repeated her plaintive protest, more shrilly than the first time, in a heart-rending voice, that seems to trail a shroud behind her.

Slowly she stroked the dead man's face; she rested it once more against the rock by the stream. And she drew herself up.

Then all is stilled: nature, trees, birds (a blackbird flying past silences its song). The faint soughing of the breeze dies away as it sweeps the ground; the five men look on helplessly, waiting, motionless. She alone . . .

A little shepherd-girl, emerging from the dust-haze of a dream-world, feels a keen solemnity inhabit her, sharp as a scythe suspended for one brief waiting moment.

One prolonged, preliminary cry has escaped her. The child rises, her body an even brighter patch in the transparent air; her voice shrills out, stumbling over the first notes, like the shudder of a sail before it is hoisted on the foremast. Then the voice cautiously takes wing, the voice soars, gaining in strength, what voice? That of the mother who bore the soldiers' torture with never a whimper? That of the little cooped-up sisters, too young to understand, but bearing the message of wild-eyed anguish? The voice of the old women of the douar *who face the horror of the approaching death-knell, open-mouthed, with palms of fleshless hands turned upwards? What irrepressible keening, what full-throated clamour, strident tremolo? . . . Is it the voice of the child whose hands are red with henna and a brother's blood?*

The partisans behind her fall back as one man with the spurting blood. They know what they must live with from now on: the rhythmic wailing of the spirits of unburied dead, the roar of invisible lionesses shot by no hunter . . . The discordant dirge of inarticulate revolt launches its arabesques into the blue.

The lament swells in an upsurge of sound: glissandos passing into vibrato; a stream of emptiness hollows out the air. Barbed wires taut above invisible torments . . . Then the thirteen-year-old suddenly starts to her feet, impelled to sway to and fro, keeping time to the rhythm of her grief; the shepherd-girl is initiated to the ritual circle. The first circle around the first one to die . . .

The men stare down at her from the edge of the ravine: standing there throughout that cry that lurches like a pall dripping with blood and flapping in the sun. The dead man swathes himself in it, using it to retrieve his memory: noxious emanations, foetid gases, borborygmic rumblings. Suffusing him in the reverberating, stifling heat. The plangent chirring, the rhythm of the cadences swaddle his flesh to protect it from decay. Voice armouring the dead man on the ground, giving him back his eyes on the edge of the grave . . .

The spent cry dies away, sloughed off like shrivelled skin. It leaves the child standing with a questioning look. She does not seem exhausted; perhaps she has been strengthened.

Awkward in his uniform, the partisan draws near; embraces his sister, strokes her hair.

Her name is Cherifa. When she tells her story, twenty years later, she mentions no interment nor any other form of burial for the brother lying in the river bed.

Aphasia of Love

[Aphasia, *Path*. Loss of the faculty
of speech, as a result of cerebral
affection. OED]

When I was a child I spent every summer in the old coastal city, filled
with Roman ruins, that are such a tourist attraction. Girls and women
of the family, of neighbouring houses and those related by marriage,
regularly visit some sanctuary or other . . . Then gaggles of squealing
females scatter over the surrounding countryside.

One or two small boys keep watch, while the little girls stay with the
veiled women. Suddenly, the alarm is given: 'There's a man coming!'

The women sitting under a fig or olive tree, or in the shade of a
clump of lentisks, with their veils slipping on to their shoulders,
hurriedly pull them back over their hair. One, who's uncovered her
chest to display her jewellery, muffles herself up again; another stands
up and tries to see without being seen, a third stifles her giggles in
agitation at each male's approach.

Sometimes it turns out to be a false alarm. 'Oh!' says one, 'it's only a
Frenchman!'

Normal modesty is no longer necessary. If the passer-by does look,
since he's a Frenchman, a European, a Christian, can he really see
anything? When the stranger is faced with all these women, whose
life's mission, whose duty, whose most sacred inheritance is to
preserve their image – when he's faced with all these women, my
aunts, cousins, my equals, does he really see them, when he pauses,
stares at them, thinking he's taken them by surprise? No, he imagines
he sees them . . .

'Poor man', one of them comments, when the stranger
passes close by and glimpses the lustre of long jet-black tresses, the

glint of mocking, kohl-rimmed eyes. 'Poor man, he's quite upset!'

For he does not know. His gaze, from the other side of the hedge, beyond the taboo, cannot touch them. There is no possible danger of being lured into any little flirtations; thus, they can enjoy their secret walks without any need to hide.

So it was for me with the French language. Ever since I was a child the foreign language was a casement opening on the spectacle of the world and all its riches. In certain circumstances it became a dagger threatening me. Should a man venture to describe my eyes, my laughter or my hands, should I hear him speak of me in this way, I risked losing my composure; then I immediately felt I had to shut him out. Make him feel by the way I started, suddenly bracing myself, shutting off my gaze, that he had made a false move, worse, he was intruding. The game of banal, flirtatious compliments couldn't take place, because it takes two to play.

Afterwards I suffered from the misunderstanding: when I protected myself from flattery or made it clear that it was ineffectual, this was not because of either virtue or prudish reserve. I discovered that I too was veiled, not so much disguised as anonymous. Although I had a body just like that of a Western girl, I had thought it to be invisible, in spite of evidence to the contrary; I suffered because this illusion did not turn out to be shared.

The compliments – harmless or respectful – expressed in the foreign language, traversed a no-man's-land of silence . . . How could I admit to the foreigner, who had sometimes become a friend or a relative by marriage, that such loaded words defused themselves as soon as uttered, that by their very nature they lost their power to touch me, and that in this case it was nothing to do with either of us? The word had simply drowned before reaching its destination . . .

I became again, in my own way, a Vestal virgin who had wandered into an outside world stripped of its magic. I was invisible, and the only thing I caught of the flattering speech was the tone of voice, sometimes the wish to please. My reply was softened by indulgence towards what I judged at that time, in my limited and naïve experience, to be an inherent fault of the European education: verbosity, an indiscreet compulsive longiloquence in these preambles to seduction. For my part, based on my own experience, I was convinced that the surfeit of sweet nothings is the crown, the fireworks after the feast which seals the satisfaction of mutual pleasuring.

I did not realize that by this assumption I was putting on a symbolic veil. I had passed the age of puberty without being buried in the harem like my girl cousins; I had spent my dreaming adolescence on its fringes, neither totally outside, nor in its heart; so I spoke and studied French, and my body, during this formative period, became Westernized in its way.

At all the regular family gatherings, I had lost the knack of sitting cross-legged: this posture no longer indicated that I was one of all the women and shared their warmth – at the most it simply meant squatting uncomfortably.

Evening parties on the terraces, from where, cooped up and invisible, the women looked down on the Andalusian musicians with their time-honoured tenor. He occupied the place of honour among the men dressed in their finery, who knew that they were being watched by the women sitting in the dark. The latter accompanied the meeting with their shrill clamour which rose up and fanned out on the air. My throat lent itself uneasily, discordantly, to this ancestral plangent cry – which is emitted by spasmodic vibrations of the glottis. Instead of arising spontaneously, it tore me apart. I preferred to listen to my mother giving voice, half cooing, half ululation, blending first with the full-throated chorus then finishing with a triumphant vocalism, a prolonged soprano solo.

My adolescent body imperceptibly breaks away from this bunch of female forms. It still participates in the collective, spasmodic dances, but the next day it knows the purer joy of dashing out into the middle of a sunny sports ground to take part in athletic contests or games of basketball. However, this body is not yet armed to face the words of others.

In this communication with the doubly opposite sex (not only male, but men of the opposing tribe), sometimes a suitor from foreign parts succeeded in touching me by his reserve. The only possible eloquence, the only weapon that could reach me was silence, not so much out of respect or shyness on the part of the man who might venture at any moment to declare his feelings; silence, because that's the only way he can make his declaration. Between the man and me, refusal of speech became both the starting point and the end point of our relationship.

When the Chevalier d'Aranda was captured in Algiers in the seventeenth century, and kept in slavery for two years, he said of the

Algerian women of that time, 'These women have no scruples in the presence of Christian slaves, because they say that they are blind.' I must admit that the effect of an identical illusion could have been the exact opposite; that confronted with the gaze or the words of the taboo-man, the unveiled woman possibly experiences a sharper pleasure in stripping herself naked, making herself vulnerable, conquered . . . Exactly, 'conquered'. The women whom d'Aranda knew accepted the love of a foreigner, maybe 'blind', but in any case a slave.

For my part, I lived at a time when, for more than a century, the vilest of men from the dominant society had imagined himself a master over us. So there was never any chance of him assuming the cloak of seducer in women's eyes. After all, Lucifer himself shares an identical kingdom with Eve.

Never did the harem, that is to say, the taboo, whether it be a place of habitation or a symbol, never did the harem act as a better barrier, preventing as it did the cross-breeding of two opposing worlds; as if my people, as if my brothers and thus, by definition, my jailers, had first been decimated, then uprooted, and finally risked the loss of their identity: curious dereliction which caused even their sexual image to become blurred . . .

The impossibility of this love was reinforced by memory of the conquest. When, as a child, I went to school, the French words scarcely made any impact on this stronghold. I had inherited this imperviousness; from the time of my adolescence I experienced a kind of aphasia in matters of love: the written words, the words I had learned, retreated before me as soon as the slightest heart-felt emotion sought for expression.

Whenever a man whose mother tongue was the same as mine ventured to make advances, speaking in French, his words formed a mask which the interlocutor had willy-nilly to adopt in the opening moves of the game. It was he, in the last resort, who put on a veil, to venture to approach.

If the whim took me to react to the man's advances, I did not need to put on some show of graciousness. All I had to do was to revert to the mother tongue: by returning to the sounds of childhood to express some detail, I was ensuring that we would agree to a spirit of good fellowship, that we might become friends and perhaps – why not? – by some miracle, we might take the mutual risk of our acquaintanceship developing into love.

With friend or lover from my own birthplace, emerging from an identical childhood, swaddled in the same indigenous sounds, anointed with the same ancestral warmth, grazed by the same sharp ridges of frustration as my cousins, neighbours, intimate enemies, still steeped in the same garden of taboos, in the same thickets of lethargy, yes, with my brothers or my lover-friends, I finally recover my power of speech, use the same understatements, interlace the allusiveness of tone and accent, letting inflexions, whispers, sounds and pronunciation be a promise of embraces . . . At last, voice answers to voice and body can approach body.

Voice

Abdelkader and the partisans began to upbraid me: 'Your brother Ahmed died a martyr! We shall be happy to enjoy a similar end!'

They led me away. I joined the other girls. They suggested I stay with them there.

'No!' I replied. 'I go wherever my brother goes!'

We left that place. In Bou Harb we met Nourredine, the leader, who pointed to me and said, 'She must put on a *kachabia*! Don't let her go among the soldiers like that!'

We met Abdelkrim, one of the political organizers. We stayed with him for about three months. Then we went to Bou Athmane where I joined two other girls; the group of Brothers came and went; we three girls started looking after the cooking. Finally they sent me, the youngest, to the field hospital for the maquis, to make myself useful.

There I met Ferhat, the doctor.

'You're going to learn to give first aid to the wounded,' he told me.

I stayed with him and his patients; I learned to give injections (but I can't do that any more, because of my health; my hands tremble).

I spent the first night in the general ward. In the morning one of the wounded, who was feverish, woke up and caught sight of me; at that time I had very long hair, which I let down over my shoulders to comb. Then, the man, who was delirious, shouted, 'Look! there's an ogress!'

And the others all laughed . . . So I stayed with them. Afterwards several men came and helped with the nursing. It was my job to wash the patients and their clothes and bed-linen; I began to give injections. I spent a whole year there.

Eventually, I suddenly didn't feel like staying any more. My elder brother only came to see me once. The others started to say, 'Why are you going? Nobody looks after the wounded as well as you do!'

'I'm not staying any longer!' I said. 'I've been here a year and I've

130

not seen a single woman, or even a child! No-one except our wounded! And my brother's only been to see me once!'

'Is that the reason?' they asked me.

'The only reason,' I retorted, 'is God! I feel as if he'd suddenly cast a shadow over this place!'

And yet I loved the patients. I even thought, 'If my mother could see me, how proud she'd be! Just look, I've learnt how to wash wounded men!' A part of the hospital was built underground: the badly wounded patients were put there; beds for the others were set up under the trees, in the forest.

The leaders came to inspect us, Slimane, Si Djelloul from Cherchel, Si Mahmoud (all of them died as martyrs). They said, 'Stay! You work well, you're all right here!'

But I kept saying no; I was bent on leaving.

'Did someone say anything to you?' they asked. By that they meant, 'Was anyone disrespectful to you?'

'Nobody said anything to me!' I replied. 'But I'm not staying! My heart isn't in this place any more.'

'Where do you want to go?'

'Anywhere you want to send me, as long as I don't stay here! I can't stand this place any more!'

So they sent me to another post. The day I left, we all wept – the patients as well as me!

They took me to the Mimoun hospital where Si Omar was in charge. It took me some time to get used to the change. Then suddenly they said to me, 'You'll have to get married!'

'No, I won't,' I replied. 'You can kill me if you like, but I won't get married!'

No matter what they said, they couldn't persuade me. The doctor who had taught me everything sided with me and Omar.

'They're really only children! Leave them alone!'

Eventually, it seems, this doctor left the maquis because of this incident. He didn't do anything, he didn't turn traitor, but he preferred to give himself up! . . .

In this marriage business, they thought of giving me to a 'chief'! A chief from Mouzaïa. I stuck to my guns. Then they said, 'If you don't want to marry this one, marry someone else, anyone you like! Choose!'

I replied, 'Did I join you just to get married? No, I won't marry anyone! These men are all my brothers!'

Eventually they left me in peace. I stayed at this second hospital. A woman came who'd worked in the city 'in the underground'. She arrived with her husband. So that she could remain with him she'd said she knew how to make uniforms, when she really didn't know how to . . . But we stayed together. I spent the night with her. Soon afterwards another woman arrived; she was married too.

A few months later, Si Djelloul arrived from Cherchel with some others, his seconds in command. They said, referring to me, 'This girl is from our region! We're not leaving her here! We're taking her back to our sector!'

They'd heard about my opposition to the marriage plan; they didn't say anything to me but they took me to Bou Hillal, to join the maquisards from my region. We stayed at the post. At night, the men slept on one side and the women, even the partisans' wives who weren't in uniform, slept on the other side . . . I remember one of the women, the oldest, who grew very fond of me. I called her 'Jedda'.

A few months later, one of the partisans gave us away. At dawn the French surrounded us. Jedda and I were the first up to perform our ablutions before the morning prayer. I could hear French spoken, not far away. I asked in surprise, 'Who's speaking French?'

The old woman said, 'One of our men, probably!'

'No,' I replied. 'You know perfectly well we're forbidden to speak French now.'

I turned round to look and spied French soldiers. I gave the alarm, shouting, 'Soldiers! Soldiers!'

I'd barely started running and shouting when the firing began. A child (some of the married women had children) had just got up and came tottering out first: a bullet hit him in the middle of the forehead and he fell down dead on the ground in front of me. Poor kid: one single step from sleep straight into death! Jedda and I started running. The other women, who weren't dressed in soldiers' uniforms, gave up the attempt at flight.

The enemy pursued us. I managed to hide. I remained hidden the whole night. But this time the enemy didn't budge; not even at night. We continued to be surrounded. And eventually they found me, huddled up among the prickly-pear bushes!

They pulled me out and when they took me to the village, a clerk from Ménacer (I didn't know him but the others told me later that he played music at weddings) said, 'That girl's the sister of the Amrounes! One of her brothers died in the fighting, the other's still in the maquis!'

They asked me if it was true. I said it was.

'Where's your brother – the one who's alive?'

'I haven't seen him!'

As I was dressed as a partisan, an officer ordered the soldiers to search me: 'She could be hiding a weapon!'

The Frenchman said that, but the *goumier* who was guarding me replied, 'No! If she's hiding anything, it's too bad! . . . Let her kill someone if she wants to!'

Another *goumier* came up and accused me: 'I know you! I was there when you and your brother and Arbouz killed twenty-eight people! You kill your own kind! That's why I left you people and gave myself up!'

'Traitor among traitors!' I retorted. 'You dare talk like that! You're the one who kills and assassinates your own people and then goes and betrays them! *We* aren't the ones who kill each other! You're the one who sells your own people and enlists for the sake of a bowl of soup!'

He was furious, he aimed his rifle at me and threatened me, 'I'll kill you!'

'Kill me,' I said, 'if you're a man! But you aren't a man, you're a *goumier*! I'm not yet a grown woman, but that makes no difference! Kill me, since you love killing!'

They kept me there for the night. The soldiers had previously decided they were going to tie me up.

'Never!' I shouted. 'Nobody's going to touch me! Several of you can guard me, if you like! Nobody's going to tie me up!'

Several of them stayed to guard me. In the morning they brought me some coffee.

'I don't drink before I've washed my face!'

They brought me some water. I performed my ablutions. They brought the coffee back.

'I'm not drinking anything!'

They offered me some biscuits.

'I'm not eating anything!'

I took the biscuits and put them on the ground.

'You've put them there for your brothers?' one of them said ironically.

'My brothers aren't like you,' I replied, 'doing anything because you're hungry!'

'Who brought you your food?'

'We got it ourselves!'

'Who brought you your clothes?'

'We made them ourselves!'

Then they brought some human bones: remains of certain people who'd 'worked' with France.

'Who killed them?'

'I never saw anything!'

'Show us where you went when you left here!'

'I don't know, I always stayed here!'

'Tell us what they're like! Describe them to us!'

'Soldiers, like you! I never look at faces!'

'What's a young girl like you doing here, away from your parents?'

'The maquisards are my brothers and they're like parents to me too!'

Then, without waiting for them to ask me any more questions, I added, 'I don't recognize France! I've been brought up according to the Arab word! The "Brothers" are my brothers!'

They took me away. When we were near a wadi, one of the *goumiers* slipped me an ammunition pouch. But an officer suddenly appeared and he immediately took the cartridges back . . . A bit further on, the one who'd accused me and insulted me approached and began to threaten me again: 'I'm going to kill her!' I defied him again and repeated what I thought of him, 'a man who'd sold himself for a bowl of soup!'

Another *goumier*, whose name was Cherif, intervened and said to the other one, 'Just leave her alone! Look at the Frenchmen; they hardly dare speak to her, young as she is, and you, her compatriot, you're trying to provoke her!'

A third one turned to me and said: 'Here, take my rifle and shoot him!'

Of course I knew he was making fun of me. But I retorted, 'D'you think I can't shoot? Give it to me and you'll soon see!'

The argument continued, but they loaded us into trucks and drove off. At Cherchel, they stopped at some barracks. They put me in a cell with a stone floor. I lay down and went to sleep. A guard came later and asked, 'You want to wash?'

They took me to a tap and gave me some soap and a towel. I washed and went back to my cell. Then they came to fetch me for questioning. It began in the early afternoon. It lasted for hours . . . I simply replied to all their questions, 'I don't recognize you! I don't recognize France!'

They tried to make me tell them where the *khatibas* were marching to and the names of their leaders. I invariably replied, 'I don't know!'

They took me from one interrogation room to another. Then they asked, 'The "Hamdaniya" *khatiba* [so called after the name of its leader, Hamdane] has broken up, hasn't it?'

I knew that this was so, but I replied with a sneer, 'No! It's still intact! You've only got to use your eyes: the other day, when you got into that skirmish with us that left the hospital full of your wounded, that was Hamdane's *khatiba*! It covers the country from the Chenoua hills to Bou Hilal!'

One of the officers lost his temper and hit me twice across the face. Then they brought a tommy-gun.

'Confess! Tell us what we want to know or we'll shoot!'

'Shoot!' I said. 'It makes no difference to me! I'm a girl, I'm not a grown woman, but I'll leave men behind me! . . . Each one of them will kill a hundred of yours! Kill me!'

They brought a whip. They beat me. They switched on the electricity for their machines. They tortured me.

'I don't recognize you!'

I didn't feel any fear: God made these Frenchmen seem like shadows in front of my eyes! And it was true, I would have preferred to die!

Suddenly one of them asked me, 'Are you a virgin? . . . We heard that X . . . [and he gave the name of the leader of the Mouzaïa] asked to marry you!'

I realized that the man who'd left the maquis and become a *goumier* had told them about the marriage business.

'I'm not married!' I replied.

Finally they took me back to the cell. They gave me a bed, a blanket. They brought me a plate of food, even some meat, some bread and a spoon. But once I was alone I suddenly started to weep: my tears wouldn't stop! 'How can God have allowed me to fall into the hands of the French?' I asked myself in despair.

A *goumier* came and opened the door.

'Come now! Don't cry!' he said. 'You're not the first girl they've caught. At first, when they question you, it's hard, but in the end they let you go.'

I wouldn't answer him. He shut the door again. I went over to the food. I picked at the meat: one or two mouthfuls only, as I was so hungry, but I didn't trust them. I didn't touch the rest. In the morning they brought me some coffee. I asked to wash first: they took me out into a courtyard where there was a tap. I washed while they looked on; I splashed water on my face, washed my arms up to my elbows, my feet and legs up to my knees: just like for my ablutions. I loosened my hair which wasn't so long any more, combed it and arranged it. And they all stood there, watching me!

'Have you finished?'

'I've finished!'

In my cell I sipped a mouthful of coffee, no more! Even though I was famished I wanted to show them, show the whole of France, that that was all I wanted!

'You've drunk your coffee? You've finished?'

'I've finished, I thank God!'

They took me to a car. The pot-bellied officer who'd slapped my face the day before came up. He asked me in Arabic, 'Do you know where you're going now?'

'How should I know?'

'Do you know Gouraya?'

'I've never heard of it!'

'You Arabs! All you can say is, "I don't know! I've never heard of it!"'

'When you're walking in a forest,' I said, 'why d'you have to know the name of the forest?'

Another Frenchman, also an officer, interposed: 'She's young. It's natural that she wouldn't know anything!'

This officer got in the car, as well as the driver and a *goumier*. A jeep followed. Every time we passed through a village, the officer who really believed that I didn't know the area told me the Arabic names of the villages. When we got to Gouraya, Bérardi, the chief of the SAS, who was well known in the locality, came out and greeted the officer who whispered to me, 'That's Bérardi!'

After Gouraya, we got to the place called the 'The Sacred Wood'. I knew that was where the biggest prison in the district was. An officer, a lieutenant called Coste, received us; he didn't speak to me, just looked me over then nodded.

'Put her in a cell!' he said. 'A cell right in the sun!'

When he'd gone, the officer in the car asked for another cell for me. A prisoner, a partisan who was probably there for questioning, managed to get near me shortly afterwards and whisper, 'Oh, sister, where did they capture you?'

I stared at him without replying. He hurriedly added, 'You know X . . . and Y . . .?' I said yes, as my distrust vanished. They took me for questioning. I answered in the same way as at Cherchel. They used electricity again. Once it went on from dawn until two in the afternoon. It was particularly hard.

They confronted me with the *goumier* who had recognized me when I was arrested and who'd threatened me. I didn't let them intimidate me: 'You can keep me in prison for twenty years if you like. I'm not giving in! What war has ever lasted twenty years? Ours won't last that long! . . . Do what you like with me!'

Finally, they left me in my cell. I was locked in day and night. One day Lieutenant Coste arrived and asked me, 'You all right?'

'No! I'm not all right! It's like an oven in here! . . . When we take your men prisoner, we don't lock them up night and day! . . . We don't act unjustly like you do!'

Then they allowed me to keep the door on to the courtyard open. If I wanted to go out for a moment, I could. At night the door was locked again. I remained there for seven months or more!

Eventually I was allowed to walk about the camp. When new prisoners arrived and their interrogation began, I went to comfort them and took them something to drink. That situation didn't last, because of a *goumier*, who came from Constantine. One night, he somehow managed to unlock the door of my cell, then he called me twice, very softly, in the dark. I went out and yelled for the guard. He disappeared.

In the morning he came and asked me to forgive him. 'I don't forgive!' I said and I went and lodged a complaint. He was sentenced to a week in the punishment cell for unlocking my door like that.

When he was let out, he came to see me again, but this time to blame me. He stood in front of me in the courtyard with a dog. I didn't say anything, I was going to open the doors of the brothers who were imprisoned there as I always did when I took them water and food. The *goumier* threatened me: 'Why did you go and complain to Lieutenant Coste? Who d'you think you are? . . . And the *fellaheen*, your brothers, they're no better than rats hiding in holes!'

In the face of this insult, I couldn't contain myself.

'Come closer, if you dare! You call us rats, so let's see if we're rats or lions!'

The quarrel got more and more bitter. Lieutenant Coste arrived with his second in command, the man who did the electric shocks during the questioning and who spoke Arabic. He translated for the lieutenant. I told him how the *goumier* had insulted me. The lieutenant forbade him to speak to me.

Two or three months later, this same *goumier* reappeared on the scene. It was one morning; I was taking coffee to the prisoners who were there for questioning. I saw him approaching me; I pointed this out to another guard. The latter, to avoid any incident, asked me to go back to my cell. It wasn't my place to give way!

'I'm not going back!' I decided. 'I don't care what happens! Today, I'm going to have it out with him!'

'You've just got to stay in your hole,' the *goumier* sniggered, 'out of sight of God's mercy!'

'I'm not going back!' I repeated.

I ran into another courtyard. He began to shout insults after me, for everyone to hear.

'You *fellaheen*, you live in the forests like wild beasts and you want to behave like savages here!'

'And where do you *goumiers* come from?' I retorted. 'You have sold your loyalties! The flag that I believe in doesn't fly above this place! It's over there, in the forests and on the mountains!'

The quarrel grew in front of everybody. It lasted for some time. Finally I grabbed a big coffee-pot and when he came too close to me I hit him as hard as I could on the shoulder.

'Damn her!' he yelled. 'She's fractured my collar-bone!'

As it happened I had a knife in my pocket: a prisoner had slipped it to me at the beginning of the quarrel. And I'd just picked up an iron bar which was lying near a railing. I'd said to myself, 'If he comes near me again, I'll hit him with the iron bar and finish him off with the knife!' And I was quite determined to do it, too! . . . It's true that at that time, I was in prime condition! When the French arrested me in the mountains, they were astonished! They just had to look at my wrists to see how strong I was . . . Alas! if any of the brothers from those days met me today, they'd swear I wasn't the same person!

A staff-sergeant and another soldier arrived. They blamed me for striking the *goumier*. I told them the truth about what happened. They tried to force me to return to my cell.

'I'm not going back!'

'You must!'

Three of them took hold of me; I resisted with all my strength: kicking, punching, butting them with my head. They let me go and left me lying on the ground, screaming hysterically . . . Lieutenant Coste's second in command arrived. He spoke to me quite gently and begged me, 'Come now, go back to your cell! Lieutenant Coste'll be along and you'll see what he'll do!'

I went back to my cell. Then they sentenced me to three days and three nights in the punishment cell, without food or drink. When the three days were up and they brought me food, I decided I wouldn't touch it, and I stayed on hunger strike for twenty days! As if I depended on them! . . . Some of the brothers who were imprisoned there managed to get a bit of bread to me, sometimes an apple (that I made last for three days); they passed a wire through a skylight with bits of food on the end . . . A soldier from Oran whom they'd won over sometimes unlocked my door and slipped the bread in for me. The main thing for me, as far as the French were concerned, was to show them I didn't need them!

Eventually, they left me in peace and I didn't see that *goumier* again.

A long time later a group of Red Cross officials came to the camp. Ten or more men in civilian clothes came to my cell and greeted me respectfully. But Lieutentant Coste intervened. 'She doesn't understand French!' he told them.

They went away. Months passed. Once an important officer came. When he entered my cell he said, 'De Gaulle has sent me to visit these prisons!'

Two *goumiers* who were accompanying him translated.

'Seeing that you're here, where were you arrested?'

I told them I'd been arrested 'in the mountains'.

'What were you doing in the mountains?'

'I was fighting!'

'Why were you fighting?'

'For what I believe in, for my ideas!'

'And now, seeing you're a prisoner?'

'I'm a prisoner, so what!'

'What have you gained?'

'I've gained the respect of my compatriots and my own self-respect! Did you arrest me for stealing or for murder? I never stole! My conscience is clear!'

They went away. I remained in the camp, but thanks to this man, probably, I was able to see my parents. They came all the way from their village to visit me. When my father saw me he wept.

Six months before the cease-fire, they managed to get me transferred to a prison near them. They had just lost Abdelkader, my eldest brother . . .

Embraces

Cherifa's voice embraces the bygone days. Tracing the fear, the defiance, the intoxication in that forgotten place. Outbursts of a recalcitrant prisoner in the sun-seared camp.

The voice recounts? Scarcely that. It digs out the old revolt. It portrays the rolling hills, so often set on fire, the ride across the russet slopes of these bare mountains that I travel through today.

Strange little sister, whom henceforth I leave veiled or whose story I now transcribe in a foreign tongue. Her body and her face are once more engulfed in shadow as she whispers her story – a butterfly displayed on a pin with the dust from its crushed wing staining one's finger.

She sits in the middle of a darkened room, crowded with bright-eyed children squatting around: we are in the heart of an orange plantation in the Tell district . . . The thin, weak voice scales the heights of so many past years, then tells of peace suddenly descending like a lead weight. She pauses, picks up the tale, a stream that disappears beneath the cactus hedges.

The words fade away . . . Cherifa is married now to a taciturn widower, a workman whom I saw leave shortly before on his tractor; he is in charge of the equipment in this agricultural co-operative. She brings up the man's five children.

She speaks slowly. Her voice lifts the burden of memory; it now wings its way towards that summer of 1956, when she was just a girl, the summer of the devastation . . . Do her words bring it to light? She braves the suspicious mother-in-law who prowls around us, hoping to discover what the hesitating narrative reveals: what exigency in the story, what secret, what sin, or simply what is missing . . .

Cherifa ageing, in poor health, is housebound. As she sets her voice free for me, she sets herself free again; what nostalgia will cause her voice to fail presently? . . .

I do not claim here to be either a story-teller or a scribe. On the territory of dispossession, I would that I could sing.

I would cast off my childhood memories and advance naked, bearing offerings, hands outstretched to whom? – to the Lords of yesterday's war, or to the young girls who lay in hiding and who now inhabit the silence that succeeds the battles . . . And what are my offerings? Only handfuls of husks, culled from my memory, what do I seek? Maybe the brook where wounding words are drowned . . .

Cherifa! I wanted to re-create your flight: there, in the isolated field, the tree appears before you when you are scared of the jackals. Next you are driven through the villages, surrounded by guards, taken to the prison camp where every year more prisoners arrive . . . I have captured your voice; disguised it with my French without clothing it. I barely brush the shadow of your footsteps!

The words that I thought to put in your mouth are shrouded in the same mourning garb as those of Bosquet or Saint-Arnaud. Actually, it is they who are writing to each other, using my hand, since I condone this bastardy, the only cross-breeding that the ancestral beliefs do not condemn: that of language, not that of the blood.

Torch-words which light up my women-companions, my accomplices; these words divide me from them once and for all. And weigh me down as I leave my native land.

Second Movement:

The Trance

The memory of my maternal grandmother appears darkly before me: a lioness grown weak, impotent, gasping for breath.

At regular intervals, about every two or three months, the matriarch would summon musicians from the city: three or four women of venerable age, one of whom was almost blind. They arrived muffled up in grimy *haïks* over their shabby lace-trimmed gowns, carrying their drums wrapped in scarves.

Kanouns filled with hot coals were hurriedly brought. Memories of the women's crimson faces as smoke began to rise . . . The servants and girls of the family placed the braziers in my grandmother's darkened room; she always remained hidden from sight from dawn.

The smell of incense gradually filled the room; the musicians let the parchment of the drums warm up, while the blind woman, seated on one corner of the high bed, droned out a funeral invocation.

This noctural quavering chant brought my cousin and me running, half uneasy, but at the same time, fascinated . . . I must have been quite young; the boy, who was a little older, had a certain prestige in my eyes; unruly, impudent, he drove his mother to distraction; she would grow hysterical and I can still see her chasing him frantically over the roof-terraces to give him a good hiding . . . the boy was nicknamed the *mejnoun*, as if he were possessed . . .

These strange days began with the musicians' ceremonial chants; then the relationship between my cousin and me was reversed. He was frightened, he grew tense; he huddled up against me, the younger one, while waiting for the show which scared him. I, on the contrary, greatly enjoyed my rôle as spectator. We sat side by side near a window and waited.

143

The *chikhats*, lady-musicians, began to strike the drums with their ringed fingers; the insidious invocation rose up in the smoke-filled room, where more and more women and children gathered.

Finally my grandmother made her dramatic entrance, as always the consummate actress. Upright, clad only in a tight-fitting tunic, her head turbaned in multi-coloured scarves, she began a slow dance. All of us onlookers could sense that, in spite of appearances, this was not the beginning of a festivity.

For one hour, two hours, the matriarch swayed her bony body from side to side; her hair came undone, and every now and then she gave out a hoarse grunt. The blind woman's chant helped to goad her on, while the chorus broke off to cry, 'Flush out the ill fortune! May the teeth of envy and covetousness not harm you, O my lady! . . . Bring out your strength and all your armoury into the light of day, O my queen!'

The others resumed their monotonous hypnotic sing-song as torpor descended on the over-heated room. The women bustled to and fro between the room and the kitchens, stoking up the fires in the *kanouns* in preparation for the climax. My cousin and I, tense with anticipation, mesmerized by the increasing frenzy of the music, felt we were witnessing the solemn prologue to a ritual act.

Finally came the crisis: my grandmother, oblivious to everything, jerked spasmodically to and fro till she went into a trance. The drums had worked up to a frenzy. The blind woman went on chanting her solo; she alone orchestrated the collective hysteria. The women of the household abandoned their cooking to hurry in: a couple of the aunts or cousins helped the weakened matriarch, supporting her on each side. The blind woman's threnody grew softer, reduced to a murmur, an imperceptible guttural groan; she finally drew near to the prancing woman and whispered scraps of the Quran in her ear.

A drum beat out the tempo for the crisis; the cries began: drawn up from the depths of her belly, perhaps even from her legs, rending her hollow chest, emerging at last in rasping squawks from the old lady's throat. Now she could hardly stand, her loosened hair, her gaudy head-scarves were tossed about her shoulders, only her head swayed from side to side as she grunted rhythmically.

At first the choking cries came thick and fast, jostling each other, then they swelled and swirled in spreading spirals, intersecting arches, tapering to needle-points. The old lady gave up the struggle, surrendering herself completely to the insistent beat of the blind

144

woman's drum: all the voices of the past, imprisoned in her present existence, were now set free and leapt far away from her.

Half an hour or one hour later she lay bunched up in her bed, an almost invisible heap, while the musicians ate and gossiped amid the smell of incense. Their magic as pagan priestesses had vanished, and now in the tardy noonday light they were simply ugly old women with faces extravagantly painted.

During the crisis, the *mejnoun* cousin sat clinging tightly to my shoulders, seeking a fragile protection, while I kept my eyes glued on my grandmother in her trance – she of whom we children were normally so much in awe. I felt I was following the dancer into some realm of frenzy.

I was conscious of the mystery: the matriarch was normally the only one of the women who never complained; she condescended to mouth the formulas of submission disdainfully; but this extravagant or derisory ceremonial which she regularly organized was her own way of protesting ... Against whom? Against the others or against fate? I wondered. But when she danced, she became indubitably queen of the city. Cocooned in that primitive music, she drew her daily strength before our very eyes.

The haughty matron's voice and body gave me a glimpse of the source of all our sorrows: like half-obliterated signs which we spend the rest of our lives trying to decipher.

Voice

The 'revolution' began and ended in my home, as every *douar* in these mountains can bear witness.

In the beginning the partisans ate up everything I had. I even took them a little pension I got. And then the corn – before the French burnt us out, we gave it to the mill, then we kneaded the flour. I owned two ovens for baking bread. They're still there, as they'd been built of concrete. After my farm had been gutted several times, it stayed without a roof; you can still see the walls . . . I had plenty of cattle then, when I lived there!

As I was saying, at first they only came to get something to eat. Then Sid Ali arrived and said, 'We're going to let the men hide here, aunt!' (He's my mother's nephew.)

'No!' I replied. 'Go and see what happened to the Kabyle, Mohand Oumous, on the main road; it's scarcely a week since you started using his place, and they've burnt down everything he had!'

But he went on, 'Aunt, don't reason like that! Don't say, "I have . . ." or "This is mine . . .", say rather, "I don't own! . . . This isn't mine! . . ." Put yourself in the hands of God and if needs must, let the fire spread and devour everything.'

So that's how they came to use my farm . . .

From then on, I didn't have to find food for them myself any more. Other people started giving. Perhaps they were afraid, at least some of them were; soon they gave so much that we all had enough to eat and there was food left over! Sometimes we even had to throw it away . . . Towards the end, everything got scarce again. Once more we were hungry and wretched! . . .

As for the number of *Moujahidine*, could you even count them? Impossible! Even when two of them walked into a house together, they seemed to fill the patio! . . . And could you ever say a word?

146

Impossible! All you could do was roll up your sleeves, knead the dough, prepare the stewpot, see to the cooking, and so on, the whole day; there were always little groups of them coming and going . . . They arranged for somebody to keep guard. I was just kept busy with the pots and pans all the time, I put the food down in front of them, then I went and sat outside and waited, ready for death . . . Yes, at the gate of the orchard! I was so frightened! I kept watch, while they ate. Suppose someone came up the hill to our place and found them there, we'd all have been wiped out, on the spot!

They used my farm for five years to hide in. Yes, five years, until the end of the 'revolution'! . . .

Once I was betrayed; it was because of a lad who happened to belong to the same tribe as me, through his father.

He was too young to understand! He must have been fifteen. His mother, a neighbour, had gone to Mount Chenoua, to see her married daughter. She asked me, 'Keep an eye on him! The lad's so young, so naïve. If he starts wandering off he'll get picked up!'

So he stayed hidden with me while his mother was away. One day he went out to irrigate the orchard. His mother had told him over and over again, 'See that you water the garden every night!' But that night he hadn't woken up; so he went out in the morning when he got up, but the sun was already high . . .

The French soldiers arrested him. They brought him back to me: I didn't recognize him at first. He was wearing a pair of European trousers instead of his father's baggy breeches. They'd smeared his face with some sort of powder. And he was wearing a hat! . . . I never thought it could be him. But when he began to speak I recognized his voice. He told them, 'That's the place . . .'

So that's when they first burnt my house down.

When his mother came back, I gave her a piece of my mind: I let her know what her son had done to me. She answered, as cool as you like, 'So what? Once the French caught him, what d'you suppose he could do? Did you want them to kill him? . . .'

When my farm was in flames a man whose house wasn't far, just on the main road, shouted, 'Well! That's God's doing! When the partisans wanted to hide in this woman's house, I advised her not to get involved. And she replied, "I am involved, until I die!" Since she claims she's in it till she dies, let's just see what happens now!'

This same peasant, when any people passed his house, he badgered them with questions, 'Aren't they still feeding the maquisards?'

What's more, his son came to see what damage had been done: they'd even smashed my cooking pots! . . . But I wouldn't give up. The following days I decided to go and make my fire between some stones and I managed to feed the partisans, just the same! 'To the bitter end,' I said to myself, 'I'll go on to the bitter end! The rest is in God's hands!'

So this neighbour spent his time spying on me. He started going to inform: 'Such and such a company has arrived at Sahraoui Zohra's! . . . Such and such *khatiba*' . . .

Alas! We can't read or write. We don't leave any accounts of what we lived through and all we suffered! . . . You'll see other people who spent their time crouching in holes and who, afterwards, told what they've told!

They didn't leave us a thing: they took the cattle, everything put by in the silos, everything. They didn't even leave us a goat! Not a thing . . .

People rented me little plots of land, then the soldiers came and asked, 'Are those Sahraoui Zohra's cows? . . . Ah, is that her crop?'

And they burnt everything, until we were absolutely destitute! Then I decided, 'I'll go down to the village!' The Brothers said, 'Don't give yourself up!'

'I'm not going to give myself up,' I said, 'I'm only going down to the village because I've nothing left here!'

'No, stay here!' they said.

I went to the village. The maquisards came down from the hills to get in touch with me. A forest guard gave me away – he saw them once passing through the forest, and wondered where they could be going. Then he realized they were coming to my place.

One morning, at daybreak, the local police came and tied me up.

'You're the one who's betraying France! Who d'you think you are? . . . Up on the mountain, you gave us enough trouble, and you're starting the same thing again here!'

They threatened me, thinking they'd frighten me. That day, I thought, 'This time, they're going to kill me!' And I felt quite calm. But, thanks to God's mercy, there was a man named Ali among them, a relative by marriage of my mother's. He exclaimed, 'What! You think this old woman could have burnt everything all over the mountains? A little old woman like this? . . . You either let her go, or I'll join the maquis myself!'

Yes, those were his exact words! You see, that man had been a maquisard, then he'd given himself up. To tell you the truth, since he'd been working with France, I was afraid of him. Seeing me living in the village, he came to see me from time to time: I agreed to do his washing and cook him a meal . . . After all, he was a relative of my mother's, wasn't he?

That time, when they arrested me, I didn't stay in prison long!

My house was almost on the edge of the forest . . . The Brothers had had this hut evacuated, deciding, 'This woman must come and live here!' The owner of the place is still alive: we didn't pay him any rent. That was his way of participating.

I lived in so many different places in those times, so many! . . . Finally, when I was let out of prison, I preferred to return to my farm. How was I to know that the next time I went down to the village I would find myself living in a tent, like a nomad!

At first, I owned thirty-one head of cattle . . . In the end, I didn't have a single one left! The soldiers took them all!

My farm was burnt down three times. Whenever they came back and found it in good repair again, they knew the Brothers had rebuilt the house for us! They brought roofing tiles they'd taken from the settlers' houses. Once again, the French soldiers destroyed everything. And again, the Brothers brought us tiles from the French settlers' houses and put a roof over our heads again . . . 'France' came again. So then we decided to do the cooking in the open air, between the walls without a roof or even in the forest.

The third time, they took us down to the village. The wadi was in spate. They didn't give us a thing, no blankets, no food, nothing. They just left us as we were. They thought we'd die. But we didn't die. We just split up, finding shelter wherever we could, some with a brother, some with a cousin. I went to Hajout, to Jennet's place. When I fled to her place, I warned her: 'Just be careful, Jennet! If anyone tells you your aunt is hiding in your place, don't admit anything! Say she's not there!'

Whenever I heard a noise, or when anyone came to the door to speak to her, I hid, I slipped under a mattress, like a snake! . . .

149

Afterwards, when they'd gone, I asked, 'Have they gone?'

'Yes!'

Because I was frightened! I knew that these people came 'in the name of God and his Prophet', in all good faith, but all the same, if they saw me when they left, they'd talk! They'd say, 'Lla Zohra from Bou Semmam is there! She's come here so that Hajout can also be burnt down!' I had to hide!

Everything that has happened to me! Oh, Lord, everything that has happened!

Murmurs

Jennet is sitting in the doorway, on the bare tiles, or on a snow-white sheepskin.

A slanting sunbeam lights up her ample form, indistinguishable under her loose gown of multi-coloured cotton. A heavy braid of black hair is coiled around her fine-featured face. She sits waiting: her husband was picked up during a military control which stopped the bus on the main road; he disappeared a year ago; where is he now, in what prison, what camp or at the bottom of what precipice? Jennet muses over the sons, the daughters that she hasn't had during twenty years of sterile married life ...

At the back of the room, her old aunt Aïcha, who has come down from the mountains, is huddled in a corner. But she rambles on in an endless lament:

'Pray they don't come, O my sister's daughter! Don't let the chattering neighbours suspect this time, curses on their cold hearts, these offspring of flayed hyenas!'

The voice, now hoarse, now sing-song, rises in regular stanzas culminating in rhymed curses. After a pause, she mutters her ritual prayer ... Jennet sits there but does not pray, even though she catches the last faint whine of the muezzin's arabesques.

She keeps watch out of habit: a child might come knocking at the outer door, she must stop him in the vestibule. The prying busybodies on the neighbouring terraces find any excuse to send to ask for an egg they're short of, a pinch of paprika, a cupful of chickpeas or caster sugar. Jennet knows that they know, these spies, these jealous women, these scandalmongers. They probably say that the old woman has come with some new scheme, proposing to arrange a marriage or organize some magic cure ... They imagine that the sterile woman without brood, the silent woman from the cities, is tormented by her recent widowhood, plagued by the solitude of the empty bed ...

Up in the hills, 'France' daily fans the fire, dispersing women and children along the muddy roads. There are more and more raids on the markets of the little town. Jennet thinks of her husband rotting in some jail or other: will a messenger come, a relative by marriage or one of God's beggars bearing a sign of good omen? . . .

Jennet sits in the doorway, waiting, while in the semi-darkness old Aïcha's moaning grows louder.

Jennet seizes the bronze pestle lying in front of her bare feet near her abandoned mules: 'Keep my hands busy, O gentle-eyed Prophet, O Lla Khadija, his beloved! Keep my hands busy to unclench the teeth of anguish!' . . .

The regular pounding of the pestle begins, crushing cloves of garlic, then fresh herbs. Despite its heavy beat Jennet can still hear the voice of the frightened fugitive: 'For three days,' she says to herself, 'the poor creature has never stopped trembling; she's trying to keep off the ill winds that beset her'; and Jennet pounds with all her might, making the metal mortar ring . . .

She gets up slowly, walks to and fro, her hands suddenly too active; she sits down again. She rests the pestle again betweeen her bare feet whose toes are stained with crimson henna. The evening draws on, the voice of the old woman lying in the back room, on the horsehair mattress, under a white sheet ('white as a shroud!' she moaned), the fugitive's voice takes up its incoherent antiphon, or sorceress's soliloquy, casting spells.

The last gleams of dusk die out above the terrace with its frail jasmin. Jennet resumes her pounding: the garlic is crushed, the coriander reduced to a powder, the cumin to dust, but as the herbs and spices scent the twilit room, Jennet decides to go on pounding till the voice in the half-darkness ceases its ravings . . .

The neighbours might hear, the busybodies on the terraces might understand, the child they send knocking on the door might have time to cross the vestibule, to reach the threshold of the room and take them by surprise; she must keep watch, she must keep guard, hour after hour, day after day.

Until the fugitive's fears are allayed, till she regains her strength and can depart, veiled, protected, to face the terrors of the adventure . . .

Plunder

In the family gatherings of former times, the matrons take their place in a circle, according to an accepted protocol. In the first place, age takes precedence over fortunes or repute. The most senior is always the first to enter the L-shaped vestibule leading out on to the patio with its bluish ceramic tiles; she is followed by her daughter-in-law, whom she calls 'her bride' even ten years after the wedding (as if her son had simply been married by proxy); next come her other daughters, widowed, divorced or still unmarried . . .

Then everyone takes a seat: the divans in the centre are reserved for the ladies who lead each procession: they are the only ones to speak aloud, to ask questions, to extend their congratulations, to distribute their blessings while they take off their veils of spotless wool and their 'brides' remove their taffeta *haïks*, and every guest settles down amid a rustle of silken skirts.

The bride in each family must spend two or three hours exhibiting her face, her antique jewels, her embroidered silks; the mother-in-law, while taking part in the exchanges, keeps an eye on her daughter-in-law to make sure she inspires compliments and envy.

I watch this ritual from the corridor or from a corner of the patio; we little girls can move around, listening out for sudden bursts of conversation or momentary pauses in the collective buzz of talk.

The younger women, married or widowed, are mostly seated uncomfortably on hard, upright chairs; they sit still, ill at ease. I can imagine what they must be suffering.

'Why don't they ever speak?' I sometimes ask.

At most they murmur thanks, compliments to the hostess on the coffee or cakes, or exchange inaudible greetings with their neighbours. Questions follow a time-honoured formula with thanks to God and to the Prophet. Sometimes the order of the courtesies is so unchanged

153

that a guest at one end of the room will simply move her lips to address another at the other end: 'How is the master of the house? How are all the children? And the Sheikh, may God grant him the pilgrimage!'

And similarly greetings and blessings are mouthed from the other end of the room, and they criss-cross in an exchange little more than mime.

The loud voices of the oldest women – a merry laugh, a chuckle, the suggestion of an obscene joke – ring out suddenly on the heady perfumed air, above the whimpering of the children who wait impatiently in the doorway or on the rug. Once coffee, tea and cakes have been handed round, the matrons can unbend; under the guise of allusions, axioms, parables, they indulge in tittle-tattle about such and such an absent family.

Then the conversation comes back to themselves or at least to their husbands, referred to by the omnipresent 'he'; rather than complain of some domestic worry, some all too familiar trouble (a repudiation, a temporary separation, a dispute over a legacy), the woman who is recounting her own experiences will end by expressing her resignation to Allah and the local saints. Sometimes the daughters take up their mother's story, elaborating it with their long-winded, whispered exegesis. Adding a vivid detail, a caustic comment, they fill in the picture of the calamity: the man coming home drunk and striking her, or, on the contrary, 'himself' overtaken by ruin, sickness, involving endless tears, debts, inexorable misery . . . So these city ladies sit there and bear witness, as best they can, to the unfolding drama of their own lives.

In these gatherings it matters little what the ladies look like in their antiquated outfits: their ribbons and *serouals* date from the beginning of the century: the golden roses quivering on their foreheads, the hennaed designs between the painted eyelids of the daughters-in-law who sit like statues – nothing of this has changed for two or three generations . . .

At every one of these gatherings, they are trapped in the web of impossible revolt; each woman who tells her tale – loud exclamations of the one, rapid whispers of another – gets something off her chest. The 'I' of the first person is never used; the time-honoured phraseology discharges the burden of rancour and râles that rasp the throat. In speaking to the listening group every woman finds relief from her deep inner hurt.

154

Similarly they are made to guess at causes for merriment or happiness; by means of understatement, proverbs, even riddles or traditional fables, handed down from generation to generation, the women dramatize their fate, or exorcize it, but never expose it directly.

The Second World War had not encroached on my country's soil, but she had sacrificed a significant contingent of her sons at the front. When it ended, the Nationalist movement flared up. A series of violent incidents even marked Armistice Day.

In my native city there was talk of a plot that was only just discovered in time: weapons stolen from the arsenal, a bomb exploding at the military hospital. The authors of these incidents were soon found and arrested.

During the following summer holidays I took part in an unusual ceremony which was just like a funeral service. My grandmother's nephew was one of the plotters arrested and sentenced to forced labour, like a brigand.

The guests arrived in their white veils; the mourning liturgy lent solemnity to the modest house where my grandmother's younger sister lived. Was this a death without a corpse? We children stood around in the vestibule, not knowing what to make of it: the matrons entered, took their seats on the mattresses, wagging their heads in sympathy and keeping time to the mother's tragic aria; she sat with a white scarf wrapped tightly round her head and gave way to her grief in spasmodic outbursts of shrill wails.

We looked on, fascinated by the curious absence of any corpse which impaired the nature of the ceremony. All that remained of the habitual ritual were the words, the women's solidarity and the resignation they affirmed over and over during the mother's monotonous lamentations . . . On the way back home we caught scraps of conversation about 'forced labour' (an unexpected sentence for this son whom they were mourning but not burying), a bomb, stolen weapons: the ladies' hushed voices, their tones of commiseration or submission, conjured up a whole romantic story.

I was struck by the verdict expressed by my grandmother: not on her nephew whom she refrained from either judging a hero or a highway robber, nor on the misfortune which had befallen her family, of which she deemed herself the mouth-piece. But she condemned her sister for exhibiting her grief too ostentatiously in front of the assembled women. Resignation was the important thing according to the matriarch: to take the rough with the smooth and always be equal to the part assigned to you by fate.

The nephew was reprieved the following year: I can't remember whether my grandmother went back on her judgement with regard to her younger sister, who had exposed her sorrow too dramatically.

In the family home, which is so little changed today, it is this memory of my late grandmother sitting in judgement which conjures up her ghost for me.

How could a woman speak aloud, even in Arabic, unless on the threshold of extreme age? How could she say 'I', since that would be to scorn the blanket-formulae which ensure that each individual journeys through life in a collective resignation? . . . How can she undertake to analyse her childhood, even if it turns out different? The difference, if not spoken of, disappears. Only speak of what conforms, my grandmother would reprove me: to deviate is dangerous, inviting disaster in its multiple disguises. Only speak of everyday mishaps, out of prudence rather than prudery, and so stave off misfortune . . . As for happiness, always too short-lived, but compact, succulent, close your eyes and concentrate all your strength on enjoying it but do not speak of it aloud . . .

My oral tradition has gradually been overlaid and is in danger of vanishing: at the age of eleven or twelve I was abruptly ejected from this theatre of feminine confidences – was I thereby spared from having to silence my humbled pride? In writing of my childhood memories I am taken back to those bodies bereft of voices. To attempt an autobiography using French words alone is to lend oneself to the vivisector's scalpel, revealing what lies beneath the skin. The flesh flakes off and with it, seemingly, the last shreds of the unwritten language of my childhood. Wounds are reopened, veins weep, one's own blood flows and that of others, which has never dried.

As the words pour out, inexhaustible, maybe distorting, our ancestral night lengthens. Conceal the body and its ephemeral grace. Prohibit gestures – they are too specific. Only let sounds remain.

Speaking of oneself in a language other than that of the elders is indeed to unveil oneself, not only to emerge from childhood but to leave it, never to return. Such incidental unveiling is tantamount to stripping oneself naked, as the demotic Arabic dialect emphasizes.

But this stripping naked, when expressed in the language of the former conquerer (who for more than a century could lay his hands on everything save women's bodies), this stripping naked takes us back oddly enough to the plundering of the preceding century.

When the body is not embalmed by ritual lamentations, it is like a scarecrow decked in rags and tatters. The battle-cries of our ancestors, unhorsed in long-forgotten combats, re-echo across the years; accompanied by the dirges of the mourning-women who watched them die.

Voice

All four of my sons took to the hills to join the maquis. The day they arrested seven of the partisans in one swoop, two of my sons were among them. They chained them together. Someone from here, one of the leaders of the *goumiers*, said, 'All this plotting, it's your mother who's behind it, O Ahmed!'

That son didn't admit anything. His other brothers got a message to him, from up in the hills: 'If we get to know that you've let one word slip, we'll come and kill you ourselves!'

They left me this last one eventually; he stayed with me . . . I had to travel to get to see the others! For a long time I didn't get any news of one of them, Malek. I thought, 'He must be dead!' A relative came to see me from the city. 'Have you any news of your sons?' he asked me.

'I've heard from all of them, except Malek,' I sighed. 'He's probably dead!'

He gave a sort of faint smile, but he didn't say anything.

'I see you smile,' I said. 'Perhaps you've got news?'

He stooped down then to kiss me on the head. 'He's in the city,' he whispered as he left. 'He's at Kaddour's, but don't say a word.'

Malek spent a long time with the maquis. He was a tailor by profession. He took my Singer sewing machine and worked for the Brothers . . . At first I made the uniforms myself. But as I had to see to the cooking, I couldn't do everything! Then Malek took the sewing machine into the hills . . . At that time the farm still brought me in a bit. I could buy another one. But the soldiers of France smashed it up eventually.

I was very proud of the uniforms I made! Without boasting, mine had the best cut! If you unfolded one of mine and hung it up, you'd think it'd been bought in a shop!

158

People still talk about the plane that the maquisards shot down. A piece of the plane was found at my place and they knew that 'the man from Kolea' was responsible for the job. That's what the local people called my eldest son.

Long before the war, he loved music, he loved gunpowder and having a good time. When Sidi Mhamed Ben Yusef, the marabout, arranged a celebration, the people said to him, 'Come with us to welcome the prefect and sub-prefect with gunpowder and music!'

'I don't like that sort of celebration!' he'd reply. 'I'll go and have a good time in Kolea, where no-one knows me. There I'll be able to have a different sort of fun!'

That's why they called him 'the friend of Kolea', when his real name's Sahraoui, the same as mine! He lives in Hajout at present. His stomach is all deformed and I can't get over it!

He was involved in a hand-to-hand fight with the soldiers, with knives! His stomach was ripped open and his intestines all fell out! A peasant gave him the cloth from his head-dress to tie his stomach up and hold everything in, more or less. Two days later, a doctor in the maquis examined him and sewed his abdomen up. It's true he didn't die but he's a cripple now!

He's still as vain as he was before the war. And as obstinate! Besides, he's still got the same bad habit he's had ever since he was a child: he's never afraid, he doesn't know what fear is! Here he is, with his belly all deformed, and he was always such a fine figure of a man! Even when he wears a fine jacket, and I know how much trouble he takes about the way he dresses, people must wonder what's he's got on his hip! . . .

The second time the soldiers burnt my house down, the fire spread and the roof collapsed . . . I went back into the fire, thinking, 'Even if I only save one mattress, I'll have that to sleep on!'

So I got one mattress out; the fire had caught one corner. I plunged it into the wadi and put the fire out. The soldiers laughed at me, saying 'Are you keeping that one for the *fellaheen*?'

They came back and set fire to the place again. They even took the clothes off our backs . . . My sister, may her soul rest in peace! she was older than me, she died, she never got over the shock! They took our clothes, and left us like that, naked as the day we were born! . . . I got a message to a relative in the village. She sent us some clothes. They came back once more and left us destitute again . . . What trials shall I tell you about, and which shall I leave to be forgotten? . . .

To the little girl I'd adopted, I kept on saying, 'If they question you, begin to cry! If they ask, "Who comes to visit your mother? What does she do?" you must begin to cry immediately . . . If you say a word, they'll ask more questions! Just cry! That's all you must do!'

And that's what she did. She burst into tears, she rolled about in the sand, she ran away in a flood of tears. When she got home I was anxious.

'Did they hit you?'

'No,' she said. 'They asked me questions; I cried, they wanted to give me money. I refused and I ran away!'

They thought she knew what money was. But paper money – she'd never seen any: true she was very little, but it was especially because she lived in the mountains. In the mountains, who ever sees a banknote?

When I came down to the village, I sent her to school; but that didn't last long . . .

In the village a boy ratted on us. He went to tell them, 'The mother of the Moujahidine has gone to Izzar! Aunt Zohra has left Ben Semmam and has gone there!'

I was asleep when they came knocking at my door and I called out, 'What's the matter?'

'The officer's asking for you: he wants to have a word with you!'

I decided to go. My little girl and my sister (it was before she died) started to follow me; they were crying.

'Don't cry,' I told them. 'Don't cry for me! I won't have anyone crying for me!'

The boy had told them everything: that I had met up with the Brothers, what they had had to eat, how many there were. The Brothers had asked me, 'Have you any news about the future movements of the French?' I told them, 'I don't know just now, but send someone to me tomorrow morning, early. I'll have the information for you!' Word for word, the boy had gone and reported to them everything we'd said! . . .

When I got back from my meeting with the Brothers, I found out in the village that the French were going to make a raid into the mountains. I had passed on the information . . . And that's how I found myself facing the French officer!

That's where I met a woman named Khadija. She was very rich: long before the war she already owned a good deal of property, then she started buying and buying! She ran a – may God preserve us! – a 'house', the wicked woman! – a bawdy house . . . in spite of that she'd been on the pilgrimage to Mecca. Then she said, 'I'll give some money to the Moujahidine. Perhaps God will forgive me!' She gave them three hundred gold pieces! . . . After that someone ratted on her: a man, apparently, who delivered medicines to the Brothers.

So I met this woman in this ante-chamber.

'What brought you here, Khadija?' I asked her.

'The same as you!' she replied. 'You've been betrayed, so have I! . . . God has willed that we meet in this place, and under these circumstances!'

This time they questioned me with electricity until . . . until I thought I'd die! I'd said, 'I don't want anyone crying over me!' If I thought they were going to question me with electricity, I wouldn't have gone, not at any price! I'd rather have died there and then.

I came back again into the mountains with my daughter. We used to go and take semolina to the Brothers. We'd look for a place in the forest where we could leave it. We also had to find a place to knead it, where we could cook it. Once, on the way back I caught sight of the soldiers in the distance.

We fled towards the wadi. We climbed down into a *guelta* that was quite deep. The house was on fire. Huge embers, as well as pieces of burning beams were hurled into the air . . . We hid, but these burning missiles fell on us. Some of them fell on my head.

The child, who was very small, was completely covered by the water of the *guelta*. I was half exposed. My hair caught fire. And the child, who was crying with fright, shouted, 'Mother, the fire's eating you up! The fire's eating you up!'

That's how I lost all my hair. I hurled myself into the water. But more burning embers fell on me. We couldn't leave the spot . . . I've still got these scars on my forehead and neck . . .

We hid the whole day in the pool. The child and I, all by ourselves! The Brothers had fled into the forest. The soldiers started to leave. I could hear the stamp of their feet. They went back to the Roman road and got into their lorries; it was nearly dusk . . . It was quite quiet for a bit.

'Fatiha,' I said, 'you're quite small. From a distance, you could be mistaken for a chicken or a little goat . . . Climb up the hill and look!'

She did as I said; she came back and told me, 'They've got back into their lorries and they're driving away. You can come out!'

I came out. We were free. We started walking. Where could we go now, it was night! We walked and walked . . . We found a *mali*. We spent the night there, near the Saint's grave. We were ashamed to go and knock on people's doors. We stayed there until it was light. Only then did we knock at the lady's door, Sid Ahmed Tahar's daughter.

'Where have you been, little mother?' she asked me.

'We've just arrived,' I replied.

I didn't want to tell her we'd spent the night in the open. I was afraid she'd laugh at us . . . Because they do laugh! They laugh and laugh, those people that nothing happens to!

I didn't want to mention the fire. Perhaps they'd even be glad about it, those people who don't know what misfortune is! I told her again, 'We've been walking in the forest . . . We've just arrived at your door!'

I must admit that she looked after us well. She made us some bread. We had as much to eat and drink as we needed. Then we left. We didn't stay the night with her. She didn't say anything and we just didn't stay. People don't like sheltering those, like ourselves, who bring 'France' behind them!

We left. We wandered about . . .

After all these misfortunes, I've got to the point where people treat me as if I'm mad. People started telling me I was mad. As a matter of fact, they were afraid.

'Here comes the mad woman, shut the door!'

It's true that after my hair all got burnt I must have been ill for several months . . . My sons took care of me. They found people to look after me. I got a bit better. I must have had a blow on my head; even now there are times when I can't remember anything . . .

The Brothers also took care of me. Thanks to them, I got better. But people still went on shutting their doors in the 'mad woman' 's face. They were afraid: that's the truth; especially the people of the village. They said, 'What are those folk doing here? They bring bad luck!'

I went to Jennet's again, in Hajout; I hadn't got a stitch to my back. I tried to find a pair of loose trousers that I could tie round my waist and cover my head with, like a veil; I couldn't find any. Who would have given me a veil?

So I decided to go to Jennet's. I had to go by bus. I took a basket of vegetables with me and . . . When God wants to help you . . . A man just happened to be wanting to buy onions. I met him and I'd got what he wanted, so I was able to pay for the bus! I arrived at Jennet's with no veil and no burnous! . . .

Embraces

Lla Zohra, from Bou Semmam, is more than eighty. I cross the threshold of the house she lives in nowadays, just on the edge of the village of Ménacer. I walk up the path through her vegetable patch that she looks after herself, and under a walnut and an apricot tree that later she points out to me proudly.

I tap softly with the knocker on the second door and the hum of the sewing machine is suspended. The white-washed rooms open on to a modest patio; from there the slopes of the mountain are visible, Pic Marceau with its observation posts that are no longer in use.

A young woman, the one who was doing the sewing, comes out first. Then the old lady, my hostess. We embrace, we touch, we tell each other how well we look. I sit down. I talk of my grandmother's death, which occurred just after independence. I hadn't seen Lla Zohra since.

'We were cousins, your grandmother and I,' she says. 'It's true I'm closer to you through your mother's father; we belong to the same fraction of the same tribe. She was related to me through another marriage, through the female line!'

I listen as she unravels the genealogical skein; the threads pass from such and such a mountain to such and such a hill, winding through *zaouia* and hamlet, and then round the heart of the city. I drink my coffee. Finally I say, 'I'm spending the night here! . . . We've plenty of time! . . .'

Her voice stirs the glowing embers of days past. The afternoon draws on, the mountainsides change colour, the sewing machine resumes its monotonous humming-song at the far end of the patio. The old woman's adopted daughter has gone back to her sewing; she doesn't want to listen or be involved. Later, she asks me how she can get a job in the nearby town, in the post-office, or in a nursery school . . .

I agree to take you up to your farm, little mother, high in the mountains. After two hours' walk on thorny paths, we found the sanctuary, which you call 'the refuge', using the French word, only slightly distorted: the walls are still standing among the rubble. Their base is blackened with traces of extinct fires, lit by present-day vagrants.

There, your voice took up your tale. The sun was still high. You let your veil fall around your waist and sat down among the gorse bushes and spring flowers. Your face, a network of fine wrinkles, was austere; you were lost for a moment in your own memories – I took a photograph of you among the poppies . . . The sun gradually sank low in the sky. We returned in the evening silence.

It is now my turn to tell a tale. To hand on words that were spoken, then written down. Words from more than a century ago, like those that we, two women from the same tribe, exchange today.

Shards of sounds which re-echo in the calm after the storm . . .

The oasis of Laghouat in the summer of 1853: the artist Eugène Fromentin has spent the preceding autumn and spring in the Sahel where peace has been restored, just as it has today, little mother.

Summer sets in. Giving way to a sudden impulse, he rushes southwards. Six months before, Laghouat had suffered a terrible siege. The oasis had been captured by the French, house by house. Traces of mass graves can still be seen under the palm trees, where Fromentin walks with a friend. And just as I listen to you unfold your tale during these few days, he hears his friend the lieutenant say, as he stops in front of a most wretched house, 'Look! Here's a miserable hut that I'd like to see razed to the ground!'

Fromentin continues: 'And as we went along, he told me the following story in a few brief words, stamped with his sad reflections on the cruel hazards of war:

' "In this house, which has changed hands since the capture of the city, lived two very pretty *Naylettes* . . ." '*

Fatma and Meriem, the *Naylettes*, earn their living in the oasis as dancers and prostitutes. They are twenty at the most. Fifteen years previously, the Amir Abd al-Qadir had attacked El-Mahdi, near

---

*Eugène Fromentin, *Un été au Sahara* (A Summer in the Sahara)

Laghouat, to try to subdue the lords of the south and unify resistance to the Christian . . . Had these women lost their father in this civil war, and some of their brothers? Let us suppose so; when we meet them in this digression into the past, they make a living out of their beauty which is in its prime . . .

If they were to live till they were forty, little mother, perhaps they would become like that woman, Khadija, with whom you kept company in the corridor of torture; wealthy sinners trying to make the pilgrimage 'to win their pardon and give money to the Partisans!'

A few months or a few weeks before the siege of Laghouat, Fatma and Meriem secretly received two officers from a French column which patrol the district: not for betrayal, but simply for a night of love, 'may God preserve us from sin!'

'After the street fighting of 4 and 5 December, the corpses were so numerous that they filled the well of the oasis!' I explained. 'And Fatma? And Meriem?' Lla Zohra interrupted, catching herself following the story as if it were a legend recounted by a bard. 'Where did you hear this story?' she went on, impatiently.

'I read it!' I replied. 'An eye-witness told it to a friend who wrote it down.'

The lieutenant, one of the officers who'd been received by the *Naylettes*, is a member of the first company which leads the attack. He fights throughout the day. 'We fought our way right into the heart of the city,' he explains. Suddenly he recognizes the district and goes with his sergeant to the dancers' house.

A soldier is just coming out, his bayonet dripping with blood. Two accomplices run out after him, their arms laden with women's jewellery.

'Too late!' the lieutenant thinks, as he enters the house which had previously welcomed him so warmly.

And night falls.

The lieutenant tells what he had seen and the artist writes it down: 'Fatma was dead, Meriem was dying. The one lay on the paving-stones in the courtyard, the other had rolled down the stairs, head first, and lay at the bottom.'

Two bodies of two young dancers lying half naked up to the waist, their thighs visible through the torn fabric of their clothes, without head-dress or diadem, without earrings or anklets, without necklaces of coral or gold coins, without glass-beaded clasps . . . In the courtyard the stove is still burning; a dish of couscous has just been served. The spindle from the loom has been put down, still wound full of wool, never to be used; only the olive-wood chest lies overturned, rifled, its hinges wrenched off.

'As Meriem died in my arms, she dropped a button she had torn off the uniform of her murderer,' sighed the lieutenant who had arrived too late.

Six months later, the officer gave his trophy to Fromentin, who kept it. Fromentin was never to paint the picture of the death of those dancers. Is it the feel of this object in his hand which transforms him from a painter of Algerian hunting scenes into the writer depicting death in words? . . . As if Fromentin's pen had taken precedence over his paint-brush, as if the story passed on to him could only find its final form in words . . .

Meriem's dying hand still holds out the button from the uniform: to the lover, to the friend of the lover who cannot now help but write. And time is abolished. I, your cousin, translate this story into our mother tongue, and tell it now to you, sitting beside you, little mother, in front of your vegetable patch. So I try my hand as temporary story-teller.

The nights I spent in Ménacer, I slept in your bed, just as long ago I slept as a child curled up against my father's mother.

Third Movement:

The Ballad of Abraham

Every gathering, for a funeral, for a wedding, is subject to rigid rules: the separation of the sexes must be rigorously respected, care must be taken that no male relative sees you, no cousin among the men crowding outside the house must run the risk of recognizing you when you go out or in, veiled amid the host of other veiled women, lost in the mob of guests concealed behind their masks.

A young girl's introduction to religious observance itself can only be through sound, never through sight: no office in which the disposition of people, the code prescribed for costume and posture, the ritual hierarchy would strike the sensibility of the female child. Any emotion that might be expressed will be inspired by music, by the worn voices of the female worshippers calling on the divine presence. At the mosque, in the corner reserved for women, only the matriarchs squat, the very old whose voices have already died.

In the transmission of Islam, an acid erosion has been at work: Tradition would seem to decree that entry through its strait gate is by submission, not by love. Love, which the most simple of settings might inflame, appears dangerous.

There remains music. I hear again the pious women chanting when, every Friday during our holidays, we children accompanied female relatives to the tomb of the city's patron saint.

Inside the primitive mud-walled hovel dozens of anonymous women from the surrounding hamlets and neighbouring farms squat on the straw mats covering the floor, and intone their plaintive chants. The noxious effluvia of mingled sweat and damp pervading the place reminds me of the ante-room of a *hammam*, with the distant trickle of fountains replaced by the murmur of rasping voices.

But as the women launch into their shrill vociferations I do not feel any mystical exaltation; the recriminations of these veiled worshippers (who barely leave a gap in the cloth covering their swollen faces), the bitterness of their lamentations, make the singers appear to me as victims ... I pity them or find them strange, or frightening. The city ladies sitting around me, and who have bedecked and beautified themselves for this outing, are not so easily put off. My mother and her cousins draw near; they hastily mumble some Quranic formulae over the saint's catafalque, blow a kiss and leave: our group remains untouched by the popular exaggerated religiosity.

We take a footpath that leads down to a sheltered creek where the women can bathe protected from onlookers.

'Going to visit the marabout' means visiting the saint whose dead presence offers solace. The dead man seems helpful to my female relatives – even seems to do them a favour – since he had the courtesy, two or three centuries ago, to come to die quite near the seashore. However, this pretext that they were going on a pilgrimage did not deceive my uncle, who during the summer became the head of the whole extended family. He was prepared to turn a blind eye to the fact that we indulged in such profane pleasures as sea-bathing rather than the religious devotions that we had announced.

My first stirrings of religious feeling go back much further: in the village, for three or four years running, the day of the 'feast of the sheep' was heralded by 'The Ballad of Abraham'.

Chilly winter mornings, when my mother, up earlier than usual, switched on the radio. The programme in Arabic invariably involved the same record in honour of the holiday: a performance by a celebrated tenor which included a dozen or so verses telling the story of Abraham and his son.

It was listening to this ballad every year throughout my childhood that formed, I think, my feeling for Islam.

In the dawn twilight I wake to the caressing voice of the singer, a tenor whom Saint-Saëns, while spending his last years in Algiers, had encouraged when he was just starting his career as a muezzin. In the course of his performance, verse after verse, he acted out all the characters: Abraham, in a dream that troubled his nights, beholding the Angel Gabriel come in the name of God, to demand that he sacrifice his son; Abraham's wife, not knowing that her son, decked out in his ceremonial jellaba, was to be sacrificed; Isaac himself, climbing up the mountain in all innocence, astonished that the raven on the branch speaks to him of death . . .

I hung on the opening words of the Biblical drama but I do not know why the song evoked such a passionate response in me: the progress of the story to its miraculous ending, each character whose words brought them so vividly to life, the burden and the horror of Abraham's fate which weighed so heavily on him as he was constrained to conceal his anguish . . . It was as much the texture itself of the song – the variegated pattern of the phraseology – as the melancholy of the singer's voice (making me curl up more tightly under the sheets) which cast such a spell over me: the unfamiliar terms, the reticence of the Arabic dialect, veiling the direct reference with a wealth of imagery. This language which the tenor's art made so simple, was vibrant with a primitive solemnity.

Abraham's wife, Sarah, had her say in the verses, just like my mother describing to us her joys, fears or forebodings. Abraham could have been my father who never expressed his own feelings aloud, but who, it seemed to me, might have . . . I was deeply moved also by the son's submission: his respect for his father, the reticence with which he bore the burden of his grief, and this very perfection carried me back to a past era, both nobler and more innocent:

> *'Since thou hadst perforce to kill me, O my father,*
> *Wherefore didst thou not advise me of it?*
> *I could then have bestowed upon my mother embraces enow! . . .*
> *Take care, when thou stoopest to sacrifice me,*
> *lest my blood stain thy gown!*
> *My mother, on thy return to her, might guess my fate too hastily!'*

I loved the simplicity of Isaac's song, in whose unhurried stanzas the dramatic quality of the tale swelled to its climax. The insistent beat of this music . . .

At this same period, an aunt used to recount the life of the Prophet, with many variations: one incident inspired the same emotion in me . . .

When the Prophet first started having visions, he returned one day from the cave so upset that, in her words, 'they made him weep'; and as she spoke she almost burst into tears herself. 'To comfort him, Lalla Khadija, his wife, sat him on her lap,' my aunt explained, as if she had herself been present. 'So,' she always concluded, 'the very first Muslim, perhaps even before the Prophet himself, may Allah preserve him! was a woman. A woman was historically the first to adhere to the Islamic faith, out of conjugal love,' according to my relative.

In a triumphant voice she revived this scene time and time again; I was ten, or perhaps eleven: listening, I was struck with sudden embarrassment as I had only seen this demonstration of conjugal love in a European society: 'Is that the way for a Prophet to behave?' I asked, offended and shocked. 'Can a man who sits on his wife's lap be a Prophet?'

My aunt smiled discreetly, her heart melted . . . Years later, my heart too was melted by another detail in her tale. 'Long after Khadija's death,' so she related, 'one particular circumstance would cause Mohamed uncontrollable distress: whenever his late wife's sister approached his tent, the Prophet would be most upset, because he said the sound of the sister's footsteps was identical to that of his dead wife. At this sound, which seemed to restore Khadija to life, the Prophet could scarce hold back his tears . . .'

This story of the sound of sandalled feet would bring on a sudden yearning for Islam. A longing to embark as on a love affair, a rustling catching at my heart: with fervour and taking all the risks of blasphemy.

Voice

We were just finishing our evening meal. I handed my young son a jam-dish with a little silver spoon. I got this spoon from my father.

I'd only been married a few days – I wasn't quite fifteen – I'd gone to see my father and I was having coffee with him. Suddenly I asked him, 'Father, I'd like to take this little spoon!'

'Take it,' he replied. 'Take the cups, look around and take anything you like from here, daughter!'

'Father,' I said, 'I only want this spoon, because it's the one you always use for your coffee! It's so dear to my heart!'

I'd kept it ever since, and that was thirty years ago at least, maybe forty . . . But on the night I was talking about the partisans were at our place. They'd had something to eat and drink. Others were keeping a look-out. When I'd given them their coffee I passed the jam-dish to my son so that he could serve them and for some reason I put the silver spoon in it. He'd scarcely gone out of the room than 'France' sent her troops up into the hills and bullets started raining down all round!

And so my boy went off with them: he dropped the jam-dish but he held on to the spoon . . . As if he was taking my father's blessing with him – may God rest his soul!

And so my last-born went off with the maquisards. He was so young: barely fourteen! It's true that he was very quick and bright. Later one of my older sons who was already married came to see me and said, 'You ought to ask the maquisards to let you have him back, he's too young!'

'Listen!' I replied. 'If he comes back and the enemy questions him, suppose he couldn't hold out and he told them everything he knew? . . . We'd be dishonoured! Leave him: if he must die, he'll die a hero, and if he's destined to live, he'll live with a clear conscience!'

So Kaddour stayed in the maquis. It's true he was young, but he'd had some schooling. Of all his brothers he was the one who had the most drive . . .

Once Mustapha, another of my sons, came from Marceau.

'Mother,' he said, 'father's just been taken away; the French officer's going to question him about Kaddour. They've spotted that he isn't here any more.'

When God wants to ensure someone's salvation, he does so! Before he joined the maquis Kaddour never did any manual work about the place: he wouldn't even go and fill a can of water! . . . But then the schoolchildren went on strike: little ones and big ones. He had to stay on the farm with nothing to do. They were looking for seasonal workers to help with the grape-picking down on the plain. A Frenchwoman, the Moulios girl, was giving out work permits for the picking. Kaddour went to see her.

'Give me a permit,' he asked her, 'so that I can go and get seasonal work down on the plain! With this strike I can't bear sitting around doing nothing . . .'

The real reason he wanted a permit was so that he could move about freely. He'd no intention of going and working for other people: he was too proud for that, and as I said, as far as manual work was concerned, he was too lazy!

The Moulios girl gave him the permit. He showed it to me. 'Very well! Go and work then!' I said.

I was so afraid, when he moved around at that time, that the *goumiers* would pick him up and beat him or provoke him . . . And then there was this alarm at our house that night and he left with the Moujahidine. A few weeks later the French questioned his father: 'Where's the youngster?'

'He asked for a permit to go and work down on the plain!' his father replied and he quoted the Frenchwoman. They questioned her and she admitted that she'd given him this permit. It seems that the officer telephoned all the farms in the surrounding country, even as far as Marengo. No-one knew anything about him. So in the end they decided that he must have died somewhere.

A long time before these events I heard someone knocking repeatedly at the door in the middle of the night. I was alone at the farm, with my daughters-in-law and the children. I didn't open up.

Well, no sooner had I put my head on the pillow than I fell into a deep sleep. I had a dream which woke me up: two apparitions, like ghosts, but all lit up, stood before me and spoke to me:

'O, Lla Hajja!' (that's how they addressed me although I hadn't been to Mecca then). 'Truly you were afraid and we understand your fears;

You thought us a company of *goumiers*

But we are indeed the Prophet's heirs! . . .'

They spoke just like that, in rhymed prose, and they repeated the last bit which was what woke me up and gave me such a feeling of remorse; it's true that that night I'd not opened the door to the partisans!

They were in the habit of arriving, of eating, keeping watch and leaving again in the night. I always showed them in to the same room. In the daytime I kept this room empty. I sometimes stood in the doorway and thought, 'This room where the sons of the Revolution enter, will become green, green, green, like an unopened water-melon, and one day its walls with fresh dew shall stream!' So I was starting to express myself in rhymed prose, like the apparitions in my dream!

One night when the Moujahidine arrived, they'd brought in the mud from the roads on their boots, right into this room.

'No, no! Don't worry!' I cried. 'We'll clean it up tomorrow!'

I felt light-hearted; I wanted them to sit down and make themselves at home. I brought them all my cushions. I asked for jugs of water and soap to be brought, then the silver ewers! The next day we had to use picks to chop away the dried mud from the entrance! Yet God has always kept us safe!

Whispers

In April 1842, the Berkanis' zaouia is burnt down; women and children wander over the snow-clad mountainsides — that year the winter was very severe. Their corpses will feed the jackals.

The French leave; their commander, General de Saint-Arnaud, who has succeeded the gloomy Cavaignac, returns to his base in Orleansville, via Miliana. From his encampment on the site of the gutted zaouia, he continues his correspondence with his brother.

The following year the same soldiers return. Since death and destruction have not brought about final submission, since old Berkani, the Caliph's deputy, acting on orders from the Amir, continues to stir up resistance further to the west, Saint-Arnaud decides on more drastic measures: he will take hostages from the Deputy's own family: 'Eight of the chiefs of the three principal fractions of the Beni-Menacer tribe,' he explains to his brother.

The matriarchs whisper to the children in the dark, to the children's children crouching on the straw mat, to the girls who will become matriarchs in turn, their time for child-bearing soon past (a mere parenthesis, from the age of fifteen to thirty-five or forty). Of their bodies there remains neither belly that begets, nor clutching arms, flung wide in travail. Of their bodies, they retain only the ears and eyes of childhood which hang on the lips of the wrinkled story-teller — this matriarch who intones in the corridor, handing on the heroic saga of the fathers, the grandfathers, the paternal great-uncles. The low voice steers the words through waters awash with the dead, prisoners never to be freed . . .

Women whispering: in their beds, once the candle has been snuffed out, during the nights when the alarm has been given, once the embers of the braziers have grown cold . . . From the age of fifteen to thirty-five or forty, the body sags, the body swells, the body bursts open in childbirth, finally the leaden years are over: the body triumphs over the twilight when mouths are gagged, features masked, eyes invariably lowered . . . During this period of enforced silence, the stilled voice bides its time, groans are stifled, grievances sublimated.

Period when women are choked with desire, the burial pit – dark tunnel – of youth, when the chorus of women gaze on death and lift up shrill, convulsive voices to the blackened sky . . . Retaining their rôle of story-teller, figurehead at the prow of memory. The legacy will otherwise be lost – night after night, wave upon wave, the whispers take up the tale, even before the child can understand, even before she finds her words of light, before she speaks in her turn and so that she will not speak alone . . .

'Eight of the chiefs of the three principal fractions,' the French general writes, referring to the hostages. 'Forty-eight prisoners bound for the Island of Sainte-Marguerite: men, women and children, including one pregnant woman': so go the whispers, setting the record straight today, on the site of the gutted zaouia, where the orchards are now more sparse. Fig trees are more numerous than orange or mandarin groves: as if the water has first gone to keep memories green, and cut its irrigation channels faster over rocks!

The spoon from the jam-dish which 'the saint' – that's what they call her because, in her fervent piety, she fasts all the year round – passed to her young son when the alarm was given. The old father's loving gesture for his daughter leaving to get married long ago, is reversed thirty years on, in the gift that the daughter makes to her youngest son who disappears one night in wartime. He will return safe and sound, a few years later! . . . That spoon from the jam-dish, a luxury object in those impoverished mountains, is for me an heraldic object to be chosen for some crest . . .

The fires in the orchards gutted by Saint-Arnaud are finally extinguished, because the old lady talks today and I am preparing to transcribe her tale. To draw up the inventory of the tiny objects passed on thus, from febrile hand to fugitive hand!

When 'the saint' was a child, she listened to the tales told by her grandmother, who was the daughter-in-law of old Berkani. The historians lost sight of him, just before the Amir was forced to surrender. Aïssa el-Berkani left with his 'deira' for Morocco. Beyond Oudja, there is no more trace of him in the archives – as if 'archives' guaranteed the imprint of reality!

Long after this exodus, one of his daughters-in-law found herself a childless widow. She asked the Caliph – so the story goes – for permission to return to her family among the Beni-Menacer tribe who were now subdued. So she returned and married a cousin who took part in the second uprising in 1871 . . .

Long after this second revolt, now in her old age, she transmits her whispered story in her turn to a new circle of bright-eyed children. Then one of these little girls will in turn travel the same path and find herself clad in satin and shot-silk; nicknamed 'the saint', she too will carry on the whispering . . .

Chains of memories: is it not indeed a 'chain', for do not memories fetter us as well as forming our roots? For every passer-by, the story-teller stands hidden in the doorway. It is not seemly to raise the curtain and stand exposed in the sunlight.

Words that are too explicit become such boastings as the braggard uses; and elected silence implies resistance still intact . . .

The Quranic School

At the age when I should be veiled already, I can still move about freely thanks to the French school: every Monday the village bus takes me to the boarding school in the nearby town, and brings me back on Saturday to my parents' home.

I have a friend who is half Italian and who goes home every weekend to a fishing port on the coast; we go together to catch our respective buses and are tempted by all sorts of escapades . . . With beating hearts we make our way into the centre of the town; to enter a smart cake-shop, wander along the edge of the park, stroll along the boulevard, which only runs alongside common barracks, seems the acme of freedom, after a week of boarding school! Excited by the proximity of forbidden pleasures, we eventually each catch our bus; the thrill lay in the risk of missing it!

As a young teenager I enjoy the exhilarating hours spent every Thursday in training on the sports field. I only have one worry: fear that my father might come to visit me! How can I tell him that it's compulsory for me to wear shorts, in other words, I have to show my legs? I keep this fear a secret, unable to confide in any of my schoolfriends; unlike me, they haven't got cousins who do not show their ankles or their arms, who do not even expose their faces. My panic is also compounded by an Arab woman's 'shame'. The French girls whirl around me; they do not suspect that my body is caught in invisible snares.

'Doesn't your daughter wear a veil yet?' asks one or other of the matrons, gazing questioningly at my mother with suspicious kohl-rimmed eyes, on the occasion of one of the summer weddings. I must be thirteen, or possibly fourteen.

'She reads!' my mother replies stiffly.

Everyone is swallowed up in the embarrassed silence that ensues. And in my own silence.

'She reads', that is to say in Arabic, 'she studies'. I think now that this command 'to read' was not just casually included in the Quranic revelation made by the Angel Gabriel in the cave ... 'She reads' is tantamount to saying that writing to be read, including that of the unbelievers, is always a source of revelation: in my case of the mobility of my body, and so of my future freedom.

When I am growing up – shortly before my native land throws off the colonial yoke – while the man still has the right to four legitimate wives, we girls, big and little, have at our command four languages to express desire before all that is left for us is sighs and moans: French for secret missives; Arabic for our stifled aspirations towards God-the-Father, the God of the religions of the Book; Lybico-Berber which takes us back to the pagan idols – mother-gods – of pre-Islamic Mecca. The fourth language, for all females, young or old, cloistered or half-emancipated, remains that of the body: the body which male neighbours' and cousins' eyes require to be deaf and blind, since they cannot completely incarcerate it; the body which, in trances, dances or vociferations, in fits of hope or despair, rebels, and unable to read or write, seeks some unknown shore as destination for its message of love.

In our towns, the first woman-reality is the voice, a dart which flies off into space, an arrow which slowly falls to earth; next comes writing with the scratching pointed quill forming amorous snares with its liana letters. By way of compensation, the need is felt to blot out women's bodies and they must be muffled up, tightly swathed, swaddled like infants or shrouded like corpses. Exposed, a woman's body would offend every eye, be an assault on the dimmest of desires, emphasize every separation. The voice, on the other hand, acts like a perfume, a draft of fresh water for the dry throat; and when it is savoured, it can be enjoyed by several simultaneously; a secret, polygamous pleasure ...

When the hand writes, slow positioning of the arm, carefully bending forward or leaning to one side, crouching, swaying to and fro, as in an act of love. When reading, the eyes take their time, delight in caressing the curves, while the calligraphy suggests the rhythm of the scansion: as if the writing marked the beginning and the end of possession.

Writing: everywhere, a wealth of burnished gold and in its vicinity there is no place for other imagery from either animal or vegetable kingdom; it looks in the mirror of its scrolls and curlicues and sees itself as woman, not the reflection of a voice. It emphasizes by its presence alone where to begin and where to retreat; it suggests, by the song that smoulders in its heart, the dance floor for rejoicing and hair-shirt for the ascetic; I speak of the Arabic script; to be separated from it is to be separated from a great love. This script, which I mastered only to write the sacred words, I see now spread out before me cloaked in innocence and whispering arabesques – and ever since, all other scripts (French, English, Greek) seem only to babble, are never cathartic; they may contain truth, indeed, but a blemished truth.

Just as the pentathlon runner of old needed the starter, so, as soon as I learned the foreign script, my body began to move as if by instinct.

As if the French language suddenly had eyes, and lent them me to see into liberty; as if the French language blinded the peeping-toms of my clan and, at this price, I could move freely, run headlong down every street, annex the outdoors for my cloistered companions, for the matriarchs of my family who endured a living death. As if . . . Derision! I know that every language is a dark depository for piled-up corpses, refuse, sewage, but faced with the language of the former conquerer, which offers me its ornaments, its jewels, its flowers, I find they are the flowers of death – chrysanthemums on tombs!

Its script is a public unveiling in front of sniggering onlookers . . . A queen walks down the street, white, anonymous, draped, but when the shroud of rough wool is torn away and drops suddenly at her feet, which a moment ago were hidden, she becomes a beggar again, squatting in the dust, to be spat at, the target of cruel comments.

In my earliest childhood – from the age of five to ten – I attended the French school in the village, and every day after lessons there I went on to the Quranic school.

Classes were held in a back room lent by a grocer, one of the village notables. I can recall the place, and its dim light: was it because the time for the lessons was just before dark, or because the lighting of the room was so parsimonious? . . .

The master's image has remained singularly clear: delicate features, pale complexion, a scholar's sunken cheeks; about forty families supported him. I was struck by the elegance of his bearing and his traditional attire: a spotless light muslin was wrapped around his head-dress and floated behind his neck; his serge tunic was dazzling white. I never saw this man except sitting.

In comparison, the horde of misbehaving little urchins squatting on straw mats – sons of *fellaheen* for the most part – seemed crude riffraff, from whom I kept my distance. We were only four or five little girls. I suppose that our sex kept us apart, rather than my supercilious amazement at their behaviour. In spite of his aristocratic bearing, the *taleb* did not hesitate to lift his cane and bring it down on the fingers of a recalcitrant or slow-witted lad. (I can still hear it whistle through the air.) We girls were spared this regular punishment.

I can remember the little impromptu parties my mother devised in our flat when I brought home (as later my brother was to do) the walnut tablet decorated with arabesques. This was the master's reward when we had learnt a long *sura* by heart. My mother and our village nanny, who was a second mother to us, then let out that semi-barbaric 'you-you'. That prolonged, irregular, spasmodic cooing, which in our building reserved for teachers' families – all European except for ours – must have appeared incongruous, a truly primitive cry. My mother considered the circumstances (the study of the Quran undertaken by her children) sufficiently important for her to let out this ancestral cry of jubilation in the middle of the village where she nevertheless felt herself an exile.

At every prize-giving ceremony at the French school, every prize I obtained strengthened my solidarity with my own family; but I felt there was more glory in this ostentatious clamour. The Quranic school, that dim cavern in which the haughty figure of the Sheikh was enthroned above the poor village children, this school became, thanks to the joy my mother demonstrated in this way, an island of bliss – Paradise regained.

Back in my native city, I learned that another Arab school was being opened, also funded by private contributions. One of my cousins attended it; she took me there. I was disappointed. The buildings, the timetable, the modern appearance of the masters, made it no different from a common-or-garden French school . . .

I understood later that in the village I had participated in the last of popular, secular teaching. In the city, thanks to the Nationalist movement of 'Modernist Muslims', a new generation of Arab culture was being forged.

Since then these *medrasas* have sprung up everywhere. If I had attended one of them (if I'd grown up in the town where I was born) I would have found it quite natural to swathe my head in a turban, to hide my hair, to cover my arms and calves, in a word to move about out of doors like a Muslim nun!

After the age of ten or eleven, shortly before puberty, I was no longer allowed to attend the Quranic school. At this age, boys are suddenly excluded from the women's Turkish bath – that emollient world of naked bodies stifling in a whirl of scalding steam . . . The same thing happened to my companions, the little village girls, one of whom I would like to describe here.

The daughter of the Kabyle baker must, like me, have attended the French school simultaneously with the Quranic school. But I can only recall her presence squatting at my side in front of the Sheikh: side by side, half smiling to each other, both already finding it uncomfortable to sit cross-legged! . . . My legs must have been too long, because of my height: it wasn't easy for me to hide them under my skirt.

For this reason alone I think that I would in any case have been weaned from Quranic instruction at this age: there is no doubt that it's easier to sit cross-legged when wearing a *seroual*; a young girl's body that is beginning to develop more easily conceals its form under the ample folds of the traditional costume. But my skirts, justified by my attendance at the French school, were ill adapted to such a posture.

When I was eleven I started secondary school and became a boarder. What happened to the baker's daughter? Certainly veiled, withdrawn overnight from school: betrayed by her figure. Her swelling breasts, her slender legs, in a word, the emergence of her woman's personality transformed her into an incarcerated body!

I remember how much this Quranic learning, as it is progressively acquired, is linked to the body.

The portion of the sacred verse, inscribed on both sides of the walnut tablet, had to be wiped off at least once a week, after we had shown that we could recite it off by heart. We scrubbed the piece of wood thoroughly, just like other people wash their clothes: the time it took to dry seemed to ensure the interval that the memory needed to digest what it had swallowed . . .

The learning was absorbed by the fingers, the arms, through the physical effort. The act of cleaning the tablet seemed like ingesting a portion of the Quranic text. The writing – itself a copy of writing which is considered immutable – could only continue to unfold before us if it relied, clause by clause, on this osmosis . . .

As the hand traces the liana-script, the mouth opens to repeat the words, obedient to their rhythm, partly to memorize, partly to relieve the muscular tension . . . The shrill voices of the drowsy children rise up in a monotonous, sing-song chorus.

Stumbling on, swaying from side to side, care taken to observe the tonic accents, to differentiate between long and short vowels, attentive to the rhythm of the chant; muscles of the larynx as well as the torso moving in harmony. Controlling the breath to allow the correct emission of the voice, and letting the understanding advance precariously along its tight-rope. Respecting the grammar by speaking it aloud, making it part of the chant.

This language which I learn demands the correct posture for the body, on which the memory rests for its support. The childish hand, spurred on – as in training for some sport – by willpower worthy of an adult, begins to write. 'Read!' The fingers labouring on the tablet send back the signs to the body, which is simultaneously reader and servant. The lips having finished their muttering, the hand will once more do the washing, proceeding to wipe out what is written on the tablet: this is the moment of absolution, like touching the hem of death's garment. Again, it is the turn of writing, and the circle is completed.

And when I sit curled up like this to study my native language it is as though my body reproduces the architecture of my native city: the *medinas* with their tortuous alleyways closed off to the outside world, living their secret life. When I write and read the foreign language, my body travels far in subversive space, in spite of the neighbours and suspicious matrons; it would not need much for it to take wing and fly away!

As I approach a marriageable age, these two different apprenticeships, undertaken simultaneously, land me in a dichotomy of location. My father's preference will decide for me: light rather than darkness. I do not realize that an irrevocable choice is being made: the outdoors and the risk, instead of the prison of my peers. This stroke of luck brings me to the verge of breakdown.

I write and speak French outside: the words I use convey no flesh-and-blood reality. I learn the names of birds I've never seen, trees I shall take ten years or more to identify, lists of flowers and plants that I shall never smell until I travel north of the Mediterranean. In this respect, all vocabulary expresses what is missing in my life, exoticism without mystery, causing a kind of visual humiliation that it is not seemly to admit to . . . Settings and episodes in children's books are nothing but theoretical concepts; in the French family the mother comes to fetch her daughter or son from school; in the French street, the parents walk quite naturally side by side . . . So, the world of the school is expunged from the daily life of my native city, as it is from the life of my family. The latter is refused any referential rôle.

My conscious mind is here, huddled against my mother's knees, in the darkest corners of the flat which she never leaves. The ambit of the school is elsewhere: my search, my eyes are fixed on other regions. I do not realize, no-one around me realizes, that, in the conflict between these two worlds, lies an incipient vertigo.

A Widow's Voice

My husband was in the habit of going to Cherchel every Sunday. Once he brought a guest back with him. The next day there was a meeting of about fifteen people: they'd all come to our farm from the nearby mountains.

The guest stayed the following night and the next day he left to go back to the city. It was during Ramadan. Alas! somebody betrayed us and went to Gouraya to report the meeting.

The morning after the guest left, the gendarmes arrived. The men – my husband and his brothers – were out hunting. We had two guns and a case of ammunition, but they were buried a little further away.

The *caïd* who came with the gendarmes asked my mother-in-law, 'Why does your son go every week to the market in Cherchel?'

'To buy things and to see his parents!' she replied.

'That's not true! I know you: you've got family in Novi, not in Cherchel!'

He asked where the missing hunting rifles were. She replied that her son had sold them a long time ago, at the religious festival of Si M'hamed ben Yusef. They left without finding anything.

Soon afterwards our men were back. A few days went by; but the gendarmes returned: this time they took all the men to prison in Cherchel.

After nine months in prison my husband and one of his brothers were sentenced to death: they were accused of having a list of names of people who were working with France and who the Revolution had condemned.

There were a lot of partisans in that prison. They decided, 'We're going to take things into our own hands!'

One morning three of them managed to overcome a guard; they killed him. At another gate, they did the same thing. One of the prisoners was wounded in the leg; he told them, 'You must all get out! I'm staying! I'm going to die! You've still got a chance. Go! I shall kill and be killed!'

They got away; fifteen to twenty prisoners escaped together. That was at nine o'clock in the morning. There was even a French woman who was killed, but we never heard how it happened.

Two hours later, the soldiers turned up at our farm. One of them said to the old lady, 'Your sons have broken out of prison and killed some guards! If the other guards decided to come here, you'd all be dead, young and old, big and small, even including your cats!'

They searched everywhere; they asked again where the guns were and eventually they left. The next morning one of our relatives came to see us from another mountain. He told us that the fugitives had spent the night near the Messelmoun wadi. A nephew accompanied him; we decided that we women would in future cook extra quantities of food, in case it was needed . . .

A boy came to ask us for clothes. We agreed we'd bury the food every time. Finally I managed to see my husband; he arrived with another man, named Abdoun . . .

'France' kept on increasing the number of guards. Every time one of the men who'd escaped was sent to us, God preserved them, and us too!

One night, they all regrouped and someone took them further away, as far as Zaccar. From the next night we could get a bit more rest!

A few months later our men came to visit us; this time they were wearing the maquisards' uniform and they were armed. We embraced them joyfully, we were proud of them!

'Praise be to God! Finally you've escaped death!'

Life was never the same again. 'France' began to come up the mountain to our place nearly every morning and evening. Eventually they burned the houses, and then the people! Taking the animals away, killing human beings! . . . Can you imagine what would happen when they arrived at a house and found women alone? . . .

I decided to run away: I went to my parents who lived near another mountain. I stayed there. Later apparently one of the soldiers asked my mother-in-law, 'And the lieutenant's wife [they knew my husband was now a lieutenant with the maquisards], where's she got to?'

'Since you've taken her husband to prison, she didn't want to stay here! She's gone back to her own family!'

They never managed to find me during the whole of the war . . . From there, I began to go into the hills to help other people; we took food, we washed their uniforms, we kneaded bread . . . Until the day when, as God had willed, my husband was killed fighting!

I only learned of his death through strangers. Someone told me, a week after the ceasefire, 'Your husband fell near Miliana, in a skirmish!'

After independence the Brothers sent me a letter to tell me he'd been buried in Algiers, at Sidi M'hamed de Belcourt. I took the letter. I went to see my sister-in-law, who lived in Algiers. Her husband asked me, 'Who told you that?'

I mentioned the letter.

'Show me! Give it to me!'

Alas! You'll laugh at me perhaps, but I never saw that letter again. How could I have the courage to ask him for it back? . . . I knew my husband had been buried in Algiers, because a nurse had looked after him when he was wounded. They called her 'The-Woman-from-Cherchel'; in fact it was her husband who came from Cherchel. She went back to live in Miliana.

A year or two later I tried to find her, simply so that she could tell me about it. I decided to go to the religious festival of Sidi M'hamed, the patron saint of Miliana. I got as far as her house and decided to talk to her. I only stayed there a minute and left again.

She couldn't tell me anything as I caught her right in the middle of her housework. She was just able to confirm the facts for me: that she had looked after my husband when she was a nurse with the maquis. She was a middle-aged woman.

Embraces

It is early in summer 1843: the prisoners, Saint-Arnaud's hostages, segregated by family and sex, are herded into the holds of a steamship which leaves Bône bound for France.

I imagine you, the unknown woman, whose tale has been handed down by story-tellers over the ten decades which lead to my childhood years. For now I too take my place in the fixed circle of listeners, near the Menacer Mountains ... I re-create you, the invisible woman, sailing with the others to the Island of Sainte Marguerite, to the prisons made celebrated by 'The Man in the Iron Mask'. Your own mask, O ancestress of ancestress! the first expatriate, is heavier by far than that of romance! I resurrect you during that crossing that no letter from any French soldier was to describe ...

At Bône you walk up the gangway, mingling with the dusty crowd; the men are roped together; the women follow, shrouded in their white or blue-grey veils which envelop whimpering infants, or to which cling crying children. When the exodus begins you know you are heavy with child. Will you give birth to a fatherless babe, since the father has not been taken? You see yourself alone, without father, brother, husband to accompany you to the shores of the Infidels. You must go with the band of cousins, kin and relatives by marriage!

All the exiles sleep like you on the bare boards of the bunkers; they have never seen the sea. They thought it would be empty and flat, not this shifting abyss ... The first night of the crossing you begin to vomit; the pains begin the following day.

The second night you feel death in your belly swallowing all hope. You curl up amidst the cousins, old, young, or not so young. These women enfold you in their damp veils, as if to bind you with their prayers, their whispers ... Without a cry, you give birth to the foetus:

the night of full moon opens up, the sea is calm again, an indifferent rival.

The ship sails on, laden with the forty-eight hostages. While your companions doze, you lie still, your face turned towards the stern. You are rent with anguish: 'How can I bury the foetus, O my Prophet, my sweet Saviour!'

An old woman at your side has taken hold of it like a bundle of rags.

'My dead bird! My eyes cannot close although it is the night!'

You sob, you prepare to lacerate your cheeks, while the old woman mutters her blessings.

'Our land is theirs! This sea is theirs! Where can I shelter my dead son? Will there never be a corner of Islam again for us wretched folk?'

The sleeping women are woken by your weeping; their anger is aroused; they begin to intone a *sura*: a continuous rustle of sound, an endless monotonous chant. Eventually you fall asleep, still holding the foetus wrapped in a linen cloth. You doze, obsessed by the thought that it is your youth you are carrying thus in your arms . . . The chorus of prisoners grows louder.

Later, someone shakes you in the dark. A voice is calling you:

'Daughter of my mother's tribe, get up! You cannot keep the lamb of God any longer in your arms!'

You look without understanding at the wrinkled face of an aunt who is addressing you. Behind her, a mottled pink and grey light in the sky indicates a new dawn; it surrounds the old woman like a halo.

'What am I to do? Where shall I find a land of the believers in which to bury him?'

Once more you are overcome with despair.

'Let us go up on deck! The men are sleeping! You and I will cast the child into the sea!'

'The Christians' ocean!' you protest timidly.

'God's ocean!' the old woman retorts. 'Everywhere is God's pasture and that of his Prophet! . . . And your son lives, I am sure, like a cherub in our own Paradise!'

Two veiled figures step over the collection of sleeping women. A moment later, you cast the bundle in your arms over the ship's rail.

'At least let it be facing our own land!' you moan.

'May God guide and assist us wherever we are cast!' adds your companion, who leads you back to your place . . .

You weep no more, you will never weep again! Will you be one of the prisoners who are released ten years later and who repeat the crossing in the opposite direction to rejoin their tribe, now completely quelled?

Fourth Movement:

The Cry in the Dream

I have a recurring dream from time to time, after a day which has been fretted momentarily by some quite ordinary or possibly unusual event. I dream of my paternal grandmother; I relive the day of her death. I am at once the six-year-old child who experienced this loss and the woman who dreams and suffers, every time, from this dream.

I can see neither my grandmother's corpse nor the funeral ceremony. I have rushed out of this house where death has come knocking, and go tearing down the narrow alley. On I run, dashing headlong down the street hemmed in by hostile walls, empty houses. I race past the church and the smart residential district where my mother lives. During all the time I am running, my mouth gapes wider and wider . . . The sound in my dream however is switched off.

I am driven relentlessly onward. A scream is implanted within me; it shoots up through my limbs, swelling in my chest, rasping my larynx, fills my mouth and is exhaled in a dense silence; my legs move automatically. My whole being is inhabited by these words: 'Mamma is dead, is dead!'; I carry my grief with me, I even run ahead of it, I don't know whether I'm calling out or fleeing, but I'm screaming and this scream no longer means anything except that a child is being driven on and on . . .

I am crying out now, and my dream spills over me like a fog and seems never-ending. A cry deep as the ocean. I bear my grandmother like a burden on my shoulders, yet I can see her face displayed on the façades of the buildings that file past. And the ghost arises of the dead woman, so deep-rooted in my early childhood. When my brother was born I could no longer sleep in my parents' room; I was eighteen months old, and from then on I shared my grandmother's bed. The memory grows more vivid: to help me go off to sleep, the old lady would take hold of one of my feet in one of her hands and warm them till I fell asleep.

She died a few years later. I have no memory of this gentle woman's voice, the one who had come to rely on her youngest son. I used to call her 'my silent mother', compared with the others – mother, maternal grandmother and aunts – those proud aristocrats who always seemed to me to live in a world of music, incense and noise.

She alone, the silent one, by this action of clasping my feet, remains linked to me . . . That is why I scream; that is why, in this dream that recurs over the years, she returns persistently, though absent, and the little girl that is me runs desperately trying to find her voice.

Lower down in the town, in the opulent house with its terraces and its din, my mother's mother holds court. There, there is singing, a chorus of loud voices. If they suddenly start whispering and murmuring, seeming on the defensive, it is out of decorum or convention because the men have finally returned home to eat and sleep.

Sometimes my dream continues in these sunlit places, near the cherry tree growing next to the steps, under the jasmins on the lowest terrace. There are copper pots filled with geraniums against the banisters . . . I am sitting crushed up in the middle of a crowd of veiled visitors. I watch.

Once more I see myself running wildly, zigzagging down a narrow alley in the old hilly district. I am forced to go on screaming, though no-one hears me. I scream, not a stifled cry, but rather as if I were breathing very hard, very fast.

Bolting once more out of the house of mourning, I hurtle down towards the house of many terraces. I tell myself that my silent grandmother should be there, in this place of so many festivities, still holding my feet in her worn hands.

On the ground floor of the big house, in the dim light of the wake, my grandmother smiles at me, a tiny figure, her features softened with kindness, her face emanating goodness. She seems to be saying to me: 'They think they are burying me, they think they are coming to my death! You alone . . .'

I alone know she will be resurrected. I do not weep for her; once more I run screaming through the streets, between the white houses, and I scatter my love with my breath on the air streaming past me. The narrow street runs downhill; the little boys on their skate-boards give way before me; right at the bottom, the smell of baking betrays the only activity at the end of the day: baskets of aniseed bread are ready to be distributed for the funeral celebration.

Does this dream allow me to find the silent mother again? I seek rather to avenge her former silence, which was made more bearable by the caresses lavished on the child who shared her bed . . .

It was some time before I realized how poor my father's family was. My father started attending the French school fairly late, did brilliantly in all his classes, rapidly caught up with what he had missed and soon passed the entrance examination to the normal school: by becoming a teacher he was able to offer his mother and sisters some security, and to secure the latter's marriage before he married himself.

I was struck particularly by one scene from this past which was described to me: my father, a schoolboy of nine or ten, had to do his homework squatting at a low table, by the light of a candle . . . I knew the old house, its dark rooms, its little courtyard. The picture of my father as a studious child was engrained in my mind, in this humble setting.

One of my paternal aunts was living for a long time in an isolated room at the back. I can still see her, a pale shadow, standing in the doorway; the curtain over the door is half-raised. From the far corner of the dim room a dying man's voice calls to her, interrupted by a bout of coughing . . . For many years this aunt looked after a tuberculous husband; when he died it was not long before she followed him into the grave, infected in her turn.

My father's second sister, the youngest, occupied a more important place in my childhood.

Her house was not far from my mother's. In the summer I sometimes quarrelled with one of my cousins or a young aunt; I did not have my playmates' knack of reeling off a picturesque string of taunts in our local dialect.

Among the squawking city kids, I easily took offence because of my shyness or my pride. I had only one recourse: to stalk out of the noisy house, scorn the peacemaking efforts of my mother and her friends, busy for the most part with their embroidery. I took refuge with my paternal aunt: tall and dried up, with green eyes glinting in her thin

Berber face; although her courtyard was swarming with her own brood, she would welcome me with open arms. She made a fuss of me; took me into her best room where I was fascinated by a high four-poster bed . . . She kept the best preserves and sweets for me, sprinkled perfume on my hair and down my neck. 'Daughter of my brother', she called me, laughing proudly, and her affection warmed my heart.

Her fondness for me was probably due to my physical resemblance to my father. In our society, a marriage only perpetuates a latent, lasting rivalry between the two lines of descent . . . My parents were a modern couple and that prevented the usual tensions.

Later, when this aunt, with the same exuberance, continued to call me 'daughter of my brother', the memory of those summers came back to me, when I was comforted by her banter and her confident presence.

Did any significant hierarchy divide the society of this mountain-rimmed city, impoverished by erosion? If so, it was of minor account, compared to the discrimination made between the city-dwellers and the peasants of the surrounding area; or, more important still, the segregation introduced by the colonial settlers. Few in number, but influential, the group of Europeans of Maltese, Spanish or Provençal origin not only possessed all the power, but controlled the only lucrative activity – fishing and the use of the trawlers in the old port.

The Arab women moved around the town, white wraiths, which the visitors to the Roman ruins imagined all identical. Among the families of the notables, a subtle distinction was maintained: due partly to the importance of the man's present social position, partly dependent on one's paternal and maternal ancestors, who are constantly being invoked.

For me, the distinction between my maternal and paternal ancestry lay in one single but essential point: my mother's mother spoke to me at length of the dead, that is to say, my maternal grandfather and great-grandfather. Of my paternal grandmother I knew only this: she had been widowed very young with two children and had to marry a very old man, who died leaving her a house and two more children, one of whom was my father.

My maternal grandmother impressed me by the way she danced when she went into one of her regular trances: besides which, at every family gathering, I found myself hemmed in by her imperious, ringing voice.

The memory of my father's mother remains as green, perhaps more so, thanks to her caressing hands. Only her former silence continues to hurt me today . . .

A Widow's Voice

I lost four of my men in this war. My husband and my three sons. They took up arms at almost the same time. One of my youngsters had just three months left for the end of the fighting; he's dead. Another disappeared at the very beginning: I never heard what happened to him.

My brother was the fifth . . . I brought him back from the river. I looked for his body everywhere; I found it. He's buried in the cemetery.

When he was alive he was talking to me one day, just as we are doing, here. He suddenly said to me, 'Listen, I carried out the attack on the Ezzar Wadi. And on the Sidi M'hamed Wali. At Belazmi, that was me too . . .' He paused and then he went on, 'O daughter of my mother, see that you don't leave me for the jackals, when I die! . . . Don't let the wild beasts eat my corpse! . . .'

May his soul rest in peace! He never asked the least thing of me, except that! . . . That's what he said, and that's what happened eventually . . . In the end they caught him. One morning, the plane flew over and dropped bombs on us. In the afternoon they killed my brother. We ran away when it got dark.

My brother had a mare. He used to go backwards and forwards to organize the support networks among the people. Wherever he went, he took this mare. When he slept out of doors he tied her to his foot.

When we ran away, we got to a wadi. Someone told me that my brother's mare had been seen not far away: she was lying down and wouldn't budge. It was night.

When it got light I went to look for the animal. I'd lost hope of finding my brother. I saw the mare; she got to her feet. She must have smelt the body . . . Someone (a peasant who was killed soon afterwards) told me, 'Listen, I think your brother's lying not far away, near the stream!'

A plane came back to bomb us again. I ran and hid in the water. When the plane went away I came out; I walked slowly, slowly up the wadi until I found my brother's body. Then I ran to call the people. He was buried in the cemetery, in the same grave as my mother . . . My sons were still alive then!

Out of all the men in the family, the only ones they were able to bury were my brother and one of my nephews. That was all.

I often went up into the hills to see my sons. The youngest one in particular used to send for me. I went straight away, from one *douar* to another . . . 'I'm at this or that *douar*,' he let me know. 'Come! . . .' Or, 'I'm waiting for you at this *douar* or the other! . . . I've got nothing to wear . . . I haven't a penny! . . . I'm this . . . I'm that!'

Once, out of all our animals, I had just one lamb left! I slaughtered it (there were more and more fires and I'd have lost it anyway). I sent the whole lamb up to him so that he and his companions could eat! . . . That's the one who died, just six months before the fighting ended! . . . Have we any more tears left? No, our eyes are dry . . .

And the son I never saw again, after he went into the hills . . . One of his companions sent me the following message about him: 'Mother, be careful, if someone comes saying you must send some soap or clothes or a little money to your son! . . . You must only think about your other sons now, the ones who are still alive! . . . Don't think about this one any more!'

He was still so young and yet he could always make up his mind so easily: 'That's what must be done! . . . That's how it is!' . . . I can still hear him.

At independence, the people in the city didn't give me anything. There was one man in charge, named Allal: the day he ran away to join the maquis I hid him for a time at my place!

He was the man who allotted the empty houses after the war. As our *douar* had been destroyed I went down into the town with other people. But I couldn't face wandering around. An old man, Si el Hajj, urged me to go to this man to remind him of my case. He even came with me and knocked at Allal's door. Allal let us in: people I didn't know were in the courtyard.

I went in.

'O Allal, where are my rights?' I exclaimed. 'My sons fought from here to the Tunisian border, while you remained hidden in caves and holes!'

And it was true. And then, in front of all those townsfolk, he started talking to me in Berber! Just to emphasize that I was a country-woman! I repeated in Arabic, with the correct accent: 'Give me my rights!'

They didn't give me a thing . . . You can see where I'm living now, I had to pay to occupy this hut. 'You pay or you don't put a foot inside!' they told me.

All the men I used to depend on, all those men have gone!

Dialogues

Trees have been replanted on the foothills; the hamlets in these valleys have been rebuilt; once more mud walls and reed fences rise up between huts overrun with whining children. I stop to confer here and there at random. I push gates open, I sit down on the straw mat; beyond the little yard my gaze encounters the same mountain, with its abandoned look-out posts.

Scattered conversations in which my mother's lineage provides the link: one or other of the speakers tells me that the peasant women – repudiated wives, or those who are sterile, bereft of any future – have resumed their pilgrimages to the grave of the two saints among my ancestors (the 'old one' and the 'young one', the one 'with the black tongue' and the other, the silent one, probably his son); they come once more with their confessions, their sessions of trances to ensure the blessings and intercession of the father and son . . . The women prepare to talk to me in the same hesitant way; am I not, through my mother and my mother's father, a descendant of these two dead saints who listen and whose petrified slumber brings them solace? . . . Yes, the voices in the shadows speak to me, and I remain silent; as I drink in their words and every inflection of their voices I could feel myself to be, if not saint or sinner, at any rate mummified.

When do I ask the straightforward questions:

'How old were you? . . .' 'Where were you living? . . .' 'Were you married or single? . . .' etc.

When does the one vital question stick in my throat, unable to escape? . . . I hold it back, I cannot formulate it, except by some coded word, some soft, neutral, whispering word . . .

Faced with these four, five listening peasant women, all living out their lives as war widows . . . Must I wait for a confidential tête-à-tête? One of them has an enormous goitre on her long, flexible neck: perhaps I can pass her a hint to stay behind, giving the others to understand that I have some advice for her about surgeons or hospitals . . . each one I speak to is my alter ego:

like me condemned without hope of salvation and yet neither guilty nor victim. I must approach their unrelieved sadness, lower the voice, expressing neither resignation nor lamentation.

'My' question quivers persistently on my tongue. In order to put it into words I ought to prepare the outward appearance of my body: I sit cross-legged on cushions or on the bare tiles, palms upward in pose of humility, my shoulders hunched to forestall weakness, my lap ready to receive the flood of emotion, legs curled up under my skirt, to prevent me running off screaming through the trees.

To say the private, Arabic word 'damage', or at the most, 'hurt':
'Sister, did you ever, at any time, suffer "damage"?'

The word suggesting rape – the euphemism: after the soldiers passed close to the river, the soldiers whom the young woman lying hidden for hours could not avoid. The soldiers whom she met. And 'submitted to', 'I submitted to "France",' the thirteen-year-old shepherd-girl might have said. Cherifa, who in fact did not submit to anything, unless it be today, the present emptiness.

Once the soldiers have gone, once she has washed, tidied herself up, plaited her hair and tied the scarlet ribbon, all these actions reflected in the brackish water of the wadi, the woman, every woman, returns, one hour or two hours later, advances to face the world to prevent the chancre being opened in the tribal circle: the blind old man, the watchful matrons, the silent children with flies about their eyes, young lads already distrustful:
'My daughter, has there been "damage"?'

One or other of the matriarchs will ask the question, to seize on the silence and build a barrier against misfortune. The young woman, her hair no longer in disarray, looks into the old woman's lacklustre eyes, sprinkles scorching sand over every word: rape will not be mentioned, will be respected. Swallowed. Until the next alarm.

Can I, twenty years later, claim to revive these stifled voices? And speak for them? Shall I not at best find dried-up streams? What ghosts will be conjured up when in this absence of expressions of love (love received, 'love' imposed), I see the reflection of my own barrenness, my own aphasia.

202

The Onlookers

Yes, there is a difference between the veiled women, a difference that the eye of the foreigner can't discern; he thinks them all identical – phantoms roaming the streets, staring, examining, surveying all about them; but they possess an inherent streak of inequality: between the one who shouts, sending her voice soaring over the confined area of the patio, and the one on the other hand who never speaks, who contents herself with sighing or lets herself be interrupted until her voice is permanently stifled.

I recall one familiar expression used to condemn a woman irrevocably: worse than the poor (wealth and luxury were relative in this restricted society), worse than the widow or the repudiated wife (a fate that depends on God alone) the only really guilty woman, the only one you could despise with impunity, the one you treated with manifest contempt, was 'the woman who raises her voice'.

One or other of the neighbours, or of the women related by marriage, might wear out her patience in caring for her ever-increasing family; one or other of the city ladies might show off flashy jewellery, treat her stepchildren or daughters-in-law harshly; they could be excused as it was rare for a woman to be lucky enough to have a 'true Muslim', a hard-working, docile man for a husband. The only one who put herself straight away beyond the pale was the 'loud-mouthed woman': the one who nagged at her brood, whose voice could be heard beyond her own vestibule and out in the street, the one who railed aloud against fate instead of keeping her protests within four walls, instead of sublimating her grievances in prayer or in the whispered confidences of the story-tellers.

In short, veiled forms had the right to circulate in the city. But what were these women doing with their cries of rebellion piercing the very heavens? The only thing they were doing was to run the gravest risk.

To refuse to veil one's voice and to start 'shouting', that was really indecent, real dissidence. For the silence of all the others suddenly lost its charm and revealed itself for what it was: a prison without reprieve.

Writing in a foreign language, not in either of the tongues of my native country – the Berber of the Dahra mountains or the Arabic of the town where I was born – writing has brought me to the cries of the women silently rebelling in my youth, to my own true origins.

Writing does not silence the voice, but awakens it, above all to resurrect so many vanished sisters.

During the family celebrations of my childhood, the city ladies sit crushed beneath the weight of their jewellery, clad in embroidered velvet, their faces adorned with spangles or tattooing. Female musicians perform, pastries are handed round, children get under the feet of the visitors in their finery. The dancers heave their buxom figures sedately from their seats . . . I have eyes only for my mother, thinking probably of my dream of growing up and dancing too in this heat. The city streets are far away; men do not exist. Paradise will last for ever; slowly dancing, melancholy faces are lulled by the music . . .

One detail of the scene however introduces a harsh note: at one moment in the ceremony when coffee and cakes have circulated, the mistress of the house gives the order for the doors to be opened wide. Then the horde of 'voyeuses' swarms in; that's what the women are called who will remain veiled even in this exclusively feminine gathering; they have not been invited, but they have the right to stand in the vestibule looking on. Because they are excluded they keep on their veils; what is more, in this city where the ladies go about veiled but leave their eyes uncovered above a bit of embroidered veiling, these 'voyeuses' hide their faces completely except for one eye, so that they remain anonymous in the festivities; with their fingers they hold a curious little triangle open under the veil.

These uninvited guests are allowed into the party as spies! The tiny free eye, shrouded in white, darts from right to left, inspects the ladies' jewels, studies the way another dances, takes a good look at the bride decked out in all her finery, examining the louis d'or and pearls given as wedding gifts . . . Here are these shrouded women, right in the heart of the parade, their silent presence tolerated, the ones who enjoy the sad privilege of remaining veiled in the very heart of the harem! At

204

last I understand both why they are condemned and why they are fortunate: these women who 'shout' in their daily lives, the ones whom the matrons thrust aside contemptuously, probably typify their need to be seen, to have an audience! The hostess has let them in in order to show off, as if saying, 'Look! examine everything! I'm not afraid of gossip! My wedding celebration respects all the traditions! Let even the women I've not deigned to invite see for themselves and let everybody know!' . . . The crux of the ceremony is there, in this uneasy knot. As if the guests could no longer endure their exclusion from the outside world . . . As if they were finding a way of forgetting their imprisonment, getting their own back on the men who kept them in the background: the males – father, sons, husband – were shut out once and for all by the women themselves who, in their own domain, began to impose the veil in turn on others.

A Widow's Voice

We lived at the place called 'Milestone 40'; those *douars* were not very far from the main road. There'd been a clash with the French soldiers just there. They'd had a lot of losses. We could see the fires, the smoke, from a distance . . . Since then they came back time and time again.

One another occasion, the road was damaged not far from the French post, to stop 'France' changing the guards. The barbed wires round the post were taken down during the night. Our men had done what the partisans had come and told them to do.

One morning, the soldiers came from the post and said, 'You're the *fellaheen*! You're the ones who removed the barbed wire and damaged the road!'

Our men had to work right through the day putting back the barbed wire and repairing the road. The following night, the same thing happened with the maquisards. This time our men ran away: they didn't want to wait for the enemy's reprisals. We women were left to bear the brunt!

When the French came they only found women.

'Take everything you can carry out of your houses!' they told us.

The *goumiers* set fire to the houses. We drifted around. If you have a brother, go to your brother's place; if you have a first cousin, go to your cousin's! . . . We set off, we left our homes in ruins . . . A little way off we built shelters out of branches. The maquisards came back; they always followed us wherever we went. Our men hid food for them and worked for them at night. The French also put in their appearance again!

As soon as we young women saw the French coming we never stayed inside. The old women stayed in the houses with the children:

we went to hide in the undergrowth or near the wadi. If the enemy caught us we never said a word . . .

One night, the maquisards arrived. They had some coffee and then left. No sooner were they out of the house than 'France' descended on us: the soldiers had seen our lights from the road.

'The *fellaheen* have been here!' (They called '*fellaheen*' those we called 'Brothers').

They wanted to take my husband away. We knew that once a man's taken away in the middle of the night he never came back. I started to cry and loosen my hair and lacerate my cheeks. All the women in the house did the same thing, howling louder and louder: enough to deafen them all!

Outside, their officer heard us crying. He came into the house and said, 'Let that man go!'

They just took his papers and told him he'd got to call at the post the next day.

We were living then near the Ouled Larbi field. We didn't own anything. My husband was a day labourer. Just the same, they did kill him eventually.

They came to get him in the field. It was a Friday. He never came back. I heard later that a man named Menaia had given him away.

The French tortured him from Friday to Sunday. On the last day, someone came and told me my husband had been stood up against a pillar, right in the middle of the village square. They killed him just like that, publicly, in front of everybody.

He left me with young children. The last-born was still in my belly: I was only one and a half months gone. That son's now twenty! I'll be bringing his bride to him next week, God willing! Because my health's not very good. I thought, 'I'll die knowing he's got his own home! I'll depart with my mind at rest!' . . . When I wanted to choose him a bride, he told me, 'Go and make enquiries in that place!'

Now he'll only have her to work for. I don't need him any more! All my daughters have their own homes; once my last-born is married, my war-widow's pension will be enough for me!

Embraces

When one day in 1956 the French paratroopers and the Foreign Legion arrive at midday at the mountain village of El-Aroub, all its thousand inhabitants have disappeared. One madman wanders alone near a row of olive trees; a senile old woman remains squatting near the water-tap.

The day before, forty-five maquisards had been living there quite openly for the last month: the green and white independence flag was flying on the newly-painted mosque. The old people of the village were sorry not to see the 'Brothers' saying their prayers regularly there. But before dawn there's an indication that the French are arriving in strength: all males aged between fourteen and sixty decide to leave with the maquisards. Women, children and old men flee into the bushes and rocks of the surrounding country, in the hope that the enemy will just be passing through.

But the soldiers settle in. The infantry and the field companies remain stationed down on the plain. After three long days of waiting, the civilian population eventually come out of hiding, driven out by hunger; they drift back, waving white flags, a pitiful procession of women with empty breasts and wailing infants.

Disappointment and boredom have driven the soldiery to systematic looting. The inhabitants find their village ransacked from top to bottom, 'turned over like a ploughed field': the dried provisions have disappeared or been trodden underfoot, the linen chests have been broken open, the roofs of the houses demolished in the search for hidden arms and silver coins . . . Doors have been ripped off their hinges, wedding dresses draped derisively on the trees, hauled through the mud, hung over the empty door-frames, in a grotesque parody of a carnival.

Mothers search through this scene of plunder for something to give their starving children. Some of them, in despair, sit weeping silently in their doorways.

In the middle of this melancholy return, two men in maquisards' uniform are captured: the army give the first cheers for victory.

The officer in command of the paratroopers, an aristocratic lieutenant, asks a private, an Alsacian, to try to find out from the prisoners the whereabouts of the arms cache. The interrogation takes place in the open, under an olive tree. The Alsacian is keen to show that he knows his job as torturer. The officer, who does not soil his hands, puts on an air of indifference, not devoid of contempt.

The prisoners are soon unrecognizable. Silence, boredom, takes hold of the soldiers who had at first been attracted by the spectacle. The garments hanging on the branches suddenly seem like the sole spectators of the endless agony in the sun . . .

Finally one of the tortured men gives in. He indicates the site of the cache. Everyone rushes there. But the lieutenant remains behind, lifts a hand and the two prisoners fall under a hail of bullets.

One of the legionnaires writes of these days in El-Aroub, reliving his experiences. Sometimes he even weeps, 'but dry-eyed, having long since had no more tears to shed'.*

I come at length upon what he wrote, turn the pages at random, read as if I were shrouded in the ancestral veil; with my one free eye perusing the page, where is written more than the eye-witness sees, more than can be heard.

The day after this interrogation a peasant woman recognizes her husband as one of the two men whose bodies lie unburied.

'She rushes boldly into the middle of our encampment, weeping, heaping insults on us in a terrifying voice. She kept on shaking her bony fist at us and shouting threats.'**

The soldiers, once more at a loose end, sit looking at the sea in the distance. The beach is tempting in this scorching heat, but a dense forest runs along the shore for miles. The lynx-eyed maquisards are probably lurking there, ready to take the opportunity of attacking . . .

The orders to retreat are long in coming. The agitation and panic

---

*Pierre Leulliette, *Saint Michel et le Dragon* (Saint Michael and the Dragon) Ed. de Minuit, 1961
**Ibid

around the village subside, the women dry their tears. Then the order comes to move out the next day. The soldiers will have a full day's march to reach the sea. Lorries, preceded by armoured cars and followed by tanks, will take them to Constantine. They sleep first on the beach, 'unwashed, looking like stray dogs'; at dawn they wake up in the rain . . .

Is it in the course of this drive down to the sea, or the next day in one of the lorries of the convoy, in the rain, that a certain Bernard confides in the man who will tell the story of El-Aroub, recalling events he will never be able to forget? . . .

Yet again, one man speaks, another listens, then writes. I stumble against their words which circulate; then I speak, I speak to you, the widows of that other mountain village, so distant or so near to El-Aroub!

In the middle of the night before they leave, Bernard crawls on hands and knees, unarmed, between two sentinels, gropes his way in the dark into the village, until he finds a farm whose roof has nearly collapsed, whose door has been half dragged off its hinges.

'There,' he tells his friend, 'a pretty Fatma smiled at me during the day!'

He slips in without knocking. It must be half past one in the morning. He hesitates in the darkness, then strikes a match: facing him, a group of women squat in a circle, staring at him; they are nearly all old, or look it. They huddle close to one another; their eyes gleam with terror or surprise . . .

The Frenchman takes food out of his pockets and hurriedly distributes it. He walks around, he strikes another match; finally his eyes light on 'the pretty Fatma' who had smiled at him. He seizes her hand, pulls her to her feet.

The match has gone out. The couple find their way to the back of the vast room, where it is pitch-black. The old women squatting in a circle have not moved; companions and sisters of silence, they crouch, staring with dim pupils which preserve the present moment: could the lake of happiness exist? . . .

The Frenchman has undressed. 'I could have been in my own home,' he will admit. He presses the girl close to him; she shudders, she holds him tight, she begins to caress him.

'What if one of the old women were to get up and come and stick a knife in my back?' he thinks.

Suddenly two frail arms are round his neck, a gasping voice begins to whisper: strange, fond, warm words come tumbling out. The unknown hot-blooded girl pours these words in Arabic or Berber into his ear.

'She kissed me full on the mouth, like a young girl. Just imagine! I'd never seen anything like it! . . . She was kissing me! Do you realize? . . . Kissing me! It was that little meaningless action that I shall never be able to forget!'

Bernard returns to the camp about three in the morning. No sooner has he fallen asleep than he wakes with a start: he must leave the village for ever.

Twenty years later I report the scene to you, you widows, so that you can see it in your turn, so that you in turn can keep silent. And the old women sit motionless, listening to the unknown village girl giving herself.

Silence spanning nights of passion and words grown cold, the silence of the watching women, that accompanies the quivering kisses in the heart of the ruined hamlet.

Fifth Movement:

The Tunic of Nessus

My father, a tall erect figure in a fez, walks down the village street; he pulls me by the hand and I, who for so long was so proud of myself – the first girl in the family to have French dolls bought for her, the one who had permanently escaped cloistering and never had to stamp and protest at being forced to wear the shroud-veil, or else yield meekly like any of my cousins, I who did deliberately drape myself in a veil for a summer wedding as if it were a fancy dress, thinking it most becoming – I walk down the street, holding my father's hand. Suddenly, I begin to have qualms: isn't it my 'duty' to stay behind with my peers in the gynaeceum? Later, as an adolescent, well nigh intoxicated with the sensation of sunlight on my skin, on my mobile body, a doubt arises in my mind: 'Why me? Why do I alone, of all my tribe, have this opportunity?'

I cohabit with the French language: I may quarrel with it, I may have bursts of affection, I may subside into sudden or angry silences – these are the normal occurrences in the life of any couple. If I deliberately provoke an outburst, it is less to break the unbearable monotony, than because I am vaguely aware of having been forced into a 'marriage' too young, rather like the little girls of my town who are 'bespoke' in their earliest childhood.

Thus, my father, the schoolteacher, for whom a French education provided a means of escape from his family's poverty, had probably 'given' me before I was nubile – did not certain fathers abandon their daughters to an unknown suitor, or, as in my case, deliver them into the enemy camp? The failure to realize the implications of this

213

traditional behaviour took on for me a different significance: when I was ten or eleven, it was understood among my female cousins that I was privileged to be my father's 'favourite' since he had unhesitatingly preserved me from cloistering.

But marriageable royal princesses also cross the border, often against their will, in terms of treaties which end wars.

French is my 'stepmother' tongue. Which is my long-lost mother-tongue, that left me standing and disappeared? . . . Mother-tongue, either idealized or unloved, neglected and left to fairground barkers and jailers! . . . Burdened by my inherited taboos, I discover I have no memory of Arabic love-songs. Is it because I was cut off from this impassioned speech that I find the French I use so flat and unprofitable?

The Arab poet describes the body of his beloved; the Andalusian exquisite composes treatise after treatise, listing a multiplicity of erotic postures; the Muslim mystic, dressed in woollen rags and satisfied with a handful of dates, expresses his thirst for God and his longing for the hereafter with a surfeit of extravagant epithets . . . The prodigality of this language seems to me somewhat suspect, consoling with empty words . . . Wealth squandered while they are being dispossessed of their Arab heritage.

Words of love heard in a wilderness. After several centuries of cloistering, the bodies of my sisters have begun to come out of hiding here and there over the last fifty years; they grope around, blinded by the light, before they dare advance. Silence surrounds the first written words, and a few scattered laughs are heard above the groans.

'*L'amour, ses cris (s'écrit)*': my hand as I write in French makes the pun on love affairs that are aired; all my body does is to move forward, stripped naked, and when it discovers the ululations of my ancestresses on the battlefields of old, it finds that it is itself at stake: it is no longer a question of writing only to survive.

Long before the French landed in 1830, the Spanish established their *presidios* (garrison posts) at strategic points along the Maghribin coast – Oran, Bougie, Tangiers, Ceuta; the indigenous rulers in the interior continued to resist and the occupying forces frequently found their food supplies cut off; thus they adopted the tactics of the *rebato*: an isolated spot would be chosen from which to launch an attack, and to which they could retreat and use in the intervals between hostilities for farming or for replenishing supplies.

This type of warfare, rapid offensives alternating with as swift retreats, allowed each side to continue the fight indefinitely.

After more than a century of French occupation – which ended not long ago in such butchery – a similar no-man's-land still exists between the French and the indigenous languages, between two national memories: the French tongue, with its body and voice, has established a proud *presidio* within me, while the mother-tongue, all oral tradition, all rags and tatters, resists and attacks between two breathing spaces. In time to the rhythm of the *rebato*, I am alternately the besieged foreigner and the native swaggering off to die, so there is seemingly endless strife between the spoken and written word.

Writing the enemy's language is more than just a matter of scribbling down a muttered monologue under your very nose; to use this alphabet involves placing your elbow some distance in front of you to form a bulwark – however, in this twisted position, the writing is washed back to you.

This language was imported in the murky, obscure past, spoils taken from the enemy with whom no fond word was ever exchanged . . . French – formerly the language of the law courts, used alike by judges and convicted. Words of accusation, legal procedure, violence – that is the oral source of the colonized people's French.

As I come to the inevitable ceasefire at the end of every war, my writing is washed up on the deserted seashores of the present day and looks for a place where a linguistic armistice can be arranged, a patio with fountains playing where people come and go.

This language was formerly used to entomb my people; when I write it today I feel like the messenger of old, who bore a sealed missive which might sentence him to death or to the dungeon.

By laying myself bare in this language I start a fire which may consume me. For attempting an autobiography in the former enemy's language . . .

After five centuries of Roman occupation, an Algerian named Augustine undertakes to write his own biography in Latin. Speaks of his childhood, declares his love for his mother and his concubine, regrets his youthful wild oats and tells how he was eventually consumed with passion for a Christian God. And his writing presses into service, in all innocence, the same language as Caesar or Sulla – writers and generals of the successful 'African Campaign'.

The same language has passed from the conquerors to the assimilated people; has grown more flexible after the corpses of the past have been enshrouded in words . . . Saint Augustine's style is borne along by his ecstatic search for God. Without this passion, he would be destitute again: 'I have become to myself the country of destitution.' If this love did not maintain him in a blissful transport, his writing would be a self-laceration!

After the Bishop of Hippo Regius, a thousand years elapse. The Maghrib sees a procession of new invasions, new occupations . . . Repeated raids by the Banu Hilal tribesmen finally bleed the country white. Soon after this fatal turning point, the historian Ibn Khaldun, the innovatory author of *The History of the Berbers*, as great a figure as Augustine, rounds off a life of adventure and meditation by composing his autobiography in Arabic. He calls it *Ta'arif*, that is to say, 'Identity'.

As with Augustine, it matters little to him that he writes in a language introduced into the land of his fathers by conquest and accompanied by bloodshed! A language imposed by rape as much as by love . . .

Ibn Khaldun is now nearly seventy years of age: after an encounter with Tamerlane – his last exploit – he prepares to die in exile in Egypt. He suddenly obeys a yearning to turn back on himself: and he becomes the subject and object of a dispassionate autopsy.

For my part, even where I am composing the most commonplace of sentences, my writing is immediately caught in the snare of the old war between two peoples. So I swing like a pendulum from images of war (war of conquest or of liberation, but always in the past) to the expression of a contradictory, ambiguous love.

My memory hides in a black mound of decomposing debris; the sound which carries it swirls upward out of reach of my pen. 'I write,' declares Michaux, 'to undertake a journey through myself.' I journey through myself at the whim of the former enemy, the enemy whose language I have stolen . . .

Autobiography practised in the enemy's language has the texture of fiction, at least as long as you are desensitized by forgetting the dead that writing resurrects. While I thought I was undertaking a 'journey

216

through myself', I find I am simply choosing another veil. While I intended every step forward to make me more clearly identifiable, I find myself progressively sucked down into the anonymity of those women of old – my ancestors!

I am forced to acknowledge a curious fact: the date of my birth is *eighteen hundred and forty-two*, the year when General Saint-Arnaud arrives to burn down the *zaouia* of the Beni Menacer, the tribe from which I am descended, and he goes into raptures over the orchards, the olive groves, 'the finest in the whole of Algeria', as he writes in a letter to his brother – orchards which have now disappeared.

It is Saint-Arnaud's fire that lights my way out of the harem one hundred years later: because its glow still surrounds me I find the strength to speak. Before I catch the sound of my own voice I can hear the death-rattles, the moans of those immured in the Dahra mountains and the prisoners on the Island of Sainte Marguerite; they provide my orchestral accompaniment. They summon me, encouraging my faltering steps, so that at the given signal my solitary song takes off.

The language of the Others, in which I was enveloped from childhood, the gift my father lovingly bestowed on me, that language has adhered to me ever since like the tunic of Nessus: that gift from my father who, every morning, took me by the hand to accompany me to school. A little Arab girl, in a village of the Algerian Sahel . . .

Soliloquy

I have been moving freely outside the harem since my adolescence, but every place I travel through is nothing but a wilderness. In cafés, in Paris or elsewhere, I am surrounded by murmuring strangers: I spend hours eavesdropping on faceless voices, catching snatches of dialogue, fragments of stories, an impenetrable mumble of sounds detached from the magma of faces, preserved from probing eyes.

The sharp ploughshare of my memory digs its furrows through the darkness behind me, while I tremble in broad daylight to find myself among women who mix with men, with impunity . . . They call me an exile. It is more than that: I have been banished from my homeland to listen and bring back some traces of liberty to the women of my family . . . I imagine I constitute the link, but I am only floundering in a murky bog.

My night stirs up French words, in spite of the resurrected dead . . . I thought when I grasped these words they would be doves of peace, in spite of the ravens hovering over the charnel houses, in spite of the snarling jackals tearing flesh to pieces. Cooing turtle-dove-words, chirruping robin-red-breasts like those that wait in opium-smokers' cages . . . The first strains of a dirge well up, penetrating the barriers of oblivion, at once a plaintive song and song of love in the first light of dawn. And every dawn is brighter because I write.

My fiction is this attempt at autobiography, weighed down under the oppressive burden of my heritage. Shall I sink beneath the weight? . . . But the tribal legend criss-crosses the empty spaces, and the imagination crouches in the silence when loving words of the unwritten mother-tongue remain unspoken – language conveyed like the inaudible babbling of a nameless, haggard mummer – crouches in this dark night like a woman begging in the streets . . .

I shelter again in the green shade of my cloistered companions' whispers. How shall I find the strength to tear off my veil, unless I have to use it to bandage the running sore nearby from which words exude?

Tzarl-rit:

(Finale)

tzarl-rit:

    – to utter cries of joy while smacking the lips with the hands (of women)
Eng. trans. of entry in Beaussier, Arabic-French Dictionary

    – shout, vociferate (of women when some misfortune befalls them)
Eng. trans. of entry in Kazimirski, Arabic-French Dictionary

Pauline . . .

Paris, the beginning of June, 1852. Ten women, including one whose Christian name is Pauline, are woken abruptly a little before dawn in the prison of Saint-Lazare.

'Get up! We're leaving for Algeria!'

The nuns hustle them to get ready. It is not yet daylight; soldiers tramp through the high grey corridors which resound with the clash of steel.

'We're leaving for Algeria,' a timid voice repeats.

So the name of my country rings like a death-knell for these prisoners. Quickly their bundles must be tied, the prison register must be signed, and then they must be on their way, on foot . . . Permission is grudgingly given for one of the women to be carried as she is too ill to walk.

The group of prisoners and soldiers crosses Paris in the faint dawn light, to be greeted by bawdy remarks from belated revellers, who take the women for prostitutes. They reach the embarkation point on the Seine. A few hours later they leave for Le Havre; from there the voyage continues to the savage land. For that is where the Parisian tribunals send the diehards of the '48 Revolution, after the coup d'état of 2 December . . . Hundreds of men and women are deported thus . . .

Among this 'people' – as the story-tellers of my homeland would say – is Pauline Rolland. A forty-eight-year-old schoolteacher who 'fights for her faith and her principles', to take up the words of the shepherd-girl from my mountains. Poor like her; like her, humble and too proud . . .

On 23 June 1852 Pauline Rolland lands near Oran. Four months later, on 25 October, she embarks at Bône on her way back to France; she is ill and has not long to live. All that summer she had been shunted from west to east, from town to town, never let out of sight, always spied on . . .

Moved from Mers el-Kebir to Oran, from Oran to Algiers, from Algiers to Bougie – in these cities Pauline sees nothing except soldiers and her jailers; from Bougie Pauline travels by mule along the roads that border unsubjugated Kabylia to Sétif, where she ekes out a living as a seamstress. Two months later, she is sent to a fortress in Constantine; finally she is brought back to Bône, where she receives permission to return to France – out of compassion, so it is claimed – has she not three children? – although she is, at the same time, considered a 'dangerous agitator'.

She is very ill when she embarks. On the boat, she remains lying on the deck, often swept by the waves of a stormy sea. When she lands at Marseille, Pauline cannot get to her feet. In Lyons, where friends take her in, she is already dying and when her eldest son, a young man covered in academic honours, hurries to see her, she is in a coma. In fact, she was delirious when she left Algeria . . . Our country became her grave: her true heirs – Cherifa hiding in her tree, Lla Zohra wandering among the fires that ravaged the countryside, the chorus of anonymous women of today – could pay homage to her with that ancestral cry of triumph, the ululation of convulsive sisterhood!

Throughout the four months of her Algerian travels, Pauline wrote letter after letter to her friends in the struggle, to her family, her relatives . . .

I met this woman on the terrain of her writings: she and I are now clasped in each other's arms, our roots entwined in the rich soil of the French vocabulary. I re-read these letters sent from Algeria: one sentence catches my eye, lovingly inscribed, covering Pauline's life:

'In Kabylia,' Pauline writes in July 1852, 'I have seen women treated as beasts of burden, and others odalisques in a rich man's harem. I have slept at the side of the former on the bare ground, and beside the latter amid gold and silk . . .'

Affectionate words from a woman, pregnant with the future: they give off light before my eyes and finally set me free.

The *Fantasia*

In this same month of October 1852, while Pauline Rolland is leaving Bône to die, Eugène Fromentin begins his travels in this country that has been crushed beneath the weight of twenty-two years of unremitting war. This elegant tourist, this peaceful aristocrat, with a known fondness for the hunt and autumnal landscapes, arrives in Algeria.

A generation of bloody confrontations, cries of 'Havoc!', dogs of war unleashed in hot pursuit – these twenty years are drawing to a close. Kabylia and the South are still inviolate: Fromentin only travels along the borders of these regions. In the North, the scenes that form the subjects for his canvases, the places where he walks with eyes and ears alert, might be one vast game-park that has been over-hunted. He is met by gentle, fragile creatures, ghosts of some lost ceremonial . . . They are trying to re-create a life, in spite of the defeat, and these near-moribund inhabitants of a conquered country, where rebellion is limited to circumscribed regions, remember the fighting but pretend to sleep, to day-dream in the sun, to smoke hashish.

A calm sets in: the settlers have not yet taken possession of the country that later their seasonal workers will trample in the dust. Despite the past shocks, the aspect of the countryside is a revelation to the artist: the North with its illusive tints, the South with its brash vibrant contrasts.

Above all, Fromentin falls in love with the light; he is enamoured of the muted, pearly greys; all this he tries to convey to us in his canvases. This consummate draughtsman, who excels in hunting scenes, portrays our ancestors surrounded by this soft glow and makes them seem the sad accomplices of his melancholy.

Eugène Fromentin keeps a journal of his stay in Algeria; he entitles one of these fragments *Chronique de l'Absent* ('Chronicle of the Missing'). For he finds the Sahel of my childhood a garden where everything in fact speaks of absence.

'Oh, my friend, you have killed me!'

Such are the dying words of Haoua, a young woman who has come one autumn day with her friend, a dancer from Blida, to watch the *Fantasia* of the Hajouts; one of the riders, a lover she'd rejected, wheels round and bears down on her. The charger kicks her in the face and she falls mortally wounded; while she lies dying the murderer disappears over the horizon, beyond the mountains of Muzaïa. Fromentin portrays this festivity that has turned to tragedy.

Can no love-story ever be evoked in these regions except by its tragic consequences? The fury of this Hajout warrior's love when, jilted by Haoua, he strikes her down. Then, too, the French artist's secret love for the mysterious Moorish woman which he expresses in the colours of his costumes, in the faint whisper of his birdlike voice . . . The first Algerian heroine to make a brief appearance in a story written in French, the first to murmur a word in the margin, pretending not to realize she is trespassing . . .

Haoua must have been born just before or just after the capture of the City. Her childhood, her adolescence fed on the sound of fighting, were spent among ambushes, laid for the French by the Hajouts – this redoubtable tribe which, five years after the subjugation of Abd al-Qadir, is decimated and slowly dies. And this is the real tragedy of the *Fantasia* which Fromentin resurrects: a gesture in honour of the vanished victory, recognition of the bodies left lying in the sun as the horse's hooves pound into the distance . . .

The preceding spring Haoua openly received a Frenchman – a fact which is public knowledge in the nearby town. This man, wandering about in the dust and silence of the roads, is a lover of twilight-scenes. The countryside all around, with its livid skies, its birdlife on the brink of extinction, the last of its camels, is bled dry . . . The Hajouts, allies of the Amir, the 'brigands' who have kept up their raids on the invaders from the City, see their tribe disappear, just as twenty years later, the magnificent Halloula Lake with its countless birdlife is to disappear.

'Oh, my friend, you have killed me!' sighs the young woman dying in the tent.

And such is the burden of the sighs heaved by the whole plain, men and beasts, throughout the length of the Sahel, once the fighting is over.

Air on a *Nay*

And then I intervene, with nomad memory and intermittent voice. Undaunted, I have travelled to the four corners of my native land – between the captured City and the ruins of Caesaria, it stretches from Mount Chenoua, in the shadow of the Muzaïa Peak, a languid plain whose wounds have not yet healed. I intervene to greet the painter who has accompanied me throughout my wanderings like a second father figure. Eugène Fromentin offers me an unexpected hand – the hand of an unknown woman he was never able to draw.

In June 1853, when he leaves the Sahel to travel down to the edge of the desert, he visits Laghouat which has been occupied after a terrible siege. He describes one sinister detail: as he is leaving the oasis which six months after the massacre is still filled with its stench, Fromentin picks up out of the dust the severed hand of an anonymous Algerian woman. He throws it down again in his path.

Later, I seize on this living hand, hand of mutilation and of memory, and I attempt to bring it the *qalam*.

Twenty years have elapsed since a recent uprooting. I travel back and forth across my native land, in the customary silence which follows the funeral lamentations; I enter the village homes where the muffled women retell their stories of the cavalcades of a more recent past, before they seem to lapse once more into sleep: to give birth behind the shutters, closed against the midday sun.

What shore awaits me as I continue my travels and my day-dreams, discovering the mutilated hand which the painter threw away? . . . What feast is being prepared, to be haunted by the chants of vanished tribes? What hennaed hands are busying themselves amid the acrid smell of roasting and the drums warming up on the smoking braziers . . .

I wait amid the scattered sheaf of sounds, I wait, foreseeing the inevitable moment when the mare's hoof will strike down any woman who dares to stand up freely, will trample all life that comes out into the sunlight to dance! Yes, in spite of the tumult of my people all around, I already hear, even before it arises and pierces the harsh sky, I hear the death cry in the *Fantasia*.

Paris/Venice/Algiers
(July '82–October '84)

Be sure to read the companion to Assia Djebar's
Fantasia --

Sister to Scheherazade

"A subtle, sharp, and moving novel." -- City Limits

Isma and Hajila are both wives of the same man, but they are not rivals.
Isma, older, vibrant, passionate, emancipated -- is in stark contrast to the
passive, cloistered Hajila. In alternating chapters, Isma tells her own story
in the first person, and then Hajila's in the second person. She tells how
she escaped from the traditional restraints imposed upon the women of her
country -- and how, in making her escape, she condemns Hajila to those
very restraints. When Hajila catches a glimpse of an unveiled woman,
she realizes that she, too, wants a life beyond the veil, and it is Isma who
offers her the key to her own freedom.

Death of an Ex-Minister
Nawal El Saadawi
Translated from the Arabic by **Shirley Eber**

In his mother's arms, a government minister describes an encounter with a junior employee who would not lower her eyes in his presence. This incident shatters his preconceived notions of acceptable behavior, and ultimately leads to his breakdown, dismissal, and death. This cunning tale of fear of authority, instilled in childhood, transmuted into tyranny over those perceived to be weaker, is the first in this superbly subtle collection of stories by one of Egypt's leading writers. While writing of Arab society, her themes are universal. These are sympathetic and powerful stories of sexual politics in today's society.

Fall of the Imam
Nawal El Saadawi
Transalted from the Arabic by **Sherif Hetata**

"This is a tale of women suffering under harsh Islamic rule, but it could be about women anywhere there is cruelty and bullying. This novel is unlike any other I have read, more like a poem or lamenting ballad, with something hypnotic about it, with its rhythmic, keening language, returning again and again to the same incident, a woman killed in the name of religion by the men who have used her.

"This is a wonderful book, and I hope a great many people will read it."
> --Doris Lessing

**Available from your bookstore,
or call 1 800 541-2086.**

A Nail, A Rose
Madeleine Bourdouxhe
Translated from the French and introduced by **Faith Evans**

In 1949, Simone de Beauvoir praised the work of the young Madeleine Bourdouxhe in her classic book, *The Second Sex*. Bourdouxhe's writing has remained wonderfully alive because of the striking modernity of her style, and her keen-sighted but tender understanding of sexual relationships. *A Nail, A Rose* describes women in the margins, working class women who say little and whose lives seem to be constrained by domestic tasks. But it's only on the surface that they are calm, passive, resigned; as they retreat into a fantasy world, surreal images illuminate and distort their everyday existence. Most of the stories in this collection were written in the forties, with the war ever present, most dramatically in the autobiographical final story about Bourdouxhe's escape from a Brussels hospital with her newborn daughter in her arms -- the day after the German invasion.

Sleeping Rough: Stories of the Night
Christina Dunhill, Frances Gapper, Andie Hawthorn, Linda Leatherbarrow, Helen Sandler, Pushpa Sellers, Robyn Vinten, Wendy Wallace

Angelic prose meets devilish wit in this collection of 14 stories by eight women of stylish imagination. Mythical figures wander the streets, lions speak, wolves gather, and vampires hone their seductive arts. Women enter sinister marriages, borrow children and scale new peaks of cunning and adventure.

These are stories of love, lycanthropy, drugs, and Fun-Fotos; sexual liaisons in North Africa and the North Pole; engagements with the Virgin. The exhilarations, fears, and visions of the night bind these stories together. This is an anarchic, erotic, melan-comic combination of high fantasy and gritty realism -- a landmark collection of writing for the nineties.